THE DOUBLE PERSPECTIVE OF
YEATS'S AESTHETIC

IRISH LITERARY STUDIES

THE DOUBLE PERSPECTIVE
OF
YEATS'S AESTHETIC

Okifumi Komesu

Irish Literary Studies 20

1984
COLIN SMYTHE
Gerrards Cross, Bucks.

BARNES & NOBLE BOOKS
Totowa, New Jersey

Copyright © 1984 by Okifumi Komesu

First published in 1984 by Colin Smythe Limited
Gerrards Cross, Buckinghamshire

British Library Cataloguing in Publication Data

Komesu, Okifumi
The double perspective of Yeats's
aesthetic.—(Irish literary studies,
ISSN 0140-895X;20)
1. Yeats, W. B.—Criticism and interpretation
I. Title   II. Series
821'.8   PR9507

ISBN 0-86140-158-1

First published in the U.S.A. by Barnes & Noble Books
Totowa, N.J.07512

Library of Congress Cataloging in Publication Data

Komesu, Okifumi, 1931—
The double perspective of Yeats's aesthetic.
Bibliography: p.
Includes index.
1. Yeats, W. B. (William Butler), 1865-1939—
Aesthetics.   2. Yeats, W. B. (William Butler), 1865-
1939—Philosophy.   3. Yeats, W. B. (William Butler), 1865-
1939—Knowledge—East.   4. Dualism in literature.
5. Polarity (Philosophy) in literature.   6. East and West
in literature.   I. Title.
PR5908.A35K65   1984   821'.8   84-14637

ISBN 0-389-20506-0

Produced in Great Britain
Photoset by Grove Graphics, Tring, Hertfordshire,
and printed and bound by Billing & Sons Limited,
Worcester

CONTENTS

ACKNOWLEDGEMENTS

The works by W. B. Yeats that are quoted in this volume are published by kind permission of Michael B. Yeats and Macmillan London, Ltd., and for North America by kind permission of Anne Yeats and the Macmillan Publishing Co. Inc., New York.

PREFACE

The question as to whether or not W. B. Yeats was a visionary poet has perplexed generations of his critics. Though recent criticism has shifted its focus from the topic, the question still remains unresolved. The difficulty of making a conclusive appraisal of an artist is frequently the measure of his greatness. Such an appraisal of Yeats is, however, problematical, for, in a sense, he invites obscurity and division by vacillating in his own convictions and by shifting emphases in his underlying philosophy. Concerning the question, for instance, as to whether or not he believes in what he says in his visionary document, *A Vision*, he says:

To such a question I can but answer that if sometimes, overwhelmed by miracle as all men must be in the midst of it, I have taken such periods literally, my reason soon recovered; and now that the system stands out clearly in my imagination I regard them as stylistic arrangements of experience comparable to the cubes in the drawing of Wyndham Lewis and to the ovoids in the sculpture of Brancusi. They have helped me to hold in a single thought reality and justice.[1]

A variety of conclusions have been drawn from such equivocation as this. Some critics declare the book to be no more than a catalogue of poetic metaphors while others regard it as a genuine apocalyptic document, replete with traditional ideas and symbols of visionary experience. Furthermore, Yeats's infatuation with Eastern mystical thought and art complicates the matter. Some critics find in his Eastern quest what amounts to an initiation into a totally new world of art and ideas, while others discern no more than a confirmation of his own beliefs.

This kind of equivocation, which Yeats makes throughout his works, is rooted in far deeper intellectual and aesthetic grounds than a mere love of mystification. At the base of his thinking there is a deep-rooted dualism — a dualism of a very sophisticated type. He is a dualist in the sense that he believes in antinomy as the basic principle of reality; he is a dualist in setting up two worlds in his universe — the world of names and forms and the world of unity;

7

he is a dualist in trying to be both a saint and an artist; he is a dualist in his belief in aristocracy and peasantry; but above all, he is a dualist in the very sense that he adopts a dualistic mode of thinking while maintaining monistic aspirations in his poetic endeavour. This double perspective characterises his aesthetic theory and his whole attitude as a creative artist. On the one hand, he envisages his work as an embodiment of a genuine aesthetic and spiritual experience; on the other hand, he is obsessed with the idea that a literary work can never free itself from abstract ideas. In other words, Yeats is concerned with the perennial question about the nature of art that has plagued Western artists and theorists for centuries: Is art cognitive or affective? Placed in this context, the above statement on *A Vision* becomes clear: Yeats was exercising both his cognitive and affective faculties in writing the book, and the book is meant to be both 'the map' and 'the country' of his universe — to borrow the expressions he used in his letter to his father.[2] In this context, his visionary aspirations and aesthetic claims become intelligible. His interest in Eastern thought and art should be examined in this context as well.

This two-part study of Yeats deals with the problem of the two conflicting perspectives that the poet maintained as a man and an artist. The first part, comprising Chapters One through Three, discusses the problem in the context of the poet's own development and against the background of the Western tradition; the second part discusses the significance of the poet's encounter with the East, particularly with Hindu thought and Japanese Noh aesthetic, in the light of his Western heritage. Those whose interest lies solely in the East-West relationship in Yeats's art and thought may proceed directly to Chapter Four. It is my belief, however, that the true significance of Yeats's schooling in Eastern thought and aesthetics can be understood better on the basis of the conclusions drawn in the first three chapters. Although I am not a whole-hearted believer in recent hermeneutical criticism, I do accept its thesis that understanding is historically situated and that any interpretation involves mediation. In the case of Yeats, the historical context in which he was situated was the Western intellectual tradition particularly in the pattern I have delineated in the earlier chapters. His interpretation of Eastern thought and aesthetics was mediated by assumptions derived from that tradition.

For the publication of this study I am deeply indebted to the kind encouragement given by Professor A. Norman Jeffares, who read parts of my manuscript.

Okinawa, Japan   Okifumi Komesu
December, 1982

1. INTRODUCTION

A question is frequently raised as to whether it is an experience or a knowledge that is derived by the reader from a literary work. The question is a radical one vis-à-vis the nature of art in general: Is art affective or cognitive; or to put it in another way, is art experiential or representational? If it is affective or experiential it demands an act of participation on the part of the audience in aesthetic or spiritual experience; if it is representational or cognitive it provides the audience with a knowledge, or challenges it to an interpretation, of some kind of order, be it society, humanity or eternity. The answer to this question is always ambivalent. One answer might follow Walter Pater's suggestion that it is aesthetic experience that matters in poetry or fiction; another answer might emulate Matthew Arnold's declaration that literary work represents a criticism of life. Yet again one answer might assert with William Blake the Vision of Eternity to be an embodiment of art; and still another might prefer Aristotelian universals of human action as the valid theme of art.

The ambivalence is perennial. It is as old and as new as literary theory and criticism themselves. It was Plato, the progenitor of the mimetic theory of art, who argued on the one hand that art was a (false) copy of nature, yet conceded that it was endowed with a magical power magnetising one reader after another like a loadstone attracts pieces of metal into a magnetic chain. In modern times Susanne Langer and Susan Sontag are proponents of the experiential theory of art, while a host of critics deriving their positions from structuralism and semiology are exponents of literature on cognitive grounds.

The polarity of perspectives represented by these divergent views of literature is inherent in the theory of art of the West and has served as the powerhouse out of which various theories of art have been generated. When the cognitive pole is predominant we find a theory of art which views literature basically as a genre with the object of understanding as its content, a quasi-philosophy. When, on the other hand, the experiential or affective pole has its sway, we have on our hands a theory which burdens art with the autonomous world of vision and experience. The classical theory of art, which placed art along with philosophy on one side and history on the other, heralded the cognitive theory of literature, while the Romantic theory, with its emphasis on feeling, represented the experiential theory. There is, however, a polarity of perspectives in either school. In fact, there is a definite tradition in the history of aesthetic theory of the West which represents an endeavour to reconcile the conflicting claims of the two theories. Thus we encounter in the writings of such neoclassicists as Dryden, Johnson, and Reynolds a persistent, if apologetic, appeal to 'delight' in aesthetic experience. Conversely, we find the Romantics falling back on intellect and 'powers of observation and description' as legitimate guides to creative success. W. B. Yeats was addressing himself to this tradition when he expressed his views on the secret powers of art in his much-discussed poem, 'The Statues':

> Pythagoras planned it. Why did the people stare?
> His numbers, though they moved or seemed to move
> In marble or in bronze, lacked character.
> But boys and girls, pale from the imagined love
> Of solitary beds, knew what they were,
> That passion could bring character enough,
> And pressed at midnight in some public place
> Live lips upon a plummet-measured face.

Here we have a position which concedes the formative role to abstraction (the object of understanding) in art while emphasising the role of passion for enticing the viewers into participating in the aesthetic experience afforded by the work of art. Yeats was an artist in whom the conflicting claims for art created an acute tension. This tension in turn fuelled his creative energy, and produced some of the finest poetic utterances of the century. His infatuation with Eastern mysticism and Japanese Noh Drama must be considered, along with his interest in various philosophical doctrines of the West, in the context of this tradition. Yeats was trying to create poetry informed by a genuine vision of history and reality, which, at the same time, would lead him and his reader to a spiritual liberation. But before we discuss the Yeatsian tension and reconciliation of, or failure to reconcile, the conflicting poles of aesthetic perspective, a brief survey of the tradition in which our poet may be properly placed is necessary. Such a survey must necessarily be selective, however, since a complete or even adequate treatment of the subject would demand a book in itself. Suffice it here to dwell on two notable instances in which the polarity manifests itself, namely, the mimetic theory of art represented by the classical and neoclassical school and the expressive theory represented by the Romantic school. Chapter Two will give a close attention to the topic, while the remainder of the present chapter will explain the theoretical framework for our discussion.

II

The mimetic orientation of art criticism, which dates back to classical times, finding its first theoretical formulation in the dialogues of Plato, is generally assumed to have dominated the history of literary criticism down to the eighteenth century and to have waited till the age of the Romantics to meet its rival theory. The theoretical basis upon which this historical view and the antithetical positing of the two rival positions stand is the belief, resulting from the dichotomous view of nature and the artist, that the so-called mimetic theory of art allows only a passive role for the artist while the Romantic theory stresses the role of the artist as an active creating agent. The analogues that these conflicting views of art have found for the role of the artist are the mirror and the lamp — a passive reflector of the objects of reality on the one hand and a radiant projector revealing, and even improving, the hidden secrets of reality on the other.[1]

This historical and antithetical view of art criticism provides answers to many questions about art and aesthetics in their historical perspective. However, it leaves unanswered some vital questions as well. How, for instance, would such a view treat the epistemological discrepancy that exists between the Platonic view that denies access to reality to the artist and the neoclassical view that holds that nature and wit are one and the same? Also, it would seem rather difficult to classify the neo-Platonists under the broad category of mimeticists. In fact, it would seem difficult, in my opinion, to include anyone except Plato himself in this category, as long as the dichotomy of nature and the artist remains central to the consideration of the question.

Plato alone strictly adhered to this epistemological creed in his assessment of the role of the artist; all the subsequent theorists professing allegiance to the Platonic doctrine of mimesis deviate from the doctrine one way or another. Plato may be said to have gone to the extreme on the possible spectrum of the critical views that contend that art endeavours to embody nature: he simply denied nature to art. By defining art as semblance-making (*phantastike*) Plato flatly denied the artist any access to the intelligible world. In his well-known attack on the artist in Book X of the *Republic* Plato berates the artist by declaring that the artist appeals to the baser part of the soul by working through the senses in his imitative act, thereby proving himself to be detrimental to the education of the youth in the ideal republic. The nobler part of the soul, the rational faculty of man, does not fall within the artist's domain. It is impossible for the artist, therefore, to know anything of true existence.[2] Strict fidelity to the Platonic doctrine of mimesis demands that this epistemological position be persistently maintained. Any retreat from this position would result in a deviation from the truly mimetic contention.

We see this retreat in Aristotle's *Poetics*. When he recognised the imitation of the universal as an end of art, Aristotle conceded to the artist much more respectable a status than Plato granted him — a status which was subsequently glorified by the Renaissance critics in their penchant for didacticism to the point where the artist came to enjoy supremacy over the philosopher for his ability to instruct people by presenting truth in a delightful manner. The status of the artist was exalted even higher by the eighteenth-century poets and critics who stressed the importance of poetic imagination by declaring that 'the basis of all wit is truth'. At this point the artist and nature achieved a perfect balance in their relative importance. From here it was only a small step to the Romantic concept of art which tipped the balance in favour of the artist in the dichotomy of nature and artist.

If the Platonic view of art occupies one end on the spectrum of aesthetic criticism in its denial to the artist of access to truth and nature, the neo-Platonic view goes to the other extreme. This it does not only by endowing the artist with the ability to imprint the forms of nature on the material of art but also by going so far as to equate the beautiful with the good, Beauty with the Supreme Deity, and in the case of Plotinus, even by obliterating the distance between the artist and the Supreme Deity, the One, through what he calls the Intellectual Principle. In the Platonic view of art the artist can never reach the realm of the Idea, whereas in the neo-Platonic view the artist is capable of achieving blissful union with the Supreme Being, that is, he can become the Idea itself.

The cardinal difference between Plato and Plotinus in their views of art arises out of the difference in their epistemological views as applied to art and the artist.

For Plato, the artist belongs to the sensible world and is primarily concerned with the appearances of things. Of the four ascending phases of knowledge in Platonic epistemology, the last and highest — the discursive understanding of mathematical truths and the intuitive and true knowledge of *eide* (*dianois* and *noesis*) — is found wanting in the artist. To him is accorded the lowest phase, *eikasia*, in which only the knowledge of sensory images is available. In the famous analogy of the carpenter and the painter of a bed, given in Book X of the *Republic*, the carpenter enjoys a position superior to the painter, since the object of his art, the bed, is a copy of the form created by God, which places him at two removes from God and truth, whereas the painter is thrice removed from God, as he, in painting the bed, makes a copy of the copy that the carpenter made of the God-created form. The painter occupies the lesser position, because he is engaged in the act of imitation of things not as they are but as they appear.

In the *Sophist* Plato sets up two modes of image-making. One is the making of likeness in which the imitator endeavours to produce a copy of the original in its true proportions and dimensions. Since this mode of image-making produces a likeness (*eikon*) of the original, it is called *eikastike*. The other mode of image-making is one that concerns those sculptors and painters whose main business is making their works appear true and not to make them correspond to the originals in their real proportions and dimensions. Since their effort is directed to the making of *phantasma* (semblance), their art is called *phantastike*. The semblance-making artist is not interested in things as they are. He would even resort to exaggeration and falsification in order to bring about a desired effect in his work. When he is working on an object of colossal size, for instance, he would make the upper part larger than it would be in the true proportion in an effort to avoid a diminutive impression on the viewer in relation to the lower part. The semblance-making artist, therefore, 'knows nothing of the reality but only the appearance'.[3]

Since the appearances of things fall neither within the domain of the discursive understanding of mathematical truths nor within that of the intuitive knowledge of the world of the Idea, but rather come under the control of the opinion and the feeling, they are necessarily restricted to the evanescent world of becoming. Nor is the artist's work conducive to the exciting of the soul for the pursuit of wisdom and virtue, as it appeals to the inferior part of the soul. The imitative artist's fault is thus two-fold: He is guilty not only of telling lies but also of impairing the reason by awakening and strengthening the feeling. 'Mimetic art, then, is an inferior thing cohabiting with an inferior and engendering inferior offspring'.[4]

The epistemological rating that the Platonic doctrine gives to the imitative artist is low indeed. The moral and political strictures on him as an undesirable member of an ideal republic are based on the epistemological views concerning the imitative art. Platonic epistemology would not allow a respectable place for the imitative artist in the ideal state.

It is clear, then, that Plato has the imitative artist utterly divorced from the world of true existence. The case is quite contrary with Plotinus. In the first place Plotinus considers the world of intelligence and the world of senses as a continuum. In the Plotinian system the whole of existence may be viewed as a gigantic river in which there are two currents flowing in opposite directions. The one flowing from the Creator (the One) constitutes the created world and the other is a regressive movement of that world to the source of creation. The two currents, however, are not separate existences. They are actually one current flowing from and toward God at the same time. Viewed in one way, it is a spiritual procession originating in the Supreme Deity and ending in the sensible world. In another way, it is an ascending movement of that spiritual procession consummating its reunion with the Supreme Being. The soul, which is part of this great procession, finds itself midway between the Spiritual World and the Sensible. In it are represented all metaphysical principles that control the entire spiritual procession emanating from and regressing to the One. In other words, the soul is a microcosm of the whole universe. It contains the last *logos* of the Spiritual World and the first *logos* of the Sensible World. By virtue of the former it participates in the world of intelligence; through the latter it works as an organising force to the world of senses. There is, however, no qualitative difference between the two *logos*, as they have their origin in the One. Sensation is not different from spiritual perception save in degree, for the fact of sensation is no less than evidence of the living unity of nature, a spiritual sympathy arising out of the awareness of the vital force embracing the whole existence (*Enneads*, 4–5–2).[5] Plato ruled out sense-perception as a path to knowledge in *Theaetetus*. Plotinus, however, has it as an active power of the soul occupying a legitimate position in the unbroken chain of perceptions leading from the lowest level of existence to the Supreme Being (*Enneads*, 4–6–3).[6]

Imagination, too, is not at all different qualitatively from the rational faculty of man. Again it is found midway between sensation and reasoning (*Enneads*, 4-3-30, 31). It borders on the realm of reasoning on one side and on the realm of sensation on the other. When there is an impact on the rational part of the soul from the spiritual world on which the soul borders, then the intellectual imagination will be set to work.

Thus there is a double feature in every phase of existence in the Plotinian system. This double feature is, in reality, a single feature. That is to say, when a person speaks of one feature he automatically speaks of the other feature as well. The soul proceeds from the One, yet remains in the one at the same time. It participates in the world of Intelligence and organises the world of matter at the same time, forcing the *logos* of the former on the latter. It proceeds from and participates in the Intelligible. It represents an eternal process of emanation and return.

The artist who engages in imitative work is promised a return to the One. Since all things in nature do proceed from the Ingelligible they have every claim for participation in the world of Intelligence. Arts, too, find themselves on the continuous procession from the One and therefore have a promise of return. Therefore, arts should not

be slighted on the ground that they create by imitation of natural objects; for to begin with, these natural objects are themselves imitations; then, we must recognise that they give no bare reproduction of the thing seen but go back to the Ideas from which Nature itself derives. . . . (*Enneads* 5-8-1).[7]

The artist is not a liar, as Plato would have him, but an active participant in the realm of truth and beauty. Any natural material touched by the hands of the artist is beautiful not in itself 'but in virtue of the form or idea introduced by the art'.[8] The form is inherent not in the material but in the mind of the designer before it is introduced into the material; 'and the artificer holds it not by his equipment of eyes and hands but by his participation in his art'.[9] The artist is neither a liar nor simply a holder of a mirror against nature, but an active participant in the Intellectual Beauty. Art is one way for him to return to the One from which he has proceeded.

From the foregoing it may be rightly inferred that for Plotinus there is no distinction between art, philosophy, and religion. The way of art is the way to the knowledge of true existence; and the way of true knowledge is the way of true religious experience. They are discrete modes that experience assumes as the soul goes through the phases of emanation and return in the continuous spiritual procession from and to the Supreme Being. Art therefore is by no means inferior to philosophy or religion in the attainment of the true knowledge and the vision of God. In the words of Plotinus:

> It is principle with us that one who has attained to the vision of the Intellectual Beauty and grasped the beauty of the Authentic Intellect will be able also to come to understand the Father and Transcendent of that Divine Being.[10]

It is clear that Plotinus stands in a position diametrically opposed to Plato in his views of art and the artist. The former unites nature and the artist while the latter severs them.

III

The difference between Plato and Plotinus in their views of art and its relationship to nature suggests the possibility of the following theoretical model for criticism of art. The dichotomy of nature and artist gives rise to the polarity of perspectives by which the role and weight that the artist enjoys in relation to nature are viewed. It is possible at one extreme of the critical position to envisage the world of art as basically a dualistic one in which nature is clearly out of the reach of the artist, whose work consists in the cognitive treatment of the things in nature. In this perspective the artist may or may not be a successful imitator. If he is endowed with the faculty whereby he may grasp the things of nature, he is a successful imitator; if not, he becomes a contemptible falsifier. Plato refused this gift to the artist. The neoclassicist in general granted it to him. This way of looking at art is characterised by a dualistic orientation in its metaphysical premise in which the intelligible world is set apart from the sensible. It is also characterised by an epistemological bias that views the role of the artist as being basically cognitive rather than creative.

At the other extreme we may place the Plotinian criticism of art which envisages the world of art as basically a monistic one in which the distance between the artist and nature is obliterated and in which the world of art is finally equated with the world of truth and the good. The artist here is not an imitative artificer confined to the sensible world, but a visionary who searches within, instead of looking without, for a vision of intellectual beauty and of the supreme deity. His world is not one of cognition within the subject-object framework, but one of experience where all epistemological considerations cease to have meaning.

These critical views are diametrically opposed to each other, having antipodal metaphysical and epistemological premises, which result in totally different emphases on the role and importance of the artist. The Platonic perspective of art criticism builds a wall around nature, which the artist finds hard to penetrate. The Plotinian perspective, on the other hand, gives all importance to the artist, who is not only endowed with the ability to imprint the forms of nature on the matter of the sensible world but is also capable of absorbing or being absorbed into nature itself. The former perspective is rationally and cognitively oriented while the latter has a strong mystical colouring. Any criticism of art, as long as it is based on the dichotomous view of nature and the artist, will find its position somewhere between these extremes. Some may lean towards the dualism and the purely cognitive perspective of Plato, and others towards the monism and the purely experiential pole of Plotinus. The degrees of their inclination determine the scope and weight of the artist vis-à-vis nature.

2. KNOWLEDGE OR EXPERIENCE

I

That Aristotle is an exponent of the mimetic theory of art is a commonplace of literary studies. However, how he differed from Plato in the epistemological consideration of the relationship of nature and the artist is not always made clear. That he re-defined the Platonic concept of imitation by bringing the object of artistic imitation from the realm of metaphysical forms down to the realm of human action has been repeatedly pointed out. Little has been said, however, about the implications that the difference in their epistemological views has for the concept of the artist held by these ancient philosophers.

Unlike Plato Aristotle maintained that individual perceptible things were real, that the whole process of cognition took place in the mundane world of the senses, and that the mind, through perception and reasoning, fathomed the essence of things. Thus the ground upon which the artist may make contact with the real states of things was prepared.

In *Nicomachean Ethics* Aristotle stipulates five states by virtue of which the soul knows the things of true existence. They are art, scientific knowledge, practical wisdom, philosophic wisdom, and intuitive reason. It is not necessary for our present purposes to go into detail for each of the five states mentioned. It may be helpful, however, to discuss scientific and intuitive reason together with art.

Scientific knowledge is the knowledge of things that are of necessity in the unqualified sense. It is the knowledge of things that cannot be other than what they are. The object of scientific knowledge, therefore, is subject to demonstration by induction or syllogism. Scientific knowledge is thus a state of capacity to demonstrate with the limitation that the starting points must be known before the conclusion is drawn. Since things that are of necessity in the unqualified sense are eternal, ungenerated, and imperishable, the object of scientific knowledge is invariable.

The starting points from which what is scientifically known follows are the object of intuitive knowledge. They are the first principles which are independent of demonstration and which have existence prior to and are the cause of the conclusion. The object of intuitive knowledge is also invariable.

If scientific knowledge and intuitive knowledge are concerned with things invariable, art is concerned with the variable. Included in the variable are things made and things done. Art is concerned with things made. Art thus is not concerned with the true states of being but with coming into being, that is, 'contriving and considering how something may come into being which is capable of either being or not being.'[1] Furthermore, art is not concerned with things that are or come into being by necessity, since these have their origin in themselves, and this means that they are not made. Thus the object of art is a product of chance, its origin being not in nature but in the mind of the maker. The object of art, however, is not in a state of chaos. It involves a reasoning process in the course of making, although that process is not inherent in the object itself but external to it. Art in the final analysis

is a state concerned with making, involving a true course of reasoning and lack of art on the contrary is a state concerned with making involving a false course of reasoning; both are concerned with the variable.[2]

Three things become clear from the discussion above. To begin with, art is not concerned with the Platonic forms but with the dynamic process in which things come into being; in other words, it is concerned with the universals of becoming. Secondly, art is a *logos* of making. Architecture, for instance, represents essentially 'a reasoned state of capacity to make'.[3] In other words, art represents the universals of artifice. Thirdly, art resides in the mind of the artist. This point is significant in that it dignifies the artist as the creating agent.

It may be well to keep these points in mind when one considers the theory of art that Aristotle develops in his *Poetics*, for although it is by no means an epistemological treatise but purely an aesthetic discussion, the *Poetics* undoubtedly subsumes Aristotle's views of knowledge.

In the first place, Aristotle confines the object of imitative art to the sensible world. It is not the Platonic forms that art imitates but 'men in action'.[4] This means that art must present the actions of men in the sensible world in a sensible way. It is for this reason that the plot is the soul of tragedy. Tragedy, says Aristotle, 'is an imitation, not of men, but of an action and of life, and life consists in action, and its end is a mode of action, not a quality'.[5] Now an action implies personal agents; and since their happiness or the reverse depends on how they act, tragedy must first and foremost be concerned with their actions, which come into being in the arrangements of the incidents, namely, the plot. 'Hence the incidents and the plot are the end of a tragedy; and the end is the chief thing of all.'[6] Thus Aristotle emphatically endorses art that presents men in a sensible way.

It should not be hastily concluded, however, that Aristotle, by restricting the imitative act of the artist to the sensible world, banished the artist from the world of real things. For Aristotle believed that individual perceptible things were real and the true knowledge of things as they are was available in the mundane world of the senses. Further, he believed that the instinct of imitation was deeply imbedded in human nature and that it was instrumental to learning especially in childhood. The pleasure that is derived from imitation is also attributed to the satisfaction that we feel in finding ourselves learning or inferring. Still further, Aristotle did not consider the series of events as things in themselves. They were the effect that premised a cause, actuality derived from potentiality.

The last point brings up the question of the universals in Aristotle's theory of art. There are two phases to this question. One is that which concerns the coming into being of action, that is, the particulars of men's action in life; and the other is that which concerns the coming into being of the object of art, that is, the creative process of art. Aristotle uses the analogy of art and the practical and the theoretical sciences to clarify the parallelism as well as the discrepancy that exist between them. Art and ethic are like nature in that their objects are produced in accordance with the logos proper to them. As natural objects are produced by nature through the necessary course of reasoning inherent in it, so are objects of art and action produced through a true course of reasoning inherent in each. Art, which imitates men's action, involves two analogous courses of reasoning, two parallel *logoi*, which in turn parallel the *logos* of nature.

Human action, which is the object of imitative art, is the product of the inherent qualities in individual persons. The internal qualities that individuals possess are natural causes from which actions spring. Thus it is possible in actual life to determine these qualities and the course of reasoning through which actions flow from them. It is this 'law of probability or necessity' that art imitates. 'It is not the function of the poet,' says Aristotle, 'to relate what has happened, but what may happen, — what is possible according to the law of probability or necessity.'[7] Thus it is clear that art is not a documentary treatment of the particulars of human action as history is but 'a more philosophical and a higher thing than history.'[8] The logos that binds the qualities and actions of men Aristotle calls the universal, which, it may be noticed, is the logos of human action, which properly falls within the domain of practical science. And this universality is what art imitates:

By the universal I mean how a person of a certain type will on occasion speak or act, according to the law of probability or necessity; and it is this universality at which poetry aims in the names she attaches to the personages.[9]

The analogy between ethic and nature is paralleled by another between art and nature. Art is like nature in the way it produces its objects, for the objects of art are produced through a certain course of reasoning analogous to that of nature. Art is not a passive reflector held up to nature in the Platonic fashion but an active force of creation. It is in this sense that it imitates nature. However, there is an important difference between art and nature. The internal cause of nature that produces natural objects is inherent in the objects themselves, while in art the cause that produces artistic objects is first in the mind of the artist as a form and subsequently imposed upon matter. Thus the cause is external to the object of art. Hence art involves not necessity as in scientific knowledge but chance as in practical wisdom.

The two phases of imitative art, discussed above, involving the logos analogous to nature, have, in my opinion, implications of vital importance to the essence of art and nature. For they place the artist in an ambivalent position vis-à-vis nature in terms of the imitative function that Plato makes so much of. Since the artist is concerned with the universal, he need no longer be seen as a debased corruptor of reason, pernicious to the spiritual well-being of the state. He could be a discoverer of the truths about human action and a propounder of the good. Granted that the kind of knowledge that falls within the artist's domain does not concern itself with things of necessity or with the first principles, it is nonetheless classed in the *Nicomachean Ethics*, together with scientific knowledge and intuitive reason, among the legitimate forms of true knowledge, and in the *Poetics* Aristotle considers art as more than a passive reflector of things and the artist as being gifted not with the faculty of perception alone but also with the rational and reflective faculty.

The artist, however, is not completely cleansed of the taint of being an illusion-maker. There are two counts on which one may be justified in calling the Aristotelian type of artist an illusion-maker. Firstly, Aristotle places the cause of the object of art in the mind of the maker. In order for the artist to be a dispenser of truth, it is mandatory that he be identified with the Creator himself, or the truth he embodies in the object will be only an illusion; and it is precisely the identity of the artist and the Creator that we find in Plotinus' theory of art. So long as he is distanced from the Creator, the artist cannot become a creator of the universal or the ideal beauty; he is at best an imitator of forms created by a transcendental deity. Secondly, the logos of art in Aristotle's theory is analogous to that of nature, but not identical. The logos, again, is in the mind of the artist and is external to the object of art. It has little to do with the reality of the object. Thus the logos of art is 'probability'; hence Aristotle's repeated emphasis on probable impossibility in preference to improbable possibility:

In general, the impossible must be justified by reference to artistic requirements, or to the higher reality, or to required opinion. With respect to the requirements of art, a probable impossibility is to be prefered to a thing improbable and yet possible.[10]

What the artist must adhere to is not the logos of nature but that of art. Even falsehood is justified as long as it is in accordance with the end of art:

If [the artist] describes the impossible, he is guilty of an error; but the error may be justified, if the end of the art be thereby attained. . . if that is, the effect of this or any other part of the poem is thus rendered more striking.[11]

The requirements of art are thus independent of those of nature. When they are in conflict art has priority over nature. Ignorance of some truths is venial with the Artist while lack of art is not. 'For example, — not to know that a hind has no horns is a less serious matter than to paint it inartistically.'[12] The important thing in art is not truthful presentation but plausible representation.

Thus the artist in the Aristotelian theory is not completely free from Plato's disparagement that he is a false artificer. The reasons are, to recapitulate, that (1) the *logos* of art is in the mind of the artist, and not in nature, and (2) the *logos* of art is external to the object of art, that is, it has nothing to do with the reality of the object.

We are forced, then, to draw conflicting conclusions about the nature of the artist. In the first place, the artist is confined to the sensible world, yet is capable of grasping the universal. This Aristotle establishes by positing the sensible and the universal as continuous in the framework of cause and effect. Secondly, the artist is an imitator of the universal, and yet he is a creator of the object of art. This second point cannot be logically established as long as the dichotomy of nature and the artist is maintained as a theoretical basis, for the universal of human actions, which is the object of imitation, is external to the artist and, for that reason, is the object of his knowledge and imitation; whereas the law of probability as the *logos* of art is within the mind of the artist and, for that reason, is inherent in him yet external to the object of his art. The identity of the opposites is not a logical possibility, but a mystical vision. In order for the artist-imitator and the artist-creator to be identical, and for the *logos* of human action and the *logos* of art to be one and the same, the nature-artist dichotomy must be abolished and the monistic view of art must be introduced. Being a dualist, Aristotle could not go so far. Thus the Aristotelian artist stands in the anomalous position of an imitator-creator.

II

In his *Essay Concerning Human Understanding* John Locke says: '*Reason* is *natural revelation*, whereby the eternal Father of light and fountain of all knowledge, communicates to mankind that portion of truth which he has laid within the reach of their natural facul- ties. . . .'[13] This statement, made in depreciation of enthusiasm, has been frequently quoted as an utterance representative of an age which showed strong aversion to the view of the universe that was based on mystery and divine inspiration, an age whose climate of opinion was enhanced so strongly by reason that even faith itself was 'entirely built upon ratiocination'. Historically speaking, there is no denying that Locke's attitude is typical of his age which had succeeded in banishing from nature the supernatural in both its divine and diabolical forms and which was now intent on sanctifying nature as God's work in which they found a rational order. The scientists of the sixteenth and seventeenth centuries, who were also pious men, some being clergymen, played an all-important role in deifying as well as rationalising nature.[14] They believed, partly in a defensive attempt to justify their scientific scrutiny of nature in fear of committing the sin of curiosity, that they were doing the greatest service to God by studying his work, which to them was as pious a pursuit as the study of his word. The scientists of the sixteenth and seventeenth centuries thus brought forth a new nature, divested of all its mysterious qualities and sanctified anew as another sacred book containing divine wisdom. Nature thus divested and thus sanctified was at once the external object of scrutiny and cognition and the holy realm of truth, good, and beauty to which men aspired. The matter of religion thus came to be placed on a rational basis.

The significance of Locke's statement quoted above, however, has a totally different bearing when put in the context of the aesthetic aspirations of the poets and critics of the age. For what Locke advocated was to internalise nature and the divine instead of externalising them as the objects of scientific scrutiny and cognition as his predecessors had done. To be sure, he attacked enthusiasts in the genuine spirit of reason, and he viewed revelation rationally. But he urged that we look within, not without, for God. In Chapter Ten of Book Four in *An Essay Concerning Human Understanding* Locke says that while God admittedly has given us no innate ideas of himself, he has furnished us with those faculties our minds are endowed with, so that to demonstrate

that we are capable of *knowing*, i.e. *being certain* that there is God, and *how we may come* by this certainty, I think we need go no further than *ourselves*, and that undoubted knowledge we have of our own existence.[15]

The rational mind of man is perfectly capable of grasping the secrets of the divine without mediation.

The internalisation of the divine, or the deification of the inner faculties of man, is a crucial theme with the neo-classicists, and that put them in a peculiar dilemma in their aesthetic views. For the deification of the inner faculties of man is a corollary of the deification of nature; that is, the men of the neo-classical age thought that if there was a rational order in nature, then man, whose position was to be found in the great chain of being, must also be rational. Coupled with this is the derivation of their aesthetic views from the classical sources, which made them firm believers in imitation as the main function of art. In this connection they held the artist in rather low esteem — lower, perhaps, than their classical authorities held him, for they reduced him to a state of being an imitator of not only nature but also the classical writers whom Plato disparaged for being falsifiers. On the other hand, the neo-classicists exalted the status of the artist much higher than the classical theorists had by endowing him with the faculties with which he could come into direct contact with nature. The artist-imitator is a mere mimic who follows, selfless, the standards inherent in nature and the models set by the classical writers, while the exalted artist is a possessor of wit capable not only of revealing truth in nature but, frequently, of improving it. Thus Dryden says in his 'Essay of Dramatic Poesy': 'A serious play . . . is indeed the representation of Nature, but 'tis Nature brought up to an higher pitch'.

Another factor that led the neo-classicists to the dilemma of the artist-imitator/exalted artist is their respect for nature as the all-important standard for art and their simultaneous reverence of the ancients, who they believed represented nature faithfully. On the one hand, by deifying nature and the ancients simultaneously they reduced their own status as poets to that of mere mimics. On the other hand, by equating nature and the ancients' poetic genius they almost deified the latter. Thus we hear from Pope:

> Those Rules of old discover'd, not devis'd,
> Are Nature still, but Nature methodiz'd,
>
> Nature and Homer were, he [Virgil] found, the same.
>
> Learn hence for ancient rules a just esteem;
> To copy nature is to copy them.
> ('An Essay on Criticism.' ll. 88–9, 135, 139–40.)

It is not very difficult, however, for this idealised state to be extended to the moderns also, for Pope concedes that

> If, where the rules not far enough extend,
>
> Some lucky Licence answer to the full
> Th' intent propos'd, that Licence is a rule.
> (*Ibid.*, ll. 146, 148–9.)

It was not the ancients alone that grasped nature successfully. Dr Johnson speaks in a similar vein when he praises Shakespeare for being an original poet:

Shakespeare, whether life or nature be his subject, shews plainly, that he has seen with his own eyes; he gives the image which he receives, not weakened or distorted by the intervention of any other mind. . . .[16]

The neo-classicists' attitude to the ancients is curious indeed. They are at once respectful and sceptical toward their authorities. Dryden, also, had shown a similarly mixed attitude, though in a different context, by saying:

I grant you, that the knowledge of nature was the original rule; and that all poets ought to study her, as well as Aristotle and Horace, her interpreters. But then this also undeniably follows, that those things, which delight all ages, must have been an imitation of Nature.[17]

Dryden, who was sceptical about the infallibility of the ancients, was a staunch believer in the progress of poetry. Reflecting the spirit of an age which believed in progress, Dryden wrote:

I hope I shall not be thought arrogant when I enquire into their [the ancients'] errors. . . . and I profess to have no other ambition in this Essay, than that poetry may not go backwards, when all other arts and sciences are advancing.[18]

Dryden's scepticism of the classical authorities is so deep that he even goes so far as to deny Plato's basic creed by declaring boldly that the artist's task is to make semblances of nature so as to satisfy his premeditated effect. 'To take every lineament and feature', wrote Dryden in his 'Defence of an Essay of Dramatic Poesy',

is not to make an excellent piece, but to take so much only as will make a beautiful resemblance of the whole; and, with an ingenious flattery of nature, to heighten the beauties of some parts, and hide the deformities of the rest.[19]

A similar position is taken by Dr Johnson when he approves of Shakespeare's breach of unities. He wrote in 'Preface to Shakespeare':

Delusion, if delusion be admitted, has no certain limitation; if the spectator can be once persuaded, . . . he is in a state of elevation above the reach of reason, or of truth, and from the heights of empyrean poetry, may despise the circumscriptions of terrestrial nature. There is no reason why a mind thus wandering in extasy should count the clock, or why an hour should not be a century in that calenture of the brains that can make the stage a field.[20]

This is a far cry, one must admit, from the classical concept of mimesis. Of course, Johnson repeatedly pleads for 'just representation of general nature'[21] and Dryden, too, grants that he knows 'no other foundation of dramatic poesy than the imitation of nature',[22] but they concede to the artist far more ground than the classical authorities did in the nature-artist dichotomy. In fact, their attention is directed more frequently to the psychic effect that the artist achieves on the audience than to the imitation of nature.

The neo-classicists dignified the artist considerably in the nature-artist dichotomy. It is only just however, to say that their aesthetic belief was basically dualistic. The imitation of nature was still the main function of the artist; the aesthetic experience of the artist had not become a matter of their consideration; and the value of art was primarily cognitive, although the affective value was also beginning to be recognized. The extinction of the distance between nature and the artist was yet to be achieved. Nevertheless, a tendency toward the monistic-experiential view of art is evident in the neo-classicists' effort to merge wit with nature, in their faith in the imaginative faculty of the artist, and in their growing interest in the affective element in art.

III

To begin the discussion of the Romantic tension of conflicting claims for literature by taking up Sir Joshua Reynolds's *Discourses on Art* may appear somewhat extraordinary especially to those who remember that the *Discourses* suffered a scathing attack from William Blake. The *Discourses* are of interest, however, because we can trace in them the evolution of ideas on art in a mind representative of the generation immediately preceding the Romantics. In Reynolds we can see a clear shift of interest from the cognitive view of art to the experiential. In his earlier Discourses Reynolds focussed his interest on the rational principles through which ideal art is created; in the later Discourses he shifted his interest to the emotional appeal that art makes to 'the sparks of divinity which we have within',[23] or the faculty of imagination.

The shift does not mean, however, the total abandonment by Reynolds of his earlier position. It indicates, rather, a shift of emphasis within the polarity of aesthetic perspectives which he maintains throughout the *Discourses*. When he takes a cognitive point of view he considers art reducible to a set of certain principles which may be acquired by the student of art through experience and education; when he takes an experiential or affective viewpoint, on the other hand, he elevates art to the realm of divine inspiration which transcends the mundane confines of discursive reason and empiricism. The polarity of perspectives in Reynolds's theory of art has vexed his critics. William Blake, for instance, oblivious of his own polarised aesthetic views, violently attacked Reynolds in his marginalia on the *Discourses* writing: 'All Equivocation & Self-Contradiction!'[24]

In Discourse III (1770) Reynolds discusses what he calls 'the Grand Style'. He begins by denigrating the neoclassical emphasis upon imitating nature as the only valid approach to art. The student of art who has passed an initiate's stage of education must be told, Reynolds says, that 'a mere copier of nature can never produce any thing great', for nature is gross and needs to be improved by the artist with 'the grandeur of his ideas'.[25] It might seem that Reynolds is here demolishing the whole classical theory of art by privileging the artist at the expense of nature, but we soon discover that this is not the case. In the first place, what he means by nature is not Platonic forms, but the external nature subject to sense perception which the Romantics were subsequently to glorify. Conversely, the grand ideas which, in his view, go to produce ideal beauty are abstract principles which are akin in a curious way to Platonic forms.[26] In these grand ideas, however, we meet the polarity of Reynolds's aesthetic perspectives.

The grand ideas the artist must have in order to create an ideal beauty in art do not wholly originate in the artist. They are both heavenly and earthly in origin. There are two ways to arrive at these ideas. One way is to deduce them from the ideal beauty, which is 'a gift of heaven'. According to the ancients, Reynolds says, 'the artist is supposed to have ascended the celestial regions, to furnish his mind with this perfect idea of beauty'.[27] In this creed the moderns are in perfect accord with the ancients. Reynolds puts it enthusiastically: 'Such is the warmth with which both the Ancients and Moderns speak of this divine principle of the art'.[28]

Reynolds hastens to caution his readers, however, against the danger of excessive enthusiasm which 'seldom promotes knowledge'[29] and may even deter the progress of the artist. There is one way to avoid the danger. That is to reduce the ideal beauty to practical principles; and here is the other way to come at the grand ideas, since arriving at the practical principles means for Reynolds abstracting 'the general nature' out of mundane particulars. This abstraction makes a work of art grand. For Reynolds particular forms of nature are deformities that lack permanent character. By transcending these particularities art can enter into the realm of the permanent and ideal: 'the whole beauty and grandeur of art consists in being able to get above all singular forms, local customs, particularities, and details of every kind'.[30] Here Reynolds may mislead the reader into thinking that he is redeeming himself as a classicist. But he is speaking as an empiricist, because 'the general nature' is to be sought through experience on earth, not through the reasoning process, nor, for that matter, by the flight of imagination:

This great ideal perfection and beauty are not to be sought in the heavens, but upon the earth. They are about us, and upon every side of us. But the power of discovering what is deformed in nature, or in other words, what is particular and uncommon, can be acquired only by experience. . . .[31]

This means that a long period of laborious study and comparison of natural forms is required of the artist who aims at the grand style. 'By this means, he acquires a just idea of beautiful forms; he corrects nature by herself, her imperfect state by her more perfect.'[32] This passage and the one preceding it provoked a violent reaction from William Blake, who wrote in his annotations to the *Discourses* 'A Lie!' and 'A Folly!', and protested that 'Knowledge of Ideal Beauty is not to be Acquired'.[33]

The greatness of art thus lies, according to Reynolds, in an abstract idea that it embodies. This, however, is only half the story. Throughout the *Discourses* Reynolds alludes to the appeal of art to sensibility and imagination. Even in as early a Discourse as the Fourth (1771) he opens his discussion with: 'The value and rank of every art is in proportion to the mental labour employed in it, or the mental pleasure produced by it',[34] and again remarks: 'The great end of the art is to strike the imagination'.[35] There is a growing awareness in his mind of the significance of imagination as he progresses through the Discourses. In Discourse VII he comes to incorporate the imaginative faculty into the notion of nature, viewing it as a crucial part of the search for the ideal beauty:

My notion of nature comprehends not only the forms which nature produces, but also the nature and internal fabric and organization, as I may call it, of the human mind and imagination.[36]

Thus we hear him say further in this Discourse: 'Whatever pleases has in it what is analogous to the mind, and is, therefore, in the highest and best sense of the word, natural'.[37] And we also hear: 'All arts have means within them of applying themselves with success both to the intellectual and sensitive part of our natures'.[38]

It is in Discourse XIII, however, that we meet Reynolds's radical shift of emphasis. Here he definitely elevates imagination above the rational faculty, linking up with the maturer form of Romantic poetics. In this Discourse he observes that 'the fundamental ground' common to all arts is 'that they address themselves only to two faculties of the mind, its imagination and sensibility'.[39] This is quite a remove from his position in Discourse VII where he placed sensibility side by side with intellect as twin faculties to which art addresses itself. It is certainly a far cry from his creed in Discourse III in which he proudly announced that he had reduced the idea of perfect beauty to general principles and concluded that recourse to principle is the only guarantee against the danger of obscurity in the study of art. In Discourse XIII Reynolds has clearly come to believe that imagination is superior to reason, which is only partial in its grasp of truth. Imagination, on the other hand, is a direct path to truth.

Perhaps Reynolds's most unclassical idea is to be found in his view of how art appeals to imagination. The object of art, he declares, is 'to accommodate itself to all natural propensities and inclinations of the mind'.[40] And this it does, most significantly, by deviating from nature and by creating its own autonomous world. Plato is mistaken, Reynolds believes, when he 'speaks of painting as only an imitative art, and that our pleasure proceeds from observing and acknowledging the truth of the imitation'.[41] Plato, of course, said that art was incapable of imitating nature on the ground that it failed to appeal to reason. Reynolds's criticism of Plato therefore misses the point; it nevertheless reveals his new belief, that art is not concerned primarily with truth and knowledge but with the affective part of the mind.

If art does not imitate nature, then it creates its own coherent world in order to gratify the propensity in man's mind that craves for a sense of unity. Thus anticipating Coleridge's idea of 'Multëity in Unity', Reynolds proposes that the principle of beauty is the 'sense of congruity, coherence, and consistency'. This means in a work of art 'an agreement of the parts among themselves that one uniform whole may be produced'.[42]

Reynolds has come a long way, we must acknowledge, from his earlier neo-classical position. His new position envisages art essentially experiential in nature addressing itself to the emotive faculty of the mind. It is too soon, however, to explain him away as a Romantic convert. His empirical turn of mind is still at work in the formulation of his new aesthetic ideas. For though Reynolds holds imagination superior to reason for its immediate attainment of the knowledge of truth, it is not this faculty alone that makes this attainment possible. There is a whole mass of accumulated experience which goes into the exercise of this faculty; and it is 'this mass of collective observation'[43] that Reynolds values more than the slow fragmentary working of discursive reason. Reynolds's interest here seems to lie more in destroying the old bastion of the Cartesian rationalism than in building a new pedestal for imagination. Moreover, the refined taste to which the ideal beauty addresses itself in a work of art is not God-given; it is 'the consequence of education and habit'.[44]

Thus emerges as the base of Reynolds's new aesthetic theory a dualism — a dualism that makes art both experiential and cognitive. Art is a world of its own, organic and coherent, whose existence is justified solely by its function of gratifying the emotive faculty of the mind; yet its appeal is directed to the refined taste cultivated by education and to the imaginative faculty sharpened by experience. Such art is superior to fact-laden history, and has a dignity that reaches 'almost', Reynolds contends, to 'divinity'.[45]

Reynolds's *Discourses* were severely attacked by William Blake. Although this attack on Reynolds was biased by Blake's bitter sentiment against the establishment under which he spent his breadless youth, and the reader is expected to read 'Nothing but Indignation & Resentment', there is a genuine line of argument in his criticism which stems from the fundamental differences that lie between his ideas and Reynolds's, especially in the earlier Discourses. Blake felt most inimical to those views of Reynolds's expressing the empirical spirit of the age, which, in Blake's eyes, had come under the domination of 'a Philosophy of Five Senses' as 'Urizen wept and gave it into the hands of Newton and Locke'.[46] The practical principles for art which Reynolds abstracted from the particulars of nature and from the works of the predecessors were, to Blake, simply non-existent. Even if they existed, they would not be something that can be taught or acquired through an empirical process.

Blake loathed the spirit of passivity which lay at the base of all empirical thinking. By turning man's mind into a passive receptacle of perceptions, empiricism grounded knowledge in memory, thereby severing man from attaining a vision of the eternal world. Ideas obtained through memory are confined to this world and they must be distinguished, as in Swedenborg's philosophy,[47] from true wisdom. True wisdom is to be obtained only by imagination, which is the source of all being, and not by memory which is confined to the past. As the knowledge of a country one has visited can never enable him to obtain a knowledge of an unvisited country,[48] so memory is incapable of giving man a true vision of eternity which lies beyond the world of memory and mundane experience.

Cold principles attained from memory through an empirical process become pernicious in the hands of the would-be guardians of art, who prove to be destroyers of imagination and the eternal world.

> These are the destroyers of Jerusalem, these are the murderers
> Of Jesus, who deny the Faith & mock at Eternal Life,
> Who pretend to Poetry that they may destroy Imagination
> By imitation of Nature's Images drawn from Remembrance.[49]

In order to save poetry from the hands of the empiricists, 'the rotten rags of Memory' and 'all that is not Imagination' must be cast off.

Blake's violent reaction against empirical abstraction and generalisation is a corollary of his epistemological beliefs. He believed (1) that the knowledge of eternity is immediate; it is innate with man; and (2) that all knowledge is concrete; it rests with the particulars of our sensible world.

Immediacy of knowledge is paramount in Blake's epistemological creed. Knowledge is 'Con-Science or Innate Science'[50] with which men are born; it is not to be obtained empirically, nor is it hidden in the Platonic cave. In his annotations to Bishop Berkeley's 'Siris' he writes:

Knowledge is not by deduction, but Immediate by Perception or Sense at once. Christ addresses himself to the Man, not his Reason. Plato did not bring Life & Immortality to Light. Jesus only did this.[51]

This annotation is given to a passage in Section 303 of Berkeley's essay. It is worth quoting Berkeley at greater length than the point which Blake deals with in order to see the implications of his reaction:

Though harmony and proportion are not objects of sense, yet the eye and the ear are organs which offer to the mind such materials by means whereof she may apprehend both the one and the other. By experiments of sense we become acquainted with the lower faculties of the soul; and from them, whether by a gradual evolution or ascent, we arrive at the highest. Sense supplies images to memory. These become subjects for fancy to work upon. Reason considers and judges of the imaginations. And these acts of reason become new objects to the understanding. In his scale, each lower faculty is a step that leads to one above it. And the uppermost naturally leads to the Deity, which is rather the object of intellectual knowledge than even of the discursive faculty, not to mention the sensitive. There runs a chain throughout the whole system of beings. In this chain one link drags another. The meanest things are connected with the highest.[52]

Although it has an admittedly Platonic (neo-Platonic, more correctly) tone throughout, the passage does not discuss the Platonic Forms, nor is it right, as T. E. Jessop argues, to read any of the sections of 'Siris' as an acceptance by Berkeley of the Platonic concept of transcendental Forms. Blake's charge, therefore, is not fair to Berkeley, but it reveals his animosity to the slightest intimation of support of the Platonic Forms.

Thus there is nothing transcendental about the knowledge of the eternal world in Blake's view. This knowledge comes immediately through imagination; rather, it is one with imagination: 'This world of Imagination is the world of Eternity'.[53] Strictly speaking, there is no place for cognition in Blakean epistemology. The eternal world does not exist as the object of cognition in Blake's monistic universe. The Minute Particulars, in which the eternal world is revealed, man and eternity itself finally merge into one existence: 'General Forms have their vitality in Particulars, & every Particular is a Man, a Divine Member of the Divine Jesus'.[54] Such is the Blakean immediacy of knowledge; it is a vision, or rather an experience of the eternal world of unity, or 'the Divine Humanity who is the Only General and Universal Form/ To which all Lineaments tend & seek with love & sympathy'.[56]

The eternal realm of 'the Divine Humanity', however, is not a completely monistic world. In it each individual spirit maintains its own identity: 'In Eternity one Thing never Changes into another Thing. Each Identity is Eternal'.[57] This pluralism is also carried into Blake's idea of the Minute Particulars, the earthly reflections of the Divine Humanity. Hence his emphasis on the details of the sensible world around us as the key to our true knowledge. 'All knowledge is Particular', says Blake in his annotations to Reynolds's *Discourses*.[58] The knowledge of the eternal world, he maintains comes from the details of our ambient reality, not from the transcendental Platonic Forms nor from non-existent abstractions of the empiricists.

The Minute Particulars that Blake emphasises as the sources of true knowledge are also the proper domain of art. The correspondence between 'the Divine Humanity' and 'the Minute Particulars' has its parallel in art which embodies a vision of eternity in sensible representations of the Particularities of external reality. Now, to Blake, 'vision' is a living embodiment of eternity itself. It is different from 'Allegory' or 'Fable' which is formed out of memory, a lifeless replica. Vision is the eternal world as it exists unchangeably;

it is 'surrounded by the daughters of Inspiration'.⁵⁹ It is a world
singularly experiential in nature. It is to this vision that art addresses
itself. Lamenting the degenerative tendency of his own profession
of painting which lapses into allegorical representation of ephemeral
substances, Blake makes his point in a vehement rhetorical question:
'shall Painting . . . not be as poetry and music are, elevated into
its own proper sphere of invention and visionary conception?' The
answer, of course, is an emphatic yes: 'Painting . . . exists and exults
in immortal thoughts'.⁶⁰ Blake was especially keen about his own
vocation as a visionary artist. In 'A Vision of the Last Judgment'
he writes: 'The Nature of my Work is Visionary or Imaginative; it
is an Endeavour to restore what the Ancients call'd the Golden
Age'.⁶¹

The Golden Age or eternity, or sublimity in terms of art, is the
proper theme of the arts. This eternal theme is brought to men by
the artist in such concrete forms as characters in fiction and visible
forms in painting. The artist who reaches to the sublimity of eternal
world can create forms that transcend the mundane confines of
temporal world. Chaucer's pilgrims, for example, 'are the characters
which compose all ages and nations . . . for ever remain unaltered
and consequently are the physiognomies of lineaments of universal
human life, beyond which Nature never steps'.⁶²

Blake is never for a moment sceptical about particular forms as
Yeats is. 'Every Minute Particular is Holy', he writes in *Jerusalem*.⁶³
Again in his annotations to Reynolds's *Discourses* he writes: 'Minute
Discrimination is not accidental. All Sublimity is founded on Minute
Discrimination'.⁶⁴ What makes art grand, therefore, is not general
principles as Reynolds insists, but the artist's actual execution:
'Mechanical Excellence is the Only vehicle of Genius'.⁶⁵ The
business of the sublime artist is to create clear lineaments of concrete
artistic forms and features which are capable of serving as the
receptacles of sublime beauty. A vision is not something obscure or
vague; it is a form which is concretely organised and distinctly
articulated. In 'A Descriptive Catalogue' of his own work, Blake
comments: 'The painter of this work asserts that all his imaginations
appear to him infinitely more perfect and minutely organized than
any thing by his mortal eye. Spirits are organized men'.⁶⁶ Thus the
monistic world of eternal liberty and sublimity in which everything
is united finds its expression in the form of art in which Minute
Particulars of the sensible world are clearly delineated and structured.

The polarity of perspectives in Blake's view of art is discernible,
though not as conspicuous as it is in Reynolds's because the opposing
poles are subtly reconciled. He adopts a monistic view vis-à-vis the

vision of eternal world which art embodies. In this case, eternity, man and art merge into a single existence: 'The Eternal Body of Man is The Imagination, that is, God himself . . . It manifests itself in his Works of Art (In Eternity All is Vision)'.[67] The statement in the parentheses is of special interest, since it reveals Blake's experiential view of art — art as a creation of vision in the Blakean sense, that is, the living embodiment of eternal world into which all souls merge.

On the other hand, Blake adopts a cognitive view vis-à-vis the work of art itself. The notion that the Minute Particulars, which are the only stuff of art, are to be distinctly 'articulated' and 'organized' is certainly cognitive in nature. Coupled with the idea of the Minute Particulars as sensible details of the world around us, the notion of organisation and articulation makes it mandatory that the artist be a keen observer of our sensible world and assiduous craftsman. Viewed in this light, Blake's criticism of Reynolds's strictures against servile copying becomes intelligible. In his annotations to Reynolds's Discourse II he writes: '. . . no one can ever Design till he has learn'd the Language of Art by making many Finish'd Copies both of Nature & Art & whatever comes in his way from Earliest Childhood'.[68] A good artist who advances in his knowledge of the world around him is a keen observer and a constant improver of his craftsmanship. In his annotations to Reynolds's work Blake seldom writes favourably, but the following passage which received his approbative note tells us what point could bring the two together:

He who endeavours to copy nicely the figure before him, not only acquires a habit of exactness and precision, but is continually advancing in his knowledge of the human figure.[69]

To this passage Blake notes: 'Excellent!'

Thus, to Blake, a work of art is a clear representation of the minute details of the world around us and a fruit of keen observation and study; yet at the same time, it is a vision of eternity where the distance between the observer and the observed is obliterated in 'the Body of Jesus' or 'the Body of Man'. The more accurate and precise the artist becomes in his execution the closer will he come to that vision, for 'when a Work has Unity, it is as much in a Part as in the Whole' and 'Living Form is Eternal Existence'.[70] The conflicting claims for art are thus subtly reconciled in the Blakean aesthetic.

IV

The Blakean reconciliation of the conflicting claims for art resulted, as we have seen, in religio-aesthetic monism, in which the tripartite constituents of art, artist and eternity finally merge. This monistic perspective on art and the world was entertained generally by the Romantics, with differing emphases on the interrelationships of those constituent elements. This perspective entailed, however, a host of problems to the artist, as it is essentially a religious perspective which has little to do with artistic creation. As Yeats was later to recognise for himself, the saintly vision of a monistic world in which the subject and the object merge into a mystical entity is difficult for the artist, concerned with the evanescent images of the world of conflict, to entertain. Two of the problems which faced the Romantic poets are of particular interest to us. One is the epistemological problem in relation to the world beyond, whether concerning eternity, nature, or truth. The other problem is an ontological one concerning the reality of the artist's created world.

Both of these problems stemmed from the cognitive basis of the Romantic theory of art, inherited from the neoclassical creed of mimesis. Since in the Romantic ontology the artist and the world beyond were identified or found on a continuum, there ought to be no grounds for cognition in the framework of subject and object. However, the Romantics, who, unlike the Noh dramatists of Japan or the latter-day Western aesthetic school of art for art's sake, could not entirely relieve themselves of the burden of imitating nature inherited from their predecessors, were haunted by the presence of nature and an urge to represent it through art. Pervading the Romantic discourses on art was their concern with nature and how man attains a knowledge of it. Wordsworth, who defined poetry as 'the spontaneous overflow of powerful feelings', elsewhere said: 'Poetry is the image of man and nature'[71] and is 'the first and the last of all knowledge'.[72] A more sophisticated utterance can be heard from Shelley, who thought, in a way reminiscent of Giambattista Vico, that language and poetry had their origin in man's perception of nature and his natural propensity to express his perceptions:

In the infancy of society every author is necessarily a poet, because language itself is poetry; and to be a poet is to apprehend the true and the beautiful, in a word, the good which exists in the relation, subsisting, first between existence and perception, and secondly between perception and expression.[73]

The Romantics' inability or reluctance to dispense with nature, or an eternal order of things, brought about two divergent ways in which the poet was regarded. One way was looking upon the poet as a seer who finds himself at the empyrean height surveying the universe and fathoming its hidden secrets; the other way was ennobling the poet as a creator gifted with powerful imagination with which he could create an autonomous universe of art which is as real as the world beyond. The artist as the seer faces the epistemological problem and must answer the questions as to how he sees nature and whether what he sees in nature is true. The artist as the creator, on the other hand, faces the ontological question as to the reality of his created world of art.[74] In either case the artist must take a stance a step away from the monistic view of art in which the distance between the artist and nature is obliterated and in which the artist as the knower is indistinguishable from nature, the known.

These divergent views of the poet were not, of course, clearly distinguished by the Romantics. Both views are found in the thinking of most Romantics, who believe in the poet now as the receptive seer and now as the active creator. Shelley, for instance, expresses his ambivalence toward the question in 'Mont Blanc' in which 'the everlasting universe of things' is given a status 'out there' as an amoral power controlling the whole mutable world of matter and the human mind; while, at the same time, the mind is given a status equal to nature 'Holding an unremitting interchange/ With the clear universe of things around'.[75] Shelley's idea of the mind is thus characterised by both empiricism and idealism.

The Lockean concept of the mind as a medium through which the things of the mechanically ordered universe flow is likened, in 'A Defence of Poetry', to an aeolian lyre which moves in the blowing wind to produce ever-changing melodies. As such it is nothing but a receptacle of external stimuli. And though it can accommodate itself to the motions of the wind to produce 'not melody, alone, but harmony' (i.e. Lockean complex ideas), it cannot create anything of its own. Shelley is unequivocal when he talks about the passive mind. In 'The Necessity of Atheism' (1811) Shelley says: 'The senses are the sources of all knowledge to the mind. . . .'[76]; and in 'A Refutation of Deism' (1814): 'Mind cannot create, it can only perceive. Mind is the recipient of impressions made on the organs of sense, and without the action of external objects we should not only be deprived of all knowledge of the existence of mind, but totally incapable of the knowledge of anything.'[77] This Lockean concept of the mind was subsequently modified upon Shelley's conversion to the Berkeleyan epistemology. Internal perception rather than external nature now received the main emphasis in Shelley's belief — a shift from materialism to idealism. The shift did not, however, cause any change in his idea of the poet as the seer. For, although he now confessed that he was 'unable to refuse [his] assent to the conclusions of those philosophers who assert that nothing exists but as it is perceived',[78] he reaffirmed that the mind 'cannot create, it can only perceive'.[79] Things exist as they are perceived by the mind, but they are not subject to the mind. Berkeley had introduced God as the continuing basis for things perceived in order to avoid the pitfall of phenomenalism, but Shelley persisted in his belief in the mechanistically ordered universe which has its own order of existence independent of the mind that perceives it. He writes in 'On Life':

The relations of *things*, remain unchanged, by whatever system. By the word *things* is to be understood any object of thought, that is, any thought upon which any other thought is employed, with an apprehension of distinction. The relations of these remain unchanged; and such is the material of our knowledge.[80]

Thus Shelley's new aesthetic doctrine trails a vestige of his earlier materialism.

Shelley, however, could not rest assured with the concept of the passive mind. His essays show considerable uneasiness on his part about explaining the mind away as a passive receptacle of external stimuli. In 'Speculations on Metaphysics', for instance, he argues to the effect that the distinction between thought and the objects of thought is largely a matter of words and that 'when speaking of the objects of thought, we indeed only describe one of the forms of thought — or. . . speaking of thought, we only apprehend one of the operations of the universal system [of being].'[81] And in 'A Defence of Poetry', while explaining the passive mind by the analogy of an aeolian lyre, he likens the mind to a fading coal which re-kindles as it receives air from the passing wind. The stimulus is external, but the 'power arises from within';[82] and though the poet is one of 'those who imagine and express this indestructible order' of things outside, his poetic creation is genuinely his own. The poet who creates a world of art from within is not isolated from the rest of the universe, however. He is a participant in 'the eternal, the infinite, and the one',[83] and is gifted with an extraordinary power to approximate the beautiful and the true in nature, which he expresses for the pleasure and benefit of his fellow men.

While it may be too harsh to attribute Shelley's ambivalent views of the mind to his confusion of opposing epistemological theories,[84] he may be rightly charged with not having worked out an adequate line of argument to justify what is nothing more than a common Romantic aspiration, i.e. to have the mind both active and passive and consequently to have the poet as both the seer and the creator.[85] Thus, without establishing a theoretical link between his epistemology and ontology, Shelley erects his Janus-faced figure of the poet-seer and the poet-creator. In the poet are combined the characters of both the legislator and the prophet; he is concerned with both the present and the future. The beautiful and the true he expresses through art become not only the true foundations of the present humanity but also the germs of its future institutions. In Shelley's own trope, 'Poets are . . . the mirrors of the gigantic shadows which futurity casts upon the present'.[86]

This double feature of the poet as seer and creator can also be seen in Coleridge, although the creative function, rather than the cognitive, gets a primary emphasis in his theory of imagination. In his reaction against the doctrine of association and the passivity of the mind in the school of Locke and Hartley, Coleridge depended heavily on German idealism, particularly the Schellingian version, to restore the mind to its sovereignty over the world of matter. However, he was never oblivious to the cognitive aspect of poetry. In 'Lecture II, 1811–1812' he significantly defines poetry as 'an art . . . of representing external nature and human thought and affections'.[87] This makes poetry basically a mimetic art, whether the object of imitation is internal or external. Again in 'Treatise on Method' he warns against excessive emotionalism in the appreciation of poetry: 'Those who tread the enchanted ground of POETRY, oftentimes do not even suspect that there is such a thing as *Method* to guide their steps. . . . Let it not after this be said that Poetry . . . is not strictly Methodical; nay, does not owe its whole charm, and all its beauty, and all its power, to the Philosophical Principle of Method.'[88]

More sophisticated utterances can be heard from Coleridge in Chapter XII of *Biographia Literaria*, in which he develops epistemological ideas borrowed from Schelling which are closely connected with Coleridge's definitions of imagination and fancy formulated in Chapter XIII of the book. The double features of poetic imagination arise out of the identity of subject and object in the infinite I AM and the consequent equation of being and the act of knowing. To Coleridge, as well as to Schelling, all knowledge arises out of the coincidence of an object with a subject. The subject, which is infinite, is a sentient being; and the object, which is finite, is nature which the subject perceives. They are, therefore, beings essentially opposed to each other. They are not, however, separate entities like mind and matter; they are rather antithetical aspects of one reality, the infinite I AM. When it acts subjectively to itself it becomes the infinite subject by 'constructing itself objectively to itself'; when it acts objectively to itself it becomes the finite object by furnishing itself with the ground of knowledge. Both these acts are coinstantaneous. Hence being and the act of knowing become identical, giving rise to the Coleridgean axiom: 'Sum quia sum; I am, because I affirm myself to be; I affirm myself to be, because I am.'[89] Imagination, which derives itself from this eternal principle of the infinite I AM, is man's faculty of perception and creation and is a repetition in the human mind of the kindred principle in the infinite I AM. We need not go into the familiar distinction that Coleridge makes between imagination and fancy or between the primary imagination and the secondary. Suffice it here to note that Coleridge's theory of imagination makes the poet both a seer and a creator. What the poet comes to know and what he creates are identical and are derived from the eternal world of God's creation.

The double features of the poet were also recognised by Wordsworth, though in a far less systematic way than by Coleridge. First, the poet-seer of the Wordsworthian brand takes the stance of 'wise passiveness' toward nature and receives unilaterally the teachings that she gives him. The 'lore' that nature gives him is sweet and genuine and brings him close to the heart of things. The poet who takes this receptive stance toward nature is the 'Seer blest'[90] who is endowed with a keener sensibility and a more powerful imagination than ordinary men and who has a strong sense of delight in the passions of the mind and in the kindred passions in the universe. He is an interpreter of nature, 'a man speaking to men'.[91] The imitative character of the poet is clear: it is required of the poetic seer to see things accurately and of the interpreter to tell the story truthfully, so much so that Wordsworth names 'the powers of observation and description' as the first requisites for the poet.[92]

If the poet is seer and interpreter, his proper concern would be knowledge, and the subject of his art truth. Despite his repeated affirmation that poetry is essentially affective, Wordsworth is constantly obsessed with the cognitive function of poetry and with the idea of truth that it represents. Thus, consenting to the Aristotelian conclusion that art is the imitation of the universals of humanity, he affirms:

Aristotle, I have been told, has said, that Poetry is the most philosophic of all writing: it is so: its object is truth, not individual and local, but general, and operative: not standing upon external testimony, but carried alive into the heart by passion; truth which is its own testimony, which gives competence and confidence to the tribunal to which it appeals, and receives them from the same tribunal. Poetry is the image of man and nature.[93]

Without a systematic epistemology or ontology matching Aristotle's, however, Wordsworth's endorsement of the Aristotelian aesthetic is no more than a superficial agreement. Wordsworth is responding to Aristotle's ideas in Chapter IX, 3 of *The Poetics* where Aristotle considers poetry superior to history on the ground that the former is concerned with the universals of human nature while the latter with the particulars. But then Aristotle's universals are grounded in the law of probability according to which men *may* act. Hence a probable impossibility is preferred by Aristotle to a thing improbable and yet possible. Furthermore, Aristotle grounds art not in nature but in the mind of the poet, for art, according to him, 'is concerned with coming into being, i.e. with contriving and considering how something may come into being'.[94] Wordsworth would want a firmer ground for art as we shall see presently. Nor would he endorse the thorough-going passivity of the Eighteenth Century empiricism.[95] In *The Prelude* the poet specifically denounces the empiricist position:

> No officious slave
> Art thou of that false secondary power
> By which we multiply distinctions, then
> Deem that our puny boundaries are things
> That we perceive, and not that we have made.
> (*The Prelude*, II, ll. 215–19).

The impulses that the poet perceives from nature are not the Lockean ideas imprinted on the tabula rasa of his mind, nor are they the passing winds that blow insouciantly on the Shelleyan wind harp. They are rather 'those first affections,/ Those shadowy recollections' of the immortal world from which

> Not in entire forgetfulness,
> And not in utter nakedness,
> But trailing clouds of glory do we come. . . .
> ('Intimations of Immortality', ll. 63–5)

By gaining knowledge from nature, the poet regains the selfhood of infancy that once participated in the eternal world of God. This union of knowledge and selfhood is not dissimilar to the Coleridgean equation of being and knowing or the Schellingian fusion of subject and object. The poet's knowledge is grounded in both nature and the mind of man; poetry is an embodiment of that knowledge in visible forms through which the mind and nature interact to create a new world:

> I remember well
> That in life's everyday appearances
> I seemed about this time to gain clear sight
> Of a new world — a world, too, that was fit
> To be transmitted, and to other eyes'
> Made visible; as ruled by those fixed laws
> Whence spiritual dignity originates,
> Which do both give it being and maintain
> A balance, an ennobling interchange
> Of action from without and from within;
> The excellence, pure function, and best power
> Both of the objects seen, and eye that sees.
>   (*The Prelude*, XIII, ll. 67–78).

Wordsworth's ennobling interchange with nature was branded as an 'egotistical sublime' and was flatly rejected by Keats, who in turn was characterised by Yeats, perhaps unfairly, as a schoolboy 'with face and nose pressed to a sweet-shop window', craving for but never attaining the true knowledge of the ideal world, creating, at best, a hollow image of that world in poetry.[96] At other occasions, however, Yeats looked upon Keats as a poet of vision[97] and as one capable of attaining a unity of being.[98] Yeats's ambivalent response to Keats reflects a similar ambivalence in Keats's poetry and aesthetic. In fact, of the Romantic poets we have been discussing, Keats perhaps comes closest to Yeats in feeling the acute tension caused by the conflicting claims on art and the artist which result from the polarised perspectives of cognition and experience.

Far from being a mere sensualist, as he is sometimes regarded, Keats was a poet, who, true to the Romantic tradition, was deeply concerned with the problem of knowledge. In his letter to John Taylor he wrote: 'I find that I can have no enjoyment in the world but continual drinking of knowledge.'[99] Although this statement is somewhat exaggerated in the light of his other utterances to the contrary, there is no denying that the question of knowledge has a crucial place in Keats's poetry and aesthetic. In *Hyperion*, Apollo, the god of poetry, attains divinity through a sudden influx of knowledge 'as if some blithe wine / Or bright elixir I had drunk' (*Hyperion*, III, ll. 118–9). In *The Fall of Hyperion* the poet's imagination is likened to divine omniscience:

> A power within me of an enormous ken,
> To see as a god sees, and take the depth
> Of things as nimbly as the outward eye
> Can size and shape pervade.
> (*The Fall of Hyperion*, I, ll. 303–6).

On the human level, too, knowledge is essential for a wholesome life. Keats believed that knowledge eases 'the burden of Mystery' by enlarging man's capacity for speculation and can bring him from the depth of ignorance by providing him with a wing upon which he would navigate the air and space of chaos. Even a knowledge of the traditional disciplines — one of which, medicine, Keats had studied previously — is conducive, he believed, to the progress of the poet towards perfection. Therefore he would not give up his medical studies.[100] The kind of knowledge that poetry is concerned with, however, is that of human nature. Poets are ever trying to enlarge this knowledge. There are two chambers of human life with which Keats says he is familiar, namely, the 'Chamber of Thoughtlessness' and the 'Chamber of Maiden-Thought'. Many people rest content in the first chamber, but poets move into the second chamber where they speculate about human nature and endeavour to widen the area of enlightenment, although they soon face the darkness that lies beyond the limits of their speculative power. Notwithstanding his unfavourable tendency toward the 'egotistical sublime', Wordsworth, Keats concedes, can be counted among the poets who challenge this darkness.[101]

In spite of his emphasis on the pursuit of knowledge, Keats takes a restrictive stance against its use in poetry. Knowledge should not be forced upon the reader. It is well for Wordsworth to advance his philosophical frontiers into the domain of darkness of human knowledge, but he must not, as poet, bully the reader into accepting his philosophy. Keats demanded poetry to be unobtrusive and selfless in what it offers to the reader; it should be no more than 'fine excess' in striking the reader, expressing, in a Popian fashion, the reader's 'own highest thoughts.'[102]

If poetry should remain unobtrusive, the poet is also expected by Keats to be selfless. 'A Poet is the most unpoetical of any thing in existence', says Keats in his letter to Richard Woodhouse, 'because he has no Identity — he is continually in for — and filling some other body.'[103] In a letter to John Hamilton Reynolds Keats again recommends a receptive stance in gaining knowledge. By a curious misappropriation of metaphor he endorses the receptive way of the flower which receives 'sap and dew' from the bee that flits from

flower to flower busily collecting honey. By this probably intentional
metaphorical misappropriation Keats turns the poet into both a
receiver and a giver, for if the flower buds 'under the eye of Apollo'
by receiving the bee's visitation, it also provides the honey of
knowledge that the restless insect covets. Knowledge thus blesses
both the giver and the receiver. By way of making the point, in the
same letter to Reynolds, Keats employs an erotic metaphor of man
and woman who are equally delighted in their sexual act. Keats's
criticism of Wordsworthian 'egotistical sublime' is rooted in his fear
that knowledge thus obtained might prove lethal to the object itself.
In *Lamia*, after asking 'Do not all charms fly/ At the mere touch
of cold philosophy', Keats answers:

> Philosophy will clip an Angel's wings,
> Conquer all mysteries by rule and line,
> Empty the haunted air, and gnomed mine—
> Unweave a rainbow, as it erewhile made
> The tender-person'd Lamia melt into a shade.
> (*Lamia*, II, ll. 234–380).

Truth and beauty are likely to be destroyed by the cold analytical
operation of intellect. The fear of complete fissure between subject
and object and the resultant death of the object is persistent not only
with Keats but with other Romantics as well. The fear is expressed
by Wordsworth himself in 'The Tables Turned':

> Our meddling intellect
> Mis-shapes the beauteous forms of things:—
> We murder to dissect.
> ('The Tables Turned', ll. 26–8).

The dilemma is inherent in the Romantic aesthetic itself, which
condones a dualistic subversion of its monistic aspirations by
reverting to the neoclassical creed of mimesis vis-à-vis nature and
the artist. Equally subversive is the dualism that exists in the
relationship between the artist and his created world. Since the work
of art is something that the artist projects out of himself, his very
act of creation subverts his monistic aspirations. This problem of
dualism is countered by some Romantics who insist on the
constitutive nature of literary symbolism. The work of art, according
to their view, is not a mere allegorical replica of nature, but a living
entity co-existent and co-extensive with nature itself, its generative
force being the imagination which is identical with the creative force

of nature. The merger of the tripartite constituents of art seems thus complete. This, however, is based on an optimism about the autonomy of the created world of art that is oblivious of the semiotic nature of artistic creation, for a work of art is a projection that stands for something, whether it is feeling, as Susanne Langer argues, or *différance*, as Jacques Derrida would have it. Any attempt to obliterate the distance between a work of art and what it stands for is bound to fail. The Romantic endeavour was no exception. Thus the Romantic artist comes full circle to face the problem of mimesis as Murray Krieger's wry trope of 'the mirror of the lamp' suggests.[104]

IV

The Romantics could not, however, afford reverting completely to the neoclassical position of mimesis as the main end of art. In order to counter such a lapse, attempts were made to advance an affective theory of art, of which Wordsworth's utterance in his 'Preface' of 1850 perhaps took the crudest form:

The poet writes under one restriction only, namely, the necessity of giving immediate pleasure to a human Being possessed of that information which may be expected from him . . . as a Man.[105]

This may be termed as an affective reduction of the cognitive view of literature; the epistemological correlative of the Romantic aesthetic is here absorbed into the emotive. Or we may call it a Romantic restatement of Horatian teleology. Wordsworth always gives priority to the affective feature of poetry against the cognitive. Although he names reason and imagination as the twin attributes that constitute nature's strength,[106] Wordsworth would have the latter qualify the former, so that

> he whose soul hath risen
> Up to the height of feeling intellect
> Shall want no humbler tenderness; his heart
> Be tender as a nursing mother's heart.
> (*The Prelude*, XIV, ll. 225–8).

In 'The Preface to the Poems 1815' in which he mentions as the first requisite for the poet the ability to observe accurately and describe faithfully, Wordsworth warns against the excessive use of this ability by emphasising the subjective qualities of the mind:

This power, though indispensable to a Poet, is one which he employs only in submission to necessity, and never for a continuance of time: as its exercise supposes all the higher qualities of the mind to be passive, and in a state of subjection to external objects, much in the same way as a translator or engraver ought to be to his original.[107]

Thus, poetry in which objectivity is qualified by subjectivity would turn truth into a 'visible friend and hourly companion' whose presence all human beings enjoy in a warm spiritual communion.[108] What Wordsworth wanted was a fusion of feeling and thought.

Coleridge, who admired Wordsworth for achieving 'the union of deep feeling with profound thought',[109] speaks for himself in a similar vein in a letter to John Thelwall: 'My philosophical opinions are blended with, or deduced from, my feelings; & this, I think, peculiarized my style and writing.'[110] The union of thinking and feeling has as its corollary the fusion of truth and vision, or the merger of subjectivity and objectivity. In a letter to Thomas Poole, Coleridge says: 'My opinion is this — that deep Thinking is attainable only by a man of deep Feeling, and that all Truth is a species of Revelation.'[111]

The merger of truth and vision derives its origin from Coleridge's idea of imagination as developed in *Biographia* as we have already seen. In adapting Schelling's idealism to his aesthetic, Coleridge emulated his master in ennobling the subjective world of imagination into the universal truth of nature by fusing the subject and the object in the infinite I AM. It is interesting in this connection to see how he adapts the Kantian aesthetic to his idea of beauty developed in 'Principles of Genial Criticism', where he plays down considerably the subjective and non-cognitive implications of Kant's concept of the beautiful. One of Kant's basic conceptions concerning the judgement of taste is that an aesthetic judgement does not lead to a cognition of the object because beauty is not mediated by a concept. From the second moment of the judgement of taste, according to Kant, the beautiful may be explained as 'that which pleases universally without a concept'.[112] In a judgement of taste, though the satisfaction in the object is imputed universally because it is disinterested, no inference of the logical is possible because it lacks mediation by a concept. Hence the validity of the beautiful is of a subjective nature and cannot give rise to a cognition of the object, and makes itself known only by means of sensation.[113] Thus, according to Kant, the Beautiful is characterised by a *'subjective universal validity'*.[114] The phrase aims to emphasise both subjectivity and inter-subjectivity and their peculiar relationship that the judgement of taste involves. But Coleridge, who borrows extensively from Kant's third *Critique*, emphasises the inter-subjective (communicable) nature of the Beautiful by grounding it, against Kant's contention, not in sensation but in 'intellect', while, on the other hand, making a half-hearted reference to the subjective nature of an aesthetic judgement by saying that though we *'expect'* others to share the judgement 'we feel no right to *demand* it'.[115]

Another discrepancy between Coleridge's idea of the Beautiful and Kant's arises from Kant's third moment of the aesthetic judgement. Beauty derived from this moment is defined as 'the form of purposiveness of an object, so far as this is perceived in it without any representation of a purpose'.[116] A purpose is that whose concept furnishes the ground of the object's possibility. Purposiveness means the causality of a concept in respect of its object. Now, since an aesthetical judgement rests on the subjective grounds which do not involve a concept whereby a cognition of the object is mediated, it refers the representation of the object only to the subject; hence the purposiveness involved in an aesthetic judgement is nothing else than a formal subjective purposiveness, namely a purposiveness without a purpose.

Coleridge grounds beauty in 'the perceived harmony of an object' or 'Multëity in Unity'. This organicist theory of beauty betrays the Kantian definition of beauty derived from the third moment. Coleridge attempts to distinguish the beautiful from the good, after the Kantian fashion, by the difference of purposiveness between the two. In the debate with the prejudiced Puritan, Milton, speaking for Coleridge, says:

The GOOD consists in the congruity of a thing with the laws of the reason and the nature of the will, and in its fitness to determine the latter to actualize the former: and it is always discursive. The Beautiful arises from the perceived harmony of an object, whether sight or sound, with the inborn and constitutive rules of the judgement and imagination: and it is always intuitive.[117]

Milton's argument seems to distinguish the good and the beautiful on the grounds of objective purposiveness for the former and subjective purposiveness for the latter. The distinction, however, does not quite hold. The ground for the good is indeed the external objective purposiveness in the Kantian terms, i.e., utility. However, the ground that Milton posits for his aesthetic judgement of the beautiful is a curious mixture of subjective purposiveness and what

appears to be internal objective purposiveness. As long as the judge-
ment is made in accordance with 'the inborn and constitutive rules
of the judgement and imagination', it rests on subjective grounds,
and beauty thus represented is without a purpose. Coleridge,
however, grounds beauty also in the harmony of the object, which
would require a concept in order to be perceived. In Kant's terms
the harmony of the object would be internal objective purposiveness,
i.e., 'the perfection of the object', particularly 'the qualitative
perfection' which presupposes a concept furnishing the rule for
combining the manifold.[118] Thus in Coleridge's idea of the beautiful
we see an attempt to combine feeling and intellect or affect and
cognition. The cognitive ground which Kant refused to the aesthetic
judgement was recognised by Coleridge as the legitimate ground for
the perception of the beautiful, linking it to the world of objective
universality.

The fusion of affect and cognition is also proposed by Shelley and
Keats, though in less sophisticated a manner than by Coleridge.
Shelley, who recognised the polarity of the perceptive and the
creative (or the polarity of the visions of the outer reality and the
inner reality), recognised another polarity in art and the artist —
the polarity of the cognitive and the affective. Similar polarities were
also recognised by Keats.

Poetry, viewed on cognitive grounds, is engaged in the imitation
or creation of reality; in either case its main emphasis is the cognitive
element of literature. On the other hand, poetry viewed on affective
grounds constitutes genuine psychic experience which abolishes the
dichotomy of subject and object or makes meaningless an ontological
inquiry into the created world of art. At this pole of affect, art is
what Yeats would later call 'the drowner of dykes that separate man
from man', and the artist is a sort of a medium who entices men
into the reverie of spiritual or aesthetic experience or a mystic who
achieves oneness with the world beyond or around him. Keats said
that imagination 'may be compared to Adam's dream' whose
'empyreal reflection is the same as human Life and its Spiritual
repetition'.[119] It is not by the way of 'the bald-head philosopher' of
Lamia but by the act of imagination that the truth of nature and
man is turned into a living wisdom. Similarly, Shelley believed that
poetry turns knowledge into feeling by 'defeating the curse which
binds us to be subjected to the accident of surrounding
impressions'.[120] The Lockean passivity of our minds is thus
abolished by poetry, which in turn 'creates for us a being within our
being' and 'compels us to feel that which we perceive, and to imagine
that which we know'.[121] Through poetry the cognitive world of

knowledge metamorphoses itself into an affective world.

The principle whereby this metamorphosis is achieved is that of love. 'True knowledge leads to Love', says Shelley in a prose fragment.[122] Love, defined by Shelley as 'a going out of our own nature, and an identification of ourselves with the beautiful which exists in thought, action, or person, not our own'[123] is an urge that men universally feel for a spiritual communion in which their whole nature is drowned,[124] and in which they are connected with the whole universe.[125] The poet satisfies this universal thirst for a spiritual communion by enticing men into reverie like a nightingale that enchants people with its sweet sounds or 'the melody of an unseen musician' that makes them 'feel that they are moved and softened, yet know not whence or why'.[126] The state of trance is one to which children are more susceptible than adults, but there are people who do not lose their susceptibility as they advance in age. Such people 'feel as if their nature were resolved into the surrounding universe or as if the surrounding universe were absorbed into their being. They are conscious of no distinction.'[127] These are the states of reverie which Yeats was to call the union of the self and the anti-self at Phase One and Phase Fifteen respectively. Shelley's rather naive monism, however, repelled the mature Yeats, who grew more and more sceptical about the possibility of such states and who became critical of Shelley for not having a vision of Evil.

Keats received a similarly unfavourable comment from Yeats for his naïveté, but his affective view of poetry was not without its scepticism. Although he called 'happiness' the perfect comprehension of life and reality attained through love in the Shelleyan sense of the universal urge for going out of individuality for a 'fellowship with essence',[128] it is questionable whether Keats believed in this fusion of cognition and affect and in the permanency of the poet's happiness. It is true that the poet of *The Fall of Hyperion* comes into possession of the divine power of sight and sits himself 'upon an eagle's watch' surveying the wide universe and forgetting nothing of what he sees. Further, the poet in 'Endymion' achieves his comprehension of the spiritual reality through union with Cynthia. Against these optimistic depictions of the poet, however, we also hear Keats's sceptical, if not pessimistic, utterances.

Although it could be argued that Keats lacked a robust vision of evil, as Yeats thought Shelley did, Keats had a deep insight into the depressing contrasts that life harboured. His insight is eternalised in those exquisite expressions which we find in his lyrics such as 'Ode to a Nightingale', 'Ode on a Grecian Urn', 'Ode on Melancholy', 'La Belle Dame Sans Merci', and so on.

The poet of 'Ode to a Nightingale' cannot immerse himself permanently in the reverie evoked by the sweet song of the blissful bird. At the sound of the terrible word 'Forlorn!' the poet is brought back into the mundane world of self and time — a reversal of Yeats's sudden breaking forth into a vision at the words 'The Second Coming'!

If Keats was sceptical about the perpetuation of the state of reverie that the poet endeavours to achieve, he was equally sceptical about the identity of art and reality. In a letter to Benjamin Bailey Keats says: 'I am sometimes so very sceptical as to think Poetry itself a mere Jack a Lanthen to amuse whoever may chance to be struck with its brilliance. As Tradesmen say every thing is worth what it will fetch, so probably every mental pursuit takes its reality and worth from the ardour of the pursuer — being in itself a nothing.'[129] 'Ode on a Grecian Urn' is a study on the relationship of art and the reality it represents. Here again is manifest Keats's scepticism as to the possibility for a work of art to become co-existent with the reality represented in it. The world of 'Cold Pastoral' of the Grecian Urn is made eternal in the realm of art, but as the world of living humans it is as dead and cold as can be. There is an impassable cleavage between the urn as a work of art and the sylvan community it represents. The inhabitants of the unknown community are consigned forever to the world of art and can never return to their original abode. The urn, however, can claim eternity on their behalf, for they are made part of the aesthetic world in which truth is nothing other than beauty.

The Keatsian equation of truth and beauty is one answer to the persistent question which obsessed the Romantic poets as to the possibility for art to mediate between knowledge and experience. It acknowledges, on the one hand, art's inability to produce a cognition of its object. It affirms, on the other hand, the universal validity of the world of art which transcends the temporal limitations of human experience so long as art remains on its own terms. It is only on the aesthetic grounds that art is possible; or the *logos* that sustains the existence of art is beauty. This awareness is similar in essence to Kant's conclusion that the beautiful leads to a subjective universal validity, though it does not produce a cognition of the object.

If truth is defined as that which has objective universal validity requiring a mediation by a concept, then there is indeed no place for truth in the Keatsian world of art. Keats secures art its permanence, however, by grounding its being in beauty. In this respect, Keats is less extravagant in his claims for art and more realistic in his conceptions of the role of the artist than other Romantic poets, who believed in the possibility of reconciling the conflicting claims for art in non-aesthetic terms.

The common aspirations of the Romantic poets for the monistic world of art and nature were constantly subverted by their cognitive and mimetic stance vis-à-vis nature. In their attempt to correct this predicament, however, we can see their characteristic endeavour for a reconciliation of the conflicting claims for art, i.e. the cognitive and the experiential. Only through this reconciliation was it possible to unify art and nature.

3. THE SAINT OR THE ARTIST

I

The Keatsian scepticism as to whether or not art can be an agent of mediation between knowledge and experience takes on a more serious tone in Yeats, since he demanded more of art than Keats did. Yeats not only expected art to be a true avenue to knowledge, he also sought in art a substitute for mystical experience or occult vision. If art proves, as Yeats feared or as Sturge Moore warned him, to be nothing more than artifact discontinuous with the eternal order of the universe or destined for sure death like the natural objects of our ambient reality, then it would fail him in both ways. Not only would art deny him a knowledge of reality and history, but it would also bar him from entering into the world of eternity or refuse him a vision of eternity. Notwithstanding his misgivings, Yeats had no choice as an artist but to entrust art with his whole self in his sailing to Byzantium, though he grew increasingly uncertain about the seaworthiness of his vessel once he set sail.

In 'Lapis Lazuli', the Yeatsian counterpart to Keats's 'Urn', Yeats records his scepticism about the ability of art to encompass reality and history. In the poem reality (or history) and art are juxtaposed against each other and are characterised as 'tragic' and 'gay' respectively. The term 'tragic' is not used here in the usual Yeatsian sense of 'tragic reverie'. It is used rather in the popular sense of 'sad' or 'unfortunate'. There is a distinct cleavage between gay art and tragic reality. Art in the first stanza is criticised by the shrill-voiced women for not coming to grips with the imminent tragedy threatening Europe. Art's gaiety in the face of growing difficulty in international politics indicates its aloofness from and discontinuousness with the real and historical world in which we live. But the artists (the players in the second stanza) know well that art, though it simulates life, is essentially different from reality and history. The players would not confuse the tragedy they perform

52

with the lives they live, as what is dreadful in real life is 'transfigured' into a state of catharsis by virtue of the aesthetic distance that art keeps from life. Hence they would not stop their performance to cry; and no matter how many times the tragic scenes of Shakespearean plays are 'acted over in states unborn and accents yet unknown' (*Julius Caesar*, III, i), the tragic world *on stage* 'cannot grow by an inch or an ounce'. Viewed in a different context, however, art is part of reality and history, subject to time's destruction. In Stanza Three art represented by the work of Callimachus, a Greek sculptor of the Fifth Century B.C. who is credited as being the first to carve in marble, is found on a continuum with history in which civilisations and art alike are unable to escape the laws of mutability; but the makers of history stand aloof from the cycle of history itself. Finally, the protagonist's (or the poet's) imagination is set to work to unite art and reality by extrapolating an imaginary world of unity from the lapis lazuli, a hard sculptural medium, in which are carved three Chinamen and a long-legged bird, possibly a crane, symbolising longevity. Despite the poet's delight in imagining the world in which a link is made between art and reality, the characters in the art object are gay like Hamlet and Lear on stage. Despite the poet's endeavour to introduce temporality into the world of art by transposing the mars and scars of the medium into the organic form of art, the gaiety of art represented by the Chinese figures is doggedly retained and they never step out of the confines of their artistic world, but merely look gaily upon the 'tragic scene' of reality and history in which they have no part.[1]

Side by side with his scepticism Yeats nonetheless kept his faith alive in poetry. His faith rested in the symbolism of poetry in particular; and though this faith waned considerably in the last phase of his career, he remained a symbolist to the end of his life. In his last poem he affirms that, while 'the profane perfection of mankind' is achieved through such abstract measurements as were employed by the ancient Greek and Egyptian sculptors, the heavenly city is represented by the Quatrocento through earthly images that resemble dream images of divine revelation.

Underlying Yeats's faith in poetry, however, were his conflicting perspectives towards the nature of symbolism in poetry. On the one hand, he recognised the semiotic nature of symbols used in poetry, allowing them only an evocative function. Viewed in this light, poetic symbols work as signs, much like occult symbols, evoking certain mental states or ideas. Ideas and mental states thus evoked are mediate; and signs thus functioning may or may not be successful in evoking the ideas and the mental states. Their success depends

on the appropriateness of their form and substance as signs. Thus
Solomon muses, when a sexual union with Sheba fails to perpetuate
their spiritual unity:

> Maybe an image is too strong
> Or maybe is not strong enough.
>
> (*Collected Poems*, p. 175)

On the other hand, Yeats also saw the constitutive nature of poetic
symbols. In 'Prometheus Unbound' he says:

There is a form of meditation which permits an image or symbol to generate
itself, and the images and symbols so generated build themselves up into
coherent structures often beautiful and startling.[2]

In the same essay Yeats denounces Shelley for not being a mystic,
because

his system of thought was constructed by his logical faculty to satisfy desire,
not a symbolical revelation received after the suspension of all desire. He
could neither say with Dante, 'His will is our peace', nor with Finn in the
Irish story, 'The best music is what happens'.[3]

The world of symbols is a monistic world in which subject and object
are fused and in which pure experience remains. Shelley lacked a
vision of such a world. So Yeats turned to Blake for his model.

As a number of critics have pointed out,[4] however, Yeats warps
Blake's thought considerably to fit it into his system. In Yeats's
understanding of Blake's idea of vision there lurks his incorrigible
dualism. Yeats correctly distinguishes Blake's 'vision' from 'allegory'
by imputing the former to imagination and the latter to fancy and
by aligning the former with eternity and revelation while denigrating
the latter as belonging to the mutable world of time and memory.
But he translates Blake's idea of vision into his own idea of
symbolism. 'William Blake was the first writer of modern times', says
Yeats in an essay on Blake, 'to preach the indissoluble marriage of
all great art with symbol'.[5] Vision for Blake is, of course, a monistic
world in which the tripartite constituents of art, artist and eternity
are united in a concrete form. Yeats dislodges eternity from this
synthesis and consecrates it as transcendental essence while reducing
symbol to the state of an earthly icon of that essence. Symbol thus
becomes 'the . . . expression of some invisible essence'[6] or 'the
shadows of imperishable beings and substances'.[7] Blake would have

loathed this Platonisation of his 'Divine Humanity' and the dehydration of his 'Minute Particulars'. The Blakean synthesis is thus reduced to the mundane triad of art, artist, and eternity; and the burden of proof falls on the artist as to the validity of his symbols. In the Blakean synthesis we have seen a subtle reconciliation of the cognitive and the experiential perspectives; we fail to see this reconciliation in the Yeatsian symbolism. Instead, we witness a perpetual yearning of the cognitive for the experiential, the symbols being starved of the 'invisible essence', or the self craving for its antiself.

II

The Yeatsian dualism of the cognitive and the experiential perspectives have perplexed generations of Yeats's critics. Some critics saw a war between the two perspectives, some saw a complementary relationship between the two, others saw a final resolution of them, still others looked upon them as an aesthetic device. A new position is called for to see the dualism as a process — a process in the Yeatsian multifarious senses, philosophical, spiritual, cultural, as well as aesthetic. At one end of the process is the status quo and at the other end is the world of the ideal; stated in other terms, the self and the antiself, the conflict and the unity, the Anima Hominis and the Anima Mundi, the 'Hodos Chameliontos' and the 'Thirteenth Sphere', and so on. The two poles are not in eternal conflict like the war between Heaven and Hell, in which one or the other must triumph, but in a sort of reconciliatory war (though admittedly not a perfect reconcilement as in the Blakean vision), not killing each other, but 'dying each other's life, living each other's death'.[8] The one world implied and necessitated the other. Finding the antiself meant for one to start from the self. Climbing the ladder to Heaven meant for one to start climbing at the bottom rung of the ladder planted on earth. Yeats spent the better part of his life constructing and climbing that ladder. When, in his later years, he found that ladder gone,[9] he found himself at the spot where the ladder started.

Of the two poles the pole of unity was ideal for Yeats. To attain a unity at all levels of life — spiritual, aesthetic, cultural, philosophical, etc. — was Yeats's lifelong aim. His study of Irish mythology, his interest in Western and Eastern occultism, his imitation of the Japanese Noh Drama, his absorption of various philosophical systems were all motivated by this aim of achieving a unity out of multiplicity, a resolution of all conflict. At the spiritual

56 *The Double Perspective of Yeats's Aesthetic*

level he endeavoured to attain a Unity of Being, a turning of
consciousness into ecstatic vision; at the aesthetic level he tried to
achieve a Unity of Image, an image whereby reality is evoked; and
at the cultural level he tried to achieve a Unity of Culture, a
Byzantium where all things have oneness as if they were conceived
by a single mind.

Yeats's effort to achieve his lifelong aim culminated in the writing
of *A Vision* (1925) and ended in frustration upon reconsidering his
achievement in that book, and his confession of failure is presented
to us in the final prose section in the revised edition (1937) of the
book. Yeats felt, however, similar frustrations earlier in his life. In
'Rosa Alchemica' (1897) he writes:

I had dissolved indeed the mortal world and lived amid immortal essences,
but had obtained no miraculous ecstasy. As I thought of these things, I drew
aside the curtains and looked out into the darkness, and it seemed to my
troubled fancy that all these little points of light filling the sky were the
furnaces of innumerable divine alchemists, who labour continually, turning
lead into gold, weariness into ecstasy, bodies into souls, the darkness into
God; and at their perfect labour my mortality grew heavy, and I cried out,
as so many dreamers and men of letters in our age have cried, for the birth
of that elaborate spiritual beauty which could alone uplift souls weighted
with so many dreams.[10]

Much later, in his introduction to Shri Purohit's *An Indian Monk*
(1932), Yeats confesses that the book has given him in a complete
form what he sought after in his study of Irish folk tales, occultism,
and Christian and Pagan visionary writings:

The book lies before me complete; it seems to me something I have waited
for since I was seventeen years old. About that age, bored by an Irish
Protestant point of view that suggested by its blank abstraction chloride
of lime, I began to question the country-people about apparitions. Some
dozen years later Lady Gregory collected with my help the stories in her
Visions and Beliefs. Again and again, she and I felt that we had gotten down,
as it were, into some fibrous darkness, into some matrix out of which
everything has come, . . . but there was always something lacking. . . .
When Shri Purohit Swami described his journey up those seven thousand
steps at Mount Ginar, that creaking bed, that sound of pattens, in the little
old half-forgotten temples, and fitted everything into an ancient discipline,
a philosophy that satisfied the intellect, I found all I wanted.[11]

The book is Shri Purohit's autobiography, which describes the
author's spiritual experience. The Swami's sort of experience indeed

never came to Yeats. He knew about it, but he never attained it. That is why he advised Shri Purohit to write about it.

Presently I said: 'The ideas of India have been expounded again and again, nor do we lack ideas of our own; discussion has been exhausted, but we lack experience. Write what you have just told us; keep out all philosophy, unless it interprets something seen or done.'[12]

What Yeats lacked, then, was experience. Yeats had earlier commented that the saint had a direct passage to the antiself while the artist and the hero did not:

The poet finds and makes his mask in disappointment, the hero in defeat. . . . The saint alone is not deceived, neither thrusting with his shoulder nor holding out unsatisfied hands. He could climb without wandering to the antithetical self of the world, the Indian narrowing his thought in meditation or driving it away in contemplation, the Christian copying Christ, the antithetical self of the classic world. For a hero loves the world till it breaks him, and the poet till it has broken faith; but while the world was yet debonair, the saint has turned away, and because he renounced experience itself, he will wear his mask as he finds it.[13]

Being an artist, Yeats could not forsake the world as the saint could and, therefore, could not attain to his antiself.

Yeats envisaged the life of the saint and that of the artist as antithetical to each other. Yet he endeavoured throughout his life to live both as an artist and a saint. The two types of life were distinguished by Yeats in a short essay in the *Discoveries* (1906) in an analogy of a wheel as follows:

If it be true that God is a circle whose centre is everywhere, the saint goes to the centre, the poet and artist to the ring where everything comes round again.[14]

The saint is interested in what is fixed and eternal while the artist seeks what is perpetually recurring in the world of time and the senses. Yeats the saint endeavoured to fathom the secret of the universe and transcend the dualistic restrictions of the phenomenal world; and Yeats the poet tried to live affirmatively in the rugged world of time and the senses and concentrated on creative activity. It was mainly as the poet, however, that Yeats found his genius more fitting and productive. Although he aspired till death to achieve the saintly objective, his artist's impulse constantly checked his aspirations. Nevertheless, Yeats constantly carried within himself a polarity of perspectives, whichever type of life he pursued. In the pursuit of the saintly life he could not abandon the artist's bias, and in the pursuit of the creative life he could not dispense with the saintly aspirations.

The double perspective is clearly shown in *A Vision*, in which he exhausts his imaginative power in mapping out the realm of reality in geometric abstractions while attempting through the very effort to gain a vision of reality, a final delivery from the cycle of birth and death. *A Vision*, in this sense, is a record of an attempt and a failure of Yeats the saint. Yeats failed, because, as he well knew, he resorted to methods that did not lead to a spiritual liberation. He was caught in the geometric abstraction of his own making and was buried among a multiplicity of ideas and opinions that he borrowed from his predecessors. Instead of sinking into a meditation like an Indian monk he admired so much, he allowed himself to engage in an intellectual operation that produced a knowledge rather than an experience. Also, as he wrote the book, he was keenly conscious of his alternative as an artist, which he suggests at the closing of the prose section of the book.

The double perspective is also evident in his creative activity. Although he dealt as an artist with symbols and 'those recurring images' and believed in tragic conflict, Yeats had a firm conviction in ecstasy as the ultimate aim of art. The artist, Yeats believed, is confined by nature to the things of the earth and is permitted to work from 'desire to weariness and from weariness to desire', creating his works out of those images that recur in the world of time or of conflicting elements that symbolise the world of antinomy. The artist should, nevertheless, work toward some sort of vision or a reverie in which individuals are drowned in the Great One, Anima Mundi, a vast reservoir of tribal memory. Symbols and images are the triggers whereby the great memory is evoked. The artist must painfully work his way out of conflict toward a vision of reality. For such tragic writers as Dante and Villon, Yeats believed, a vision of reality was possible.

Yeats, however, expresses a profound pessimism over the adequacy of his approach to reality. Later in his life he casts doubt as to the possibility of ever evoking reality through images and symbols. If these images are not the same as reality itself, then they are caught in the world of time and are therefore mutable; they are withering images that have no eternal value. What is more, the so-called recurring images may not recur at all, 'for no recurring spring ever brings again yesterday's clock'.[16] If, then, the so-called recurring images do not recur at all, the artist's work comes to naught: not only will he not attain a vision of reality, but he is labouring with things that are subject to sure death. This is a horrible realisation for one whose lifelong aim has been to attain a final liberation from the mundane and the temporal.

The saint and the artist thus represent in Yeats a polarity of conflicting perspectives for life and art. Taken separately, however, each in turn carries a polarity of perspectives. The saint carries within himself the cognitive pole of the artist, while the artist carries the experiential pole of the saint. Whether as the saint or as the artist, Yeats laboured in the direction toward which his experiential pole pointed, but his attempt ended in failure because of the reverse pull of the other pole. Yeats's attempt to be a saint failed because he only tried to map out reality in cognitive terms, in geometric abstraction. So, he followed the way of art. Again in art he tried to gain an ecstatic vision, but he never abandoned his dualistic perspective, affirming the antinomial aspect of the creative process, which he thought was exemplified in Dante.

III

In spite of his confession that an apocalyptic vision is impossible in the manner which he adopted in *A Vision*, Yeats makes it clear in the closing prose section of the book that the whole purpose of writing the book was to gain such a vision. The laborious process of defining and re-defining his terms, comparing them with the ideas of his predecessors, was in the long run to lead him to a vision, the very title of the book. Day after day, he confesses, he sat in his chair playing with his symbol, trying to see if his symbol united those ideas that he learned from his predecessors, such as Plato, Plotinus, Empedocles, Heraclitus, Hegel, and the Eastern sages. The approach that Yeats chose in constructing his symbol was a mathematical one. Here is a realisation that a knowledge of reality is to be mediated by an abstraction, a product of the mind, as the physical forms of our ambient reality are mediated by mathematical abstractions. In working with the mathematical figures, however, Yeats never lost sight of his ultimate objective, that is, to draw himself 'up into the symbol' and 'find everything in the symbol',[17] forgetting the process through which the symbol was constructed. The double feature of the Yeatsian symbol is evident. On the one hand, it is an abstraction which mediates a knowledge; on the other hand, it represents a world of experience in which the poet finds everything at once. The former is mediate and the latter is immediate. The former perspective subsumes the bifurcation of subject and object while the latter is based on the monistic view of art. In the Yeatsian terms, the former looks towards the world of conflict while the latter rejoices in the world of unity. The latter perspective is not dissimilar to the Blakean immediacy and concreteness of vision. What is unique about the Yeatsian vision of unity is that, while Blake found a vision of eternity *in* the 'Minute Particulars', Yeats saw the 'Unity of Being' arise *out of* the world of conflict. The attainment of an apocalyptic vision is thus viewed as a spiritual process:

My instructors identify consciousness with conflict, not with knowledge, substitute for subject and object and their attendant logic a struggle towards harmony, towards Unity of Being. Logical and emotional conflict alike lead towards a reality which is concrete, sensuous, bodily.[18]

At the base of Yeats's theory of symbolism there is the concept of 'Anima Mundi'. It would be redundant to quote the well-known passage from his essay 'Magic' that defines his concept of Anima Mundi. Suffice it here to say that he meant that our individual memories are part of that great memory of nature. Probably the most significant premise in the concept of the Anima Mundi in connection with the theme of the saintly vision is that there is a mystical basis to the idea of the great memory. Through his own study of the country visionaries of Ireland and his association with the Theosophists and other occultists, Yeats arrived at a firm conviction that the great memory can be evoked by symbols. In the essay on Shelley's poetry, which antedates the first version of *A Vision* by a quarter of a century, he suggested a mystical basis for the evocation of the great memory:

Any one who has an experience of any mystical state of the soul knows how there float up in the mind profound symbols, whose meaning, if indeed they do not delude one into the dream that they are meaningless, one does not perhaps understand for years. Nor I think has any one, who has known that experience with any constancy, failed to find some day, in some old book or on some old monument, strange or intricate image that had floated up before him, and to grow perhaps dizzy with the sudden conviction that our little memories are but a part of some great Memory that renews the world and men's thoughts age after age, and that our thoughts are not, as we suppose, the deep but a little foam upon the deep.[19]

A knowledge of the great memory is, then, a mystical experience evoked by symbols. And though Yeats confesses as late as 1922 that he has not attained that experience, the truth he sought, he assures,

would come to him 'like the subject of a poem, from some moment
of passionate experience'. In order to achieve that experience,
however, Yeats had to find a right symbol, for he admits that 'that
passionate experience could never come — of that I was certain —
until I had found the right image or images'.[20]

That image he thought he found in the gyre. 'But nothing comes',
Yeats says in Section II of 'The End of the Cycle', 'though this
moment was to reward me for all my toil'.[21] Perhaps he is too old,
he muses, for something would come when he meditated under the
direction of the Cabalists. One cause of the failure is suggested by
Yeats at the end of Section I: '. . . it seems as if I should know all
if I could banish such memories and find everything in the symbol'.
He could not banish 'such memories' of other prophecies. Yeats had
warned himself against the danger at the time of writing *The
Trembling of the Veil* (1922) — to fall victim to the 'multiplicity of
interest and opinion', which stimulated him to conceive a Unity of
Culture in the first place: '. . . if I filled my exposition with other
men's thought, other men's investigation, I would sink into all that
multiplicity of interest and opinion'.[22] Much earlier than this Yeats
had said in the essay, 'Symbolism of Poetry' (1900), that

one is furthest from symbols when one is busy doing this or that, but the
soul moves among symbols and unfolds in symbols when trance, or madness,
or deep meditation has withdrawn it from every impulse but its own.[23]

Thus a vision of truth is not to be attained unless the mind is rid
of conflict and multiplicity and brought to a razor-sharp intensity
in its meditation.

Multiplicity and conflict, however, are not to be discarded as
completely worthless. On the contrary, they have a vital place in
Yeats's thought. In 'Hodos Chameliontos', Book III of *The Trembling
of the Veil*, he explains how a 'multiplicity of interest and opinion
drove him to conceive a Unity of Culture defined and evoked by
Unity of Image',[24] and he finds a similarly paradoxical process in
the progress of such artists as Dante and Villon. The paradox, in
fact, is universal in the spiritual progress of men. In 1927 Yeats wrote
to Mrs Shakespear and compared the paradox in him and that in
Dante:

Certainly we suck always at the eternal dugs. How well too it puts my own
mood between spiritual excitement, and the sexual torture and the knowledge
that they are somehow inseparable! It is the eyes of the Earthly Beatrice
— she has not yet put on her divinity — that makes Dante risk the fire 'like

a child that is offered an apple'. Immediately after comes the Earthly Paradise and the Heavenly Beatrice.[25]

The eternal is thus found via the earthly. Again in 'Hodos Chameliontos' Yeats writes that the personifying spirits of Anima Mundi 'contrived Dante's banishment, and snatched away his Beatrice, and thrust Villon into the arms of harlots . . . that Dante and Villon might through passion become conjoint to their buried selves. . . .'[26] Masters such as Dante and Villon deserve the name of genius, because they serve as a link that connects the individual mind with the Anima Mundi, 'a crisis that joins that buried self for certain moments to our trivial daily mind',[27] but their genius was not a natural gift but something they attained through their progress from conflict to unity. There is tragic beauty and grandeur in such masters, whom we see in awe as men re-born greater in stature:

We gaze at such men in awe, because we gaze not at a work of art, but at the re-creation of the man through that art, the birth of a new species of man, and it may even seem that the hairs of our heads stand up, because that birth, that re-creation is from terror.[28]

The re-created man, however, is also an artist, who creates out of the quarrel with himself poetry that provides us with tragic reverie in which our individual souls are supposed to lose their identities. The unity that the saint achieves for his being is thus related with the Unity of Image that the artist achieves in art. Furthermore, these unities are related to a third unity that Yeats desires to have achieved in history and civilisation — a Unity of Culture. To achieve this tripartite unity was the lifelong aim of Yeats the saint. *A Vision* represented this effort: A vision of the Unity of Culture was to be coincidental with the achievement of his own Unity of Being, which he thought was possible if only he could let himself be absorbed into the symbol he created for himself. However, nothing came. History and civilisation after all are a gigantic movement that transcends the limits of an individual artist's imagination. They are controlled by a Supreme Enchanter, as a person is controlled by an invisible Daimon of the *Thirteenth Sphere*, as they go through a cyclical movement of twelve cycles. Although, viewed from the human standpoint, a civilisation means 'a struggle to keep self-control',[29] it is only 'held together by the suggestions of an invisible hypnotist',[30] and all civilisation is subject to the gigantic cyclical movement of nature. It represents an almost superhuman effort to maintain unity and coherence; yet the effort is lost in the end and a unity is lost, the whole civilisation whirling round in the 'widening gyre' of the cyclical process of history. A time comes to any civilisation when the centre can no longer hold and 'Mere anarchy is loosed upon the world'. Any attempt to keep self-control, therefore, must be frustrated in the end. A civilisation must yield itself to fate as a tragic hero must. Yeats had earlier cast doubt over the hope of Europe's ever attaining a Unity of Culture. In 'The Tragic Generation' he wrote pessimistically:

. . . this much at any rate is certain — the dream of my early manhood, that a modern nation can return to Unity of Culture, is false; though it may be we can achieve it for some small circle of men and women, and there leave it till the moon bring round its century.[31]

Thus a civilisation is under the control of a supernatural force; any attempt to free itself from that force is hopeless, 'a struggle of the fly in the marmalade' — unless there is a revelation.

It is indeed true that Yeats expected some sort of revelation when a civilisation completes a cycle, and it seems that he likewise expected a revelation upon completion of *A Vision*, which ended in disappointment. In Book V of *A Vision*, 'Dove or Swan', he comments on the end of a cycle of a civilisation thus:

The loss of control over thought comes towards the end; first a sinking in upon the moral being, then the last surrender, the irrational cry, revelation — the scream of Juno's peacock.[32]

This is the same revelation that he expects in 'The Second Coming':

> Surely some revelation is at hand;
> Surely the Second Coming is at hand.
> (*Collected Poems*, p. 185)

And it is essentially the same revelation that is envisaged at the level of art in 'My Table' in 'Meditations in Time of Civil War':

> Our learned men have urged
> That when and where 'twas forged
> A marvelous accomplishment,
> In painting or in poetry, went
> From father unto son
> And through the centuries ran
> And seemed unchanging like the sword.
> Soul's beauty being most adored,

Men and their business took
The soul's unchanging look;
For the most rich inheritor,
Knowing that none could pass Heaven's door
That loved inferior art,
Had such an aching heart
That he, although a country's talk
For silken clothes and stately walk,
Had waking wits; it seemed
Juno's peacock screamed.
                    (*Collected Poems*, pp. 200–201)

The screaming of Juno's peacock never occurred, however, at the end of the cycle of *A Vision*. Yeats wonders how it is possible to bring about unity in Europe. Then he understands — that he has said what can be said in words. The rest is up to the *Thirteenth Cone*. The descriptive part of the job is done; what remains is experience itself, a vision of reality, a spiritual liberation. That liberation failed to come: the *Thirteenth Cone* 'has kept the secret'.[33] 'Shall we follow', Yeats asks, 'the image of Heracles that walks through the darkness bow in hand'? — a Heracles the mortal hero who was rejected by Hera, or Juno, the owner of the peacock. Or shall we, in the alternative Yeats offers, 'mount to that other Heracles, man, not image'[34] who was accepted by Hera as a god and was given Hebe, Hera's daughter by Zeus, for his bride? The choice is between the life of an artist and that of a saint. The choice, again, is between earthly bondage and freedom. From the artistic point of view, the choice is between art as a sign and art as an experience. Yeats ends his proposition with a question, leaving the whole matter in the typically Yeatsian ambiguity. Actually, however, Yeats had chosen the former.

IV

Although Yeats found his genius more suitable to the career of an artist than that of a saint, he could not completely abandon his saintly aspirations. As a result, we have an unusual type of artist in Yeats. In Yeats the artist there exists the mask of another Yeats — Yeats the saint. Yeats the artist, who is engaged in the Apollonian pursuit of artistic creation, is constantly haunted by the Dionysian desire for ecstasy. In fact, Yeats aimed to elevate the world of poetry to the sphere of religion. He had lost the 'simple-minded religion'

of his childhood under the influences of such popularisers of natural
science as T. H. Huxley and John Tyndall. In the void left by this
deprivation, which he had come to loathe, he intended to found 'a
new religion, almost an infallible Church of poetic tradition, of a
fardel of stories, and of personages, and emotions. . . .'[35] This
religion of poetry 'would find its manners of devotion in all
imaginative literature, and set before Irishmen for special manual
an Irish literature which, though made by many minds, would seem
the work of a single mind. . . .'[36] The religion of poetry that Yeats
envisages, then, is a kind of religio-aesthetic world, a Byzantium,
where men seek a unity — a world unified and made coherent by
a single myth. There 'all sounds, all colours, all forms . . . become,
as it were, one sound, one colour, one form, and evoke an emotion
that is made out of their distinct evocations and yet one emotion.'[37]
There a nation is 'distinguished from a crowd of chance comers,
bound together' by a Unity of Image. There 'the poet seeks truth,
not abstract truth, but a kind of vision of reality which satisfies the
whole being.'[38] The gates of this world would certainly open for
him, Yeats thought, as they did for Blake, Swedenborg, and Boehme,
the chief mystical authorities he recognised in 1915.[39]

What Yeats envisaged as a new religion, then, was a kind of
mystical order whose expression was to be found in imaginative
literature providing symbols which would, like occult symbols, evoke
the eternal world of the divine essence. Art under this order would
be a means of communication with the eternal world that lies beyond
the limits of the senses, and the symbols in a work of art would work
wonders when they are disengaged from the restrictions imposed on
them by the mundane factors of their original contexts:

If you liberate a person or a landscape from the bonds of motives and their
actions, causes and their effects, and from all bonds but the bonds of your
love, it will change under your eyes, and become a symbol of an infinite
emotion, a perfected emotion, a part of the Divine Essence. . . .[40]

As there is a mystical basis upon which Yeats's concept of the Great
Memory was formed, so there is a strong mystical colouring in his
idea of symbolism. The purpose of art is essentially the same as that
which religious and visionary people seek; and symbolism alone
approximates the state desired in mysticism:

Religious and visionary people, monks and nuns, and medicine-men and
opium-eaters, see symbols in their trances; for religious and visionary thought

is thought about perfection and the way to perfection; and symbols are the only things free enough from all bonds to speak of perfection.[41]

And the artist's skill must be as subtle as the Divine Essence which he seeks to grasp, for

although you can expound an opinion, or describe a thing, when your words are not quite well chosen, you cannot give a body to something that moves beyond the senses, unless your words are as subtle, as complex, as full of mysterious life, as the body of a flower or of a woman.[42]

The saintly aspirations in Yeats's religion of poetry are subverted, however, by his artistic consciousness, which became increasingly strong after the publication of *Ideas of Good and Evil* (1903) as we shall see later. Even as early as 1895 Yeats recognised the artist's interest in earthly things as part of the vital principle by which the artist is guided:

We hear much of his need for the restraints of reason, but the only restraint he can obey is the mysterious instinct that has made him an artist, and that teaches him to discover immortal moods in mortal desires, an undecaying hope in our trivial ambitions, a divine love in sexual passion.[43]

And in 1898 Yeats recognised the earthly nature of the artist's imagination compared to the mystic's:

The systematic mystic is not the greatest of artists, because his imagination is too great to be bounded by a picture or a song, and because only imperfection in a mirror of perfection, or perfection in a mirror of imperfection, delights our frailty.[44]

The artist's imagination is necessarily smaller than the mystic's, since he is concerned with the earthly things and must work from imperfection to perfection. However, the artist is a sort of medium trying to communicate with eternal spirits through earthly means. He takes the stuff of his art from earthly things and turns it into an artistic whole to the point where it touches the Divine Essence. In order to succeed he must perfect his skill; the task falls on him to turn a skeleton of a bird into a living bird.

V

The two channels through which Yeats chose to achieve his saintly aspirations were logic and image. The former involved Yeats's own intellectual approach to reality, a logical, or mathematical, mapping out of heaven[45]; it also involved a meticulous examination and understanding of wisdom presented by generations of thinkers. The latter, the way of image, Yeats hoped, would be a direct passage to the eternal world. In either case, there is no escaping dualism. Logic means a process and, therefore, implies conflict. Image, on the other hand, is only a symbol of reality, not reality itself. The two approaches were seldom used in isolation. Even in his prose writings Yeats constantly expressed himself through symbols, while he burdened his symbolic poems and plays with abstract ideas.

Of the two gates to eternity Yeats was particularly sceptical about logic. This scepticism is expressed in the form of confession in the closing section of *A Vision* that his intellectual toil failed to bring him a vision of eternity; it only helped him find the image, not eternity itself. The inadequacy of an intellectual approach as a means to attain a vision of eternity was clear to him as early as 1896. In a letter to W. T. Horton, dated May 5, Yeats writes:

I hold as Blake would have held also, that the intellect must do its utmost 'before inspiration is possible.' It clears the rubbish from the mouth of the sybil's cave but it is not the sybil.[46]

So Yeats acknowledged that intellect cleared the way for inspiration, but beyond that he was sceptical about its adequacy. Indeed, Yeats was sceptical about all human endeavour, intellectual or otherwise, to achieve perfection, since 'Adam's curse' is upon man, who must labour to be perfect, and there is no guarantee of reward for his labour.

The vain human endeavour to gain a vision of eternity is symbolised by Thoor Ballylee, the tower which Yeats acquired in 1917 and moved into two years later. The tower, though it must have been associated in Yeats's mind, as Professor Jeffares points out, with the Shelleyan romantic loneliness and search for wisdom,[47] most appropriately symbolises, with its ruined top, the frustrated human effort to gain true wisdom. In his note to *The Winding Stair and Other Poems*, Yeats explains the symbolism of the tower in the following words:

In this book and elsewhere, I have used towers, and one tower in particular, as symbols and have compared their winding stairs to the philosophical gyres, but it is hardly necessary to interpret what comes from the main track of thought and expression. Shelley uses towers constantly as symbols, and there are gyres in Swedenborg, and in Thomas Aquinas and certain classical authors. Part of the symbolism of *Blood and the Moon* was suggested by the fact that Thoor Ballylee has a waste room at the top and that butterflies come in through the loopholes and die against the windowpanes.[48]

In 'A Dialogue of Self and Soul' Yeats uses the tower as an emblem of the 'ancestral night', a spiritual liberation from the cycle of birth and death. In the poem *My Soul* urges *My Self* to quit wandering on earth and concentrate on a spiritual ascent:

> *My Soul.* I summon to the winding ancient stair;
> Set all your mind upon the steep ascent,
> Upon the broken, crumbling battlement,
> Upon the breathless starlit air,
> Upon the star that marks the hidden pole;
> Fix every wandering thought upon
> That quarter where all thought is done:
> Who can distinguish darkness from the soul?

The winding stair of the tower is used here as a symbol of spiritual ascent. Against this symbol, *My Self* poses a Japanese sword, which was given to Yeats in 1920 by Junzo Sato, a Japanese. The sword, together with the rich embroidery on the hilt, symbolises Self's determination to accept his lot on earth. The Soul argues that the sword is an emblem of love (represented by some colourful embroidery torn from a court lady's dress) and war (represented by the blade), which, taken together, imply a cyclical movement of birth (love) and death (war). The Soul then urges the Self to 'Think of ancestral night that can, / . . . Deliver from the crime of death and birth.' But the Soul, when he comes to describe the world where 'intellect no longer knows / *Is* from the *Ought*, or *Knower* from the *Known*', discovers that his 'tongue's a stone'. The Soul suddenly falls into silence and *abandons* the argument. The Self speaks on and the second section of the poem consists, in effect, of a eulogy of his own philosophy of life. The Soul abandons the argument partly because the sort of experience he is hinting at is incommunicable, but largely because Yeats the poet has almost nothing to say on that experience. The gyre of discord now dominates Yeats's mind and the gyre of concord recedes into the background. It would be a mistake to argue, as Engelberg does, that the Soul *loses* the argument because 'she offers the very permanence Self cannot accept.'[49] After all, the poem is about a dialogue, not an argument, taking place between two tendencies in Yeats's mind. For a moment two tendencies were kept in balance, but one represented by the Soul, or the gyre of concord in the terms of *A Vision*,[50] diminished as the other, the gyre of discord represented by the Self, came to the foreground. The world of eternity, the 'quarter where all thought is done', which the Soul desires is the world Yeats's self could never reach; the Self, therefore, resolves to be 'content to live it all again/ And yet again, if it be life to pitch/ Into the frog spawn of a blind man's ditch'. The Self is the predominant gyre in Yeats's mind. The very eloquence and strongly affirmative tone of the Self shows Yeats's turn of mind — at least at the time of writing the poem.

In 'Ego Dominus Tuus' and 'The Phases of the Moon' the tower image is used as a symbol of intellectual toil. The inhabitant of the tower in 'Ego Dominus Tuus' (presumably Yeats himself) leaves the tower because he seeks 'an image, not a book'. By that image he calls 'to the mysterious one', his antiself who will 'disclose/All that I seek'. The antiself will whisper a secret knowledge[51] 'as though/ He were afraid the birds', the symbol of momentary vision, 'Would carry it away to blasphemous men'. The inhabitant of the tower in 'The Phases of the Moon' has chosen to live in the tower

> Because, it may be, of the candle-light
> From the far tower where Milton's Platonist
> Sat late, or Shelley's visionary prince:
> The lonely light that Samuel Palmer engraved,
> An image of mysterious wisdom won by toil;

but his toil, Aherne and Robartes know, does not bring him what he seeks. In both poems the tower, which is used as a symbol of intellectual toil, does not satisfy its inhabitant.

In 'Blood and the Moon' a more thorough and sophisticated use is made of the tower as a symbol.

> I declare this tower is my emblem; I declare
> This winding, gyring, spiring treadmill of a stair is my
>   ancestral stair;
> The Goldsmith and the Dean, Berkeley and Burke have travelled
>   there.

Thus, the tower is an emblem of procession of great minds of the past, 'A bloody, arrogant power' that 'Rose out of the race/ Uttering, mastering' that race. It is an emblem of 'The strength that gives our blood and state magnanimity of its own desire', of the great intellectual leaders who endeavored to give the nation a Unity of Culture and who endeavored to give a rational order to the universe. On that 'ancestral stair' there is 'odour of blood', a suggestion of temporality.[52] This winding stair, which is compared to a philosophical gyre, or 'Everything that is not God consumed with intellectual fire', leads to the ruined top of the tower, where 'Upon the dusty, glittering windows cling,/ And seem to cling upon the moonlit skies,/ Tortoiseshell butterflies, peacock butterflies.' 'Is every modern nation like the tower,' Yeats muses, 'Half dead at the top?' He comes to this awareness, however, that the wisdom that the great minds who climbed the stair sought 'is the property of the dead,/ A something incompatible with life' and that the power suggested by the 'blood-saturated ground' is, like any earthly thing, 'A property of the living'. Here Yeats reverses the meaning of his symbols and does it subtly. In stanza II Yeats has the stair stand for a procession of great minds of the past. In this sense the stair is an emblem of the past glory. But then the great minds represent the shaping spirit of the entire Irish race and culture, a vitality. In stanza III blood which smelt on the stair and which saturates the ground stands for the long political struggle that Ireland had to go through, a vainly expended human endeavour. In the final stanza the stair is brought back into life again, for the power belongs to the living. Thus we see the tower in a double-exposure effect: the stair on which Goldsmith, Berkeley, and Burke trod leading to the ruined top, an emblem of the sterile wisdom of the dead, and the stair which the moderns, including Yeats himself, climb spiraling the tower half dead at the top, an emblem of a modern nation. Over the tower hangs the transcendent moon shining with its ancient purity, and 'no stain/ Can come upon the visage of the moon.'

'Blood and the Moon', then, contrasts the temporal world of struggle and power with the world of eternity. Man toils with his intellect and power upon the stair, which suggests the gyre image of *A Vision*, but his toil uplifts him only the height of the tower where it comes to the dead end; the best he can do is to 'clamour in drunken frenzy for the moon'. The poem, furthermore, is a poetic statement of what Yeats must have felt when he completed the second version of *A Vision*: he climbed the stair — or explored the gyre — but his toil was rewarded with the dead top, only to make him realise that the moon shone far above his head. T. R. Henn pointed out that Yeats correlated his endeavour in writing *A Vision* to his desire of restoring the room at the top of the tower.[53] As he was never able to restore the room in life,[54] he never attained his aim in *A Vision*.

The tower, then, symbolises for Yeats a frustrated effort in the search for reality; it is, nevertheless, also a symbol of life on earth out of which the stuff of art is derived. It is, furthermore, symbolical

of Yeats's later affirmation of the cyclical movement of life and his
resolution to be true to it. This is what he had in mind when he wrote
in 1923 these lines in 'Meditation in Time of Civil War':

> May this laborious stair and this stark tower
> Become a roofless ruin that the owl
> May build in the cracked masonry and cry
> Her desolation to the desolate sky.
> The Primum Mobile that fashioned us
> Has made the very owls in circles move;
> And I, that count myself most prosperous,
> Seeing that love and friendship are enough,
> For an old neighbour's friendship chose the house
> And decked and altered it for a girl's love,
> And know whatever flourish and decline
> These stones remain their monument and mine.

However desolate it may be, Yeats thought, the tower will endure
and remain a symbol of his life and of the gyre of life out of which
man never seems to be able to escape.

If Yeats was aware of the inadequacy of intellect as a path to
perfect wisdom, he also felt frequently frustrated in his second
approach, symbolism. Although Yeats held some hope, as Daniel
Albright argues,[55] that symbols would immortalise earthly things,
he felt frustrated as soon as he became aware of discontinuity
between art and reality. Yeats, we remember, was finally frustrated
by his symbol in *A Vision*. Indeed, Yeats is constantly aware of the
gulf that lies between reality and symbol. The symbol is nothing
unless it evokes reality — unless, in effect, it becomes one with
reality. In 'Anima Hominis' in *Per Amica Silentia Lunae*, Yeats
distinguishes what he calls 'happy art' from tragic art. 'All happy
art', he says, 'seems to me that hollow image [of fulfilled desire,
a phrase by Simeon Solomon], but when its lineaments express also
the poverty or the exasperation that set its maker to work, we call
it tragic art.'[56] The difference is aptly exemplified in Keats and
Dante. Keats's art is only a 'dream of luxury', which he never
attained, but Dante's art is made out of his spiritual conflict and is
his spiritual progress itself: '. . . while reading Dante we never long
escape the conflict, partly because the verses are at moments a mirror
of his history, and yet more because that history is so clear and simple
that it has the quality of art'.[57]

In 'Ego Dominus Tuus', which Yeats uses as the title poem in *Per
Amica Silentia Lunae* (1917), Ille, presumably Yeats himself, argues
for Dante that

> Being mocked by Guido for his lecherous life,
> Derided and deriding, driven out
> To climb that stair and eat that bitter bread,
> He found the unpersuadable justice, he found
> The most exalted lady loved by a man.

Dante found what he wanted; but what about Keats? Ille's answer is:

> His art is happy, but who knows his mind?
> I see a schoolboy when I think of him,
> With face and nose pressed to sweet-shop window,
> For certainly he sank into his grave
> His senses and his heart unsatisfied,
> And made — being poor, ailing and ignorant,
> Shut out from all the luxury of the world,
> The coarse-bred son of a livery-stable keeper—
> Luxuriant song.

The portion of 'Ego Dominus Tuus' on Keats is reproduced at the end of 'Hodos Chameliontos' in *The Trembling of the Veil* (1922) in which he deals with the idea of unity arising from conflict. Toward the end of that essay Yeats again compares Keats with Dante and Villon:

> In great lesser writers like Landor and like Keats we are shown that Image and that Mask as something set apart; Andromeda and her Perseus — though not the sea-dragon — but in a few in whom we recognize supreme masters of tragedy, the whole contest is brought into the circle of their beauty. Such masters — Villon and Dante, let us say — would not, when they speak through their art, change their luck; yet they are mirrored in all the suffering of desire. The two halves of their nature are so completely joined that they seem to labour for their objects, and yet to desire whatever happens, being at the same instant predestinated and free, creation's very self.[58]

It takes a great artist to fuse the Image and the Mask, to unite poetry and reality, to link creative effort to knowledge, to turn consciousness, in effect, into pure experience. In lesser artists such fusion is impossible. Yeats must have felt in his own art a similar inadequacy. At least, Yeats is always uncertain about the adequacy of his symbols. The instructors that gave him the systems for *A Vision* gave them in the form of abstract symbols, which were meant to enkindle his imagination and lead him to 'a reality which is concrete, sensuous, bodily':

My imagination was for a time haunted by figures that, muttering 'The great systems,' held out to me the sun-dried skeletons of birds, and it seemed to me that this image was meant to turn my thoughts to the living bird.[59]

That he did not catch that living bird, Yeats testifies at the end of *A Vision* (1937).

There are a number of poems in which the poet or the protagonist expresses his disappointment or impatience over the cleavage between the image and reality. In 'Solomon and the Witch' Solomon ascribes a failure of their love to the inadequacy of an image to bring about a resolution of 'Choice and Chance'. Solomon first explains that the strange sensation that Sheba felt in their sexual union may mean a true resolution of conflict, an announcement by a cockerel, which 'Crew from a blossoming apple bough,' that 'All that the brigand apple brought/ And this foul world were dead at last'. When Sheba points out that the foul world has not disappeared, however, Solomon replies:

> If that be so,
> Your cockerel found us in the wrong
> Although he thought it worth a crow.
> Maybe an image is too strong
> Or may be not strong enough.

In a similar context, in 'The Hero, the Girl, and the Fool', both the hero and the girl loathe imperfection of their love because the image and the true self are confused as the object of love. They are frustrated because they feel cheated out of their love: the hero loves the girl's beauty, not her; the girl loves the hero's heroism, not him; and a nun that the girl wishes to become is revered for her holiness. The fool, who is by the roadside, comments that a true love is found only when one is completely out of the human context:

> When all workers that have
> From cradle run to grave
> From grave to cradle run instead;
> When thoughts that a fool
> Has wound upon a spool
> Are but loose thread, are but loose thread:

> When cradle and spool are past
> And I mere shade at last
> Coagulate of stuff
> Transparent like the wind,

I think that I may find
A faithful love, a faithful love.

'Among School Children' is, in one sense, also a study of image
and reality. The images, which are taken from the world of Anima
Hominis and therefore subject to passage of time, break Yeats's heart,
because they are separated, due to time's destructive power, from
what they stand for. A sense of change is persistent in the poem.
Images wither with time while the 'Presences,' which are 'self-born'
and are therefore out of time, mock 'man's enterprise'. The poem
begins with a casual mention of the setting in which Yeats is
inspecting a school, but a sense of time is immediately emphasised
by a sharp contrast between the innocent children and 'A sixty-year-
old smiling public man'. The children stir Yeats's memory of his
youthful love. The 'Ledaean body' Yeats dreams of may or may not
be Maud Gonne; it is beside the point.[60] The Ledaean body with
whom Yeats was united 'Into the yolk and white of the one shell'
suggests Helen, a symbol of eternal beauty and destruction. The
process of the lovers' uniting into an egg, of course, is a reversal
of Plato's parable of the egg in the *Symposium*. The bright colour
of the children's faces, however, is driven away by her present image:

> Her present image floats into the mind—
> Did Quattrocento finger fashion it
> Hollow of cheek as though it drank the wind
> And took a mess of shadows for its meat?

If his love is now a withered image, Yeats, too, is now an old
scarecrow who is avowedly not 'of Ledaean kind'. In self-mockery
he pictures himself as an image of what stimulates a mother's dreams.
In the lines that echo the second song of *At the Hawk's Well*, Yeats
emphasises the irony which old age presents to the ideal image that
a mother seeks in her son. In his letter to Olivia Shakespear, dated
September 24, 1926, Yeats says that the poem is his 'last curse upon
old age'.[61] The poem is a sorrowful comment on the widening gulf
that time creates between image and reality.

> What youthful mother, a shape upon her lap
> Honey of generation had betrayed,
> And that must sleep, shriek, struggle to escape
> As recollection or the drug decide,
> Would think her son, did she but see that shape
> With sixty or more winters on its head,

> A compensation for the pang of his birth,
> Or the uncertainty of his setting forth?

An old man is, thus, a symbol of disillusionment of motherly affection, a withered image of reality. He breaks a mother's heart. The old man in *At the Hawk's Well*, who is forever severed from the fountain of eternal youth, would also break his mother's heart if she would see him in his present condition:

> What were his life soon done!
> Would he lose by that or win?
> A mother that saw her son
> Doubled over a speckled shin,
> Cross-grained with ninety years,
> Would cry, 'How little worth
> Were all my hopes and fears
> And the hard pain of his birth!'[62]

In the letter to Olivia Shakespear already referred to, Yeats says that the poem 'means that even the greatest men are owls, scarecrows, by the time their fame has come'. Thus, the great minds such as Plato, Aristotle, and Pythagoras, who try to find order in the flux of reality, are also subject to time, 'Old clothes upon old sticks to scare a bird'. Yeats does not include himself in the list of the great minds in this stanza, but the reader cannot but sense the irony of the poet himself who tried all his life to gain the secret from the depth of eternity but was constantly and finally thrown back on the strand of time, where he could only curse old age.

Stanza VII discusses Yeats's last category of images in the poem and suddenly erupts into a series of emotional utterances directed to the 'Presences'. The stanza runs into the next and final stanza in thought and syntax. To separate the stanzas, it seems to me, is to commit a serious critical error. It seems to misinterpret what Yeats is trying to say, or rather to ruin the emotional effect Yeats aims at here.

VII

> Both nuns and mothers worship images,
> But those the candles light are not as those
> That animate a mother's reveries,
> But keep a marble or a bronze repose.
> And yet they too break hearts — O Presences
> The passion, piety or affection knows,

And that all heavenly glory symbolise—
O self-born mockers of man's enterprise;

VIII

Labour is blossoming or dancing where
The body is not bruised to pleasure soul,
Nor beauty born out of its own despair,
Nor blear-eyed wisdom out of midnight oil.
O Chestnut tree, great-rooted blossomer,
Are you the leaf, the blossom or the bole?
O body swayed to music, O brightening glance,
How can we know the dancer from the dance?

The first four lines of stanza VII, and the fifth except 'O Presences', deal with the last category of images Yeats presents in the poem. The divine images that nuns worship are different from those that mothers worship in that they do not grow old: they 'keep a marble or a bronze repose'. And yet they are similar to those that mothers worship in that 'they too break hearts'. Here ends Yeats's enumeration of images that 'break hearts'. Then comes an eruption of emotional utterances, 'O Presences', etc. The remainder of stanza VII is an apostrophe to supernatural beings, Daimons of the thirteenth sphere. The stanza ends with a semicolon, which means that the syntactic structure and the thought content of stanza VII continue uninterruptedly to the following and final stanza. If we separate the stanzas, then we must take what the final stanza says as Yeats's 'final justification of life' that 'the poem constructs from the destructive ravage of time',[63] or as 'a proclamation that the body must not be bruised to pleasure the Soul (which is for Yeats that which seeks abstraction), and what matters is the instinctive joy of life symbolized by the chestnut tree in blossom and the body swayed to music.'[64] The stanza is addressed to the Daimons, 'self-born mockers of man's enterprise', not to the reader; it therefore represents Yeats's, or the speaker's, prayer that the image and reality be fused, not his declaration that 'we do transcend that disparity', as M. L. Rosenthal insists.[65]

Stanza VIII, then, is not a vision of reality that he gained out of his contemplation of conflict, nor is it a statement of triumph of his self over the soul. It is rather an expression of his frustration in reaching his spiritual goal. That is why the apostrophe to the 'Presences' in the middle of stanza VII is so abrupt: Yeats's sustained emotion can no longer be checked:

> And yet they too break hearts — O Presences

This is a Dantesque search for unity. It is a tragic cry in the Yeatsian sense. Yeats is crying like the tragic person he writes about in *A Vision*, 'some great tragic person, some Niobe who must display an almost superhuman will or the cry will not touch our sympathy'.[66] A similar cry, though much less tragic, is uttered by the old man of 'Sailing to Byzantium'.

'Sailing to Byzantium' is another 'curse' of Yeats's on old age. The ageing protagonist, who looks upon himself to be 'a paltry thing,/ A tattered coat upon a stick' (another scarecrow image), leaves the world of time, where 'Those dying generations' are 'at their song', because the Soul does not sing for 'its mortal dress'. He has therefore 'sailed the seas and come/ To the holy city of Byzantium.' In the city of Byzantium images have eternal life, not being subject to the destructive power of time. He prays to the sages of the city:

> gather me
> Into the artifice of eternity.

'Once out of nature' he will take his image not from natural, perishable things, but from some work of art that transcends time.

> Once out of nature I shall never take
> My bodily form from any natural thing,
> But such a form as Grecian goldsmiths make
> Of hammered gold and gold enamelling
> To keep a drowsy Emperor awake;
> Or set upon a golden bough to sing
> To lords and ladies of Byzantium
> Of what is past, or passing, or to come.

It is significant that the old man is not aspiring to be pure soul; he is not by any means choosing the Soul against the Self. Even in the natural world of time he has the soul; but that soul does not 'sing/ For every tatter in its mortal dress', that is, the soul and the image are not united. What the old man loathes is the fact that in the natural world 'Monuments of unageing intellect' are neglected and art studies only the 'Monuments of its own magnificence.' He therefore came to the holy city of Byzantium and asks the sages of the city, who stand 'in God's holy fire/ As in the gold mosaic of a wall', to gather him 'Into the artifice of eternity'. What the old man seeks, then, is an eternal image, not the soul.

In 'Byzantium', a sister piece to 'Sailing to Byzantium', Yeats is again chiefly concerned with image. What floats before the poet is an image which has nothing that man is; it is 'Shade more than man, more image than a shade'. This image, unlike the scarecrow of 'Among School Children' or 'Sailing to Byzantium', is a walking mummy that 'May unwind the winding path' and summon the spirits that have come across the seas to the holy city of Byzantium. This image, which Yeats calls 'death-in-life and life-in-death', is equivalent to the sages of 'Sailing to Byzantium' whom the old man asks to 'Come from the holy fire, perne in a gyre/ And be the singing-masters of my soul'. The next image that floats in Yeats's mind is an eternal image of a golden bird, which previously appeared in 'Sailing to Byzantium', and which is now amplified in meaning in the present poem. Yeats, stimulated by Sturge Moore's criticism, felt that the image in the earlier poem needed an explanation. The meaning of the gold bird is clarified in the present poem.

> Miracle bird or golden handiwork,
> More miracle than bird or handiwork,
> Planted on the star-lit golden bough,
> Can like the cocks of Hades crow,
> Or, by the moon embittered, scorn aloud
> In glory of changeless metal
> Common bird or petal
> And all complexities of mire or blood.

The bird is not merely a work of art, but a supernatural bird that mocks mortality.

Against these supernatural images Yeats juxtaposes the images of the 'blood-begotten spirits', which come in flood on the back of dolphins to Byzantium to dance. The flood, 'That dolphin-torn, that gong-tormented sea', is broken by 'The golden smithies of the Emperor' and by the 'Marbles of the dancing floor' of Byzantium. The 'blood-begotten spirits' sail across the sea and come to the holy city like the old man in the earlier poem.

Both 'Sailing to Byzantium' and 'Byzantium', then, have essentially the same theme. They both envisage a sailing — a sailing from the land of withering images to the land of eternal image, a sailing originated in and motivated by Yeats's mistrust of temporal images. 'The imaginative deals with spiritual things symbolised by natural things', Yeats wrote to George Russell about 1900,[67] but in the symbols taken from nature he only half believed.

In natural things Yeats only half believed. Yet he continued to sing.

Although he is aware of the limitations of the poet, sing he must. In 'Anima Hominis' he wrote:

. . . we [the poets] sing amid our uncertainty; and, smitten even in the presence of the most high beauty by the knowledge of our solitude our rhythm shudders.[68]

His resolution for creative endeavour is accompanied by this realisation:

I think that we who are poets and artists, not being permitted to shoot beyond the tangible, must go from desire to weariness and so to desire again, and live but for the moment when vision comes to our weariness like terrible lightning, in the humility of the brutes.   . . . We seek reality with the slow toil of our weakness and are smitten from the boundless and the unforeseen. Only when we are saints or sage, and renounce experience itself, can we, in imagery of the Christian Cabbala, leave the sudden lightning and the path of the serpent and become the bowman who aims his arrow at the centre of the sun.[69]

The poets and the artists, then, are bound by the cyclical movement of the gyre and cannot seem to get out of it. The confession that Yeats makes in 'The Circus Animals' Desertion' is essentially the same as the two-fold realisation of 'Anima Hominis'. In that poem he looks back on his career as an artist and confesses that he was infatuated with images, not what they stood for.

> Players and painted stage took all my love,
> And not those things that they were emblems of.

They represented a ladder from 'hodos chameliontos' to 'Anima Mundi'. Now that these images are gone he can only enumerate old themes, or be content with the heart. That is the artist's lot and he must accept it:

> Those masterful images because complete
> Grew in pure mind, but out of what began?
> A mound of refuse or the sweepings of a street,
> Old Kettles, old bottles, and a broken can,
> Old iron, old bones, old rags, that raving slut
> Who keeps the till. Now that my ladder's gone,
> I must lie down where all the ladders start,
> In the foul rag-and-bone shop of the heart.

He must pursue, to return to the last section of *A Vision*, 'the image of Heracles that walks through the darkness bow in hand', if he cannot 'mount to that other Heracles, man not image, he that has for his bride Hebe....'

4. BRAHMAN OR DAIMON

I

The main concern of Yeats the saint was the soul and its liberation. *A Vision* was a culmination of his lifelong effort in search of the soul's freedom. His meeting with the East was almost inevitable and it doubtless left a significant mark in his mind. Throughout his works Yeats makes frequent reference to Oriental thought, especially Indian and Japanese. As a number of Yeats scholars have commented, the East had a profound influence upon the progress of the poet. Indian thought, in particular contributed greatly to his cosmology, as Naresh Guha has remarked,[1] and the Japanese Noh to his dramatic theory and practice.

Yeats's debt to the East, however, has been considerably exaggerated by those critics whose active interest lies in hunting Yeats's sources. On the other hand, another line of criticism completely denies Yeats's debt to the East and establishes him as a genuinely Western thinker and poet. There is a third line of criticism that lays more emphasis on the confirmatory rather than the initiatory aspect of Yeats's schooling in Eastern thought and art. This criticism argues that Yeats had reached his conclusions long before he came to know Eastern thought and art, in which he only sought an authority for his ideas and beliefs. All these critical positions distort the true meaning of Yeats's encounter with the East, and therefore miss the possibility that a study of the relationship offers in the way of illuminating Yeats's thought and art.

Yeats was neither an Eastern convert nor a typical Westerner whose way of thinking was antithetical to the Eastern mode of thinking which is broadly termed 'mysticism'. Nevertheless, he should be placed among the ranks of such Western thinkers as Pythagoras, Plato, Plotinus, Swedenborg, and Boehme, whose mode of thinking was characterised by the double perspective of monism and dualism. He may also be placed in the tradition of Western occultism represented by the Cabala and the Rosicrucian and Hermetic traditions. Yeats's meeting with the East may be most profitably studied with this context in mind, for we should not erroneously credit Indian sources for what Yeats may have learned from European sources: Yeats's conception of sexual union as a mystical experience (a resolution of conflict), for instance, may well have been inspired by the Cabala as well as by the Tantric system of India.[2] Moreover, we can profit from the study of his relationship with Eastern thought by discovering discrepancies that exist between the two, which will in turn illuminate for us the nature of his thought and art. By discovering what he accepted and rejected or missed in Eastern thought and art, we may come close to the essence of his thought and art.

Yeats's meeting with Indian thought dates back to his late teens, when he started reading sacred books of India under the influence of his mystic friends including George Russell (AE). In 1885, at the age of twenty, he organised with Charles Johnston the Dublin Hermetic Society with a view to promoting Oriental religions and theosophy. In the following year Yeats met a Bengali Brahmin, Babu Mohini Chatterji, whose coming to Dublin coincided with the founding of the Theosophical Lodge. The Brahmin, who possessed a vast knowledge of Indian as well as Western philosophy and religion, fascinated Yeats and left in his mind ideas that haunted him for years. His new ideas found their expression in 'The Indian Upon God', 'The Indian to His Love', 'Kanva on Himself', and 'Anashuya and Vijaya'.

In 1887 Yeats joined the Theosophical Society and came to be closely associated with Madame Blavatsky after reading her book, *The Secret Doctrine*. He was soon admitted into the esoteric section of the Society, which was composed of advanced students who gathered to study the tables of esoteric symbolism. He was asked to leave the Society, however, when his desire for concrete evidence grew so strong that he attempted an experiment with other members of the esoteric section. In 1890 he withdrew from the Society and joined Macgregor Mathers's Order of Golden Dawn and thence devoted himself to the study of magic and spiritism. By joining the Order, Yeats severed himself from the Dublin group of visionaries and was never to return to it or any other similar group.

Yeats's interest in Eastern thought never waned, however. Through his association with Tagore, Shri Purohit, and Michio Ito, and by reading books of Indian philosophy, such as *The Yoga System of Patanjali* and the Upanishads, Yeats kept his interest in the East fresh. This interest found its artistic expression in a series of Noh-like dramas which he wrote in the several years after he was introduced to the genre by Ezra Pound, in 1913. It also found expression later in the translation of the ten principal Upanishads in collaboration with Shri Purohit and in a series of introductions to and essays on Indian books.

Yeats's interest in the East and mysticism in general was always stirred by his saintly aspirations. In *Reveries over Childhood and Youth* he places the thought of his father, a follower of John Stuart Mill, in an antithetical position to mysticism, and confesses that his familiarity with mysticism resulted in his breaking away from his father's influence:

It was only when I began to study psychical research and mystical philosophy that I broke away from my father's influence. He had been a follower of John Stuart Mill and so had never shared Rossetti's conviction that it mattered to nobody whether the sun went round the earth or the earth round the sun. But through this new research, this reaction from popular science, I had begun to feel that I had allies for my secret thought.[3]

And he soon angered his father by giving a definition of truth, contrary to Mill's, emphasising the subjective validity of truth.

I was soon to vex my father by defining truth as 'the dramatically appropriate utterance of the highest man.' And if I had been asked to define the 'highest man,' I would have said perhaps, 'We can but find him as Homer found Odysseus when he was looking for a theme'.[4]

Yeats's approach to Madame Blavatsky was also motivated by the same saintly aspirations. Although his meeting with Madame Blavatsky had been prepared by his youthful enthusiasm over and admiration for Indian philosophy in general and his interest in theosophy in particular, it was directly motivated by his desire to find out whether the Russian theosophist was an Ahasuerus, the Jew in Shelley's *Hellas*, of whom

> . . . 'tis said his tribe
> Dream, and are wise interpreters of dreams.[5]

The Dublin Theosophists had already affirmed to Yeats the real existence of the Jew and Yeats 'saw nothing against his reality'. So, when Madame Blavatsky came to Dublin, he decided 'to look the matter up', for he had a firm conviction that there were some people who could see into the hidden reality of things and reveal it to ordinary men as Ahasuerus the Jew did to Mahmud the Sultan:

Certainly if wisdom existed anywhere in the world it must be in some lonely mind admitting no duty to us, communing with God only, conceding nothing from fear or favour. Have not all peoples, while bound together in a single mind and taste, believed that such men existed and paid them that honour, or paid it to their mere shadow, which they have refused to philanthropists and to men of learning?[6]

Yet Madame Blavatsky and her Theosophical Society did not satisfy Yeats's expectations wholly, for he was asked to leave the Society when his desire for immediate experience of vision became stronger than the circle had permitted. Although Yeats admits that he did not separate himself from the Society by his own will, his disappointment in the 'esoteric teachings' of Madame Blavatsky is clear. He had been tired of abstraction and, under the influence of William Blake, he desired a vision of reality in concrete terms; that was why he started experimenting in ways contrary to the policies of the Society:

I had learned from Blake to hate all abstraction, and, irritated by what were called 'esoteric teachings', I began a series of experiments.[7]

Ironically, however, this abstraction is in fact what he enthrals himself to in *A Vision* and is what prevents him from attaining the secret knowledge of the *Thirteenth Cone*.

Yeats thought that abstraction held another danger for him as an artist. If an artist is wholly given to abstraction, he is likely to forget the world he lives in and his creative work will become weak and vague. While he was engaged in psychic research and the study of mysticism, Yeats was always aware of the danger, because he thought:

. . . it was my business in life to be an artist and a poet, and that there could be no business comparable to that. I refused to read books and even to meet people who excited me to generalization. . . .[8]

He was so afraid of abstraction that he 'began to pray that (his) imagination might somehow be rescued from abstraction and become preoccupied with life as had been the imagination of Chaucer'.[9]

Indian thought provided for Yeats profound wisdom and inspiration, but, at the same time, it contained a real danger if it was misused. If it brought about a true vision of reality as it promised, nothing more could be desired; however, if it gave no more than formless theory of reality, then a complete immersion in it would mean ruin for an artist. Yeats's attitude toward Indian thought is therefore ambivalent. He takes a negative attitude toward it when his artist's impulse is strong, and a positive attitude when his saint's impulse is strong. In a letter to Florence Farr, written probably in February 1906 when he was tired of his 'vague desires' and was inclined to follow the Apollonian impulse of art, he wrote negatively of the quiescent nature of Indian meditations:

I have myself by the by begun eastern meditations — of your sort, but with the object of trying to lay hands upon some dynamic and substantializing force as distinguished from the eastern quiescent and supersensualizing state of the soul — a movement downwards upon life, not upwards out of life.[10]

Much later in his life, in a conversation with an Indian, Professor Bose and Dr Wilbraham Trench of Trinity College, Yeats complained that Tagore wrote 'too much about God'. He said: 'My mind resents the vagueness of such references. Another sort of mysticism which is harmful to poetry is that of Peter Bell and the primrose.' Falling back on his tragic theory, he then added: 'I have fed upon the philosophy of the Upanishads all my life, but there is an aspect of Tagore's mysticism that I dislike. I find absence of tragedy in Indian poetry.' When he was asked if he had any message to India, he said: 'Let 100,000 men of one side meet the other. That is my message to India, insistence upon the antinomy.' He then strode across the room, and taking up and unsheathing dramatically Sato's Japanese sword, shouted, 'Conflict, more conflict'.[11]

The dualistic-cognitive perspective did not, however, dominate Yeats's mind constantly. There were moments when he aspired to direct experience of oneness with reality. Especially when in 1931 he met an Indian monk, Shri Purohit Swami, in London, his old enthusiasm for Indian thought was reawakened. He helped Shri Purohit to translate ten principal Upanishads and wrote an introduction to them when they were published by Faber and Faber in 1937. He also advised Shri Purohit to write his autobiography, which he thought, after reading it in manuscript form, represented 'the reality of which the theosophists have dreamed'.[12] The meeting with the Indian monk touched off Yeats's meditations about Indian thought, which resulted in a series of essays and introductions. They are, 'Introduction' to *An Indian Monk* by Shri Purohit (1932), 'Introduction' to *The Holy Mountain* by Bhagawan Shri Hamsa

(1934), 'The Mandudya Upanishad' (1935), 'Preface' to *The Ten Principal Upanishads* (1937) translated by Shri Purohit Swami and W. B. Yeats, and 'Introduction' to *Aphorisms of Yoga* (1938) translated into English by Shri Purohit Swami. In this series of essays Yeats definitely links his system and Indian thought.

II

In an essay entitled 'A General Introduction for my Work', written for a complete edition of his works which was never produced, Yeats briefly mentions how *A Vision* came about. He reveals two motivations in writing it. One was a conviction that 'in two or three generations it will become generally known that the mechanical theory has no reality.'[13]

The other was his belief in the unity of all mythologies knitting the natural and the supernatural together. This unity was concrete and tangible, not an abstract theory intellectually formulated nor a distant world beyond knowledge. Yeats's firm faith in this unity subconsciously motivated the writing of *A Vision*:

I was born into this faith, have lived in it, and shall die in it; my Christ, a legitimate deduction from the Creed of St Patrick as I think, is that Unity of Being Dante compared to a perfectly proportioned human body, Blake's 'Imagination,' what the Upanishads have named 'Self': nor is this unity distant and therefore intellectually understandable, but imminent, differing from man to man and age to age, taking upon itself pain and ugliness, 'eye of newt, and toe of frog.'

Subconscious preoccupation with this theme brought me *A Vision*, its harsh geometry an incomplete interpretation.[14]

What Yeats emphasises in this passage is immediacy of experience and knowledge. His Christ was to be 'not shut off in dead history, but flowing, concrete, phenomenal'.[15] *A Vision* was written with a view to knowing this Christ immediately, concretely, and permanently. But Christ failed to appear before Yeats, as he confessed at the end of the book, because he could not allow himself to be absorbed into the symbol completely. The *Thirteenth Cone* remained silent, allowing the whole book to lapse into geometric abstraction that he wished to avoid so much.

Thus, notwithstanding Yeats's saintly longing for an immediate experience of the ultimate reality, *A Vision* failed to bring him that experience. The book, in fact, is characteristically devoid of that personal vision which the title of the book envisages as its goal. The book concentrates, instead, on history and civilisation, and the souls in this world which Yeats views as antinomial; it is most incomplete, as the author admits, in its consideration of the soul and its destiny.[16] In Section V of the book Yeats acknowledges that his 'instructors' revealed to him very little about the ultimate reality and that it cannot be known but only symbolised. What his 'instructors' communicated to him, therefore, was largely about the phenomenal world rather than the secrets of the ultimate reality:

My instructors, keeping as far as possible to the phenomenal world, have spent little time upon the sphere, which can be symbolised but cannot be known, though certain chance phrases show that they have all the necessary symbols.[17]

So the book offers us very little about the ultimate reality and the soul's escape into that reality. It is only after Yeats has read Shri Purohit's autobiography and his master's book that we begin to hear his comments on the subject. As he refers to the content of *A Vision* as 'the system',[18] or 'my public philosophy',[19] the book may, as far as its visionary aspect is concerned, be regarded as an Upanishad without a Brahmanic vision.

From scattered passages referring to the *Thirteenth Cone*, however, we can reconstruct what constitutes Yeats's idea of the ultimate reality and its significance to the soul's freedom. When the passages are pieced together into a consistent whole, there emerges the crux of the whole cosmological concept of Yeats.

The idea of the *Thirteenth Cone* subsumes the Heraclitian concept of a continuity of life and the Orphic dualism of the personal God and the estranged individual souls. However, it most characteristically assumes the Upanishadic mode of thinking. The Upanishads view the ultimate reality, or the Brahman, from two viewpoints: the transcendental and the relative. *Brihadaranyaka Upanishad* (II, iii, 1–3) defines two forms of the Absolute, or Brahman:

1.   There are two forms of Brahman, the material and the immaterial, the mortal and the immortal, the solid and the fluid, sat (being) and tya (that), (i.e. sat-tya, true).

2.   Everything except air and sky is material, is mortal, is solid, is definite. The essence of that which is material, which is mortal, which is solid, which is definite is the sun that shines, for he is the essence of sat (the definite).

3. But air and sky are immaterial, are immortal, are fluid, are indefinite. The essence of that which is immaterial, which is immortal, which is fluid, which is indefinite is the person in the disk of the sun, for he is the essence of tyad (the indefinite). So far with regard to the Devas.[20]

The transcendental Brahman is the Absolute One which pervades the whole universe and yet transcends it. Let us see how the Upanishads describe it.

First of all, the Upanishads speak of the transcendental Brahman as devoid of any qualifying attributes. Since attributes are necessarily of the world of relativity, the Absolute One, which is without a second, is without them. It cannot be known except by negation. In a famous conversation between Yagnavalkya and his wife, in which the wife is bewildered about the meaning of Brahman, the husband explains that relative knowledge is possible only in the phenomenal world and that the Absolute is known only negatively:

15. For when there is as it were duality, then one sees the other, one smells the other, one tastes the other, one salutes the other, one hears the other, one perceives the other, one touches the other, one knows the other; but when the Self only is all this, how should he see another, how should he smell another, how should he taste another, how should he salute another, how should he hear another, how should he touch another, how should he know another: How should he know Him by whom he knows all this: That Self is to be described by No, no![21]

Vagasaneyi-Samhita (Isha) Upanishad describes Brahman as swifter than human thought:

4. that one (the Self), though never stirring, is swifter than thought. The Devas (senses) never reached it, it walked before them. Though standing still, it overtakes the others who are running. Matrisvan (the wind, the moving spirit) bestows powers on it.[22]

The unknowable Brahman is all-pervasive of the universe. *Svetasvatra Upanishad* (I, 16) has the following description:

16. (If he looks) for the Self that pervades everything, as butter is contained in milk, and the roots whereof are self-knowledge and penance. That is the Brahman taught by the Upanishad.[23]

This all-pervasive Brahman is all-inclusive as well:

1. Manifest, near, moving in the cave (of the heart) is the great Being. In it everything is centred which ye know as moving, breathing, and blinking, as being and non-being, as adorable, as the best, that is beyond understanding of creatures.

2. That which is brilliant, smaller than small, that on which the worlds are founded and their inhabitants, that is the indestructible Brahman, that is the breath, speech, mind; that is the true, that is the immortal.

9. In the highest golden sheath there is the Brahman without passions and without parts. That is pure, that is the light of lights, that is it which they know who know the Self.[24]

Brahman thus exists within and outside the universe at the same time. It includes and transcends the phenomenal world as we perceive it. From the transcendental standpoint, or to the illumined, there is no universe other than Brahman. Brahman is thus non-dual, absolute existence.

This non-dual Brahman, which is the absolute existence without a second, transcending all the laws of causality and relativity, makes its appearance as a knowable entity with attributes perceivable by the finite mind in the world of relativity. This appearance is made possible by the inscrutable power of Brahman itself called *maya*:

1. He, the sun, without any colour, who with set purpose by means of his power (sakti) produces endless colours, in whom all this comes together in the beginning, and comes asunder in the end — may he, the god, endow us with good thoughts.

9. That from which the maker (mayin) sends forth all this — the sacred verses, the offerings, the sacrifices, the penances, the past, the future, and all that the Vedas declare — in that the other is bound up through that maya.

10. Know then Prakriti (nature) is Maya (art), and the great Lord the Mayin (maker); the whole world is filled with what are his members.

19. No one has grasped him above, or across, or in the middle. There is no image of him whose name is Great Glory.

20. His form cannot be seen, no one perceives him with the eye. Those who through heart and mind know him thus abiding in the heart, become immortal.[25]

Things of the pheomenal world are thus conceived to emanate from the Absolute One, who is transcendental and cannot be seen. Yet the Absolute One is the home to which everything returns:

7. And, O friend, as birds to a tree to roost, thus all this rests in the Highest Atman, —*

8. The earth and its subtile elements, the water and its subtile elements,

---

* The identity of Atman and Brahman will be discussed shortly.

the light and its subtile elements, the air and its subtile elements, the ether and its subtile elements; the eye and what can be seen, the ear and what can be heard, the nose and what can be smelled, the taste and what can be tasted, the skin and what can be touched, the voice and what can be spoken, the hands and what can be grasped, the feet and what can be walked, the mind and what can be perceived, intellect (buddhi) and what can be conceived, personality and what can be personified, thought and what can be thought, light and what can be lighted up, the Prana and what is to be supported by it.

9. For he it is who sees, hears, smells, tastes, perceives, conceives, acts, he whose essence is knowledge, the person, and he dwells in the highest, indestructible Self,—[26]

The indestructible, causeless Brahman is, then, the source and the destination of all forms and names of the phenomenal world. What appears to us as real is a shadow of reality which is created by the magical power of Brahman, called *maya*. Brahman thus creates and does not create the phenomenal world. It pervades and transcends the created world. By creating the phenomenal world it does not lose its non-dual nature; it always remains one. Thus the seeming dualism of the Vedantic ontology is resolved into non-dualism as salt and water are fused into salt water.

Before we wander too far into the maze of the Vedantic wisdom, let us return to Yeats and see how his idea of the ultimate reality compares with the Vedantic concept.

Like the Upanishads, Yeats also views the ultimate reality from two standpoints: the transcendental and the relative. Viewed from the transcendental standpoint, the ultimate reality is called the *Thirteenth Sphere*. It is called a Sphere because it is phaseless. Yeats divided the historical process of the time-world into twelve cycles. Each cycle is a cone because it consists of antinomies. The *Thirteenth Sphere* transcends the twelve historical cycles. Viewed from the relative standpoint, however, the ultimate reality is a cone and the spiritual antithesis of the historical cycles and incarnate daimons. It is reflected in each lesser cycle of the time-world. Thus, Yeats's *Thirteenth Cone* or *Sphere* is both transcendental and relative as Brahman is. Its transcendental nature cannot be perceived or described by a person living in the world of relativity. It can best be symbolised:

I speak of the *Thirteenth Cone* as a sphere and yet I might say that the gyre or cone of the *Principles* is in reality a sphere, though to Man, bound to birth and death, it can never seem so, and that it is the antinomies that force us to find it a cone. Only one symbol exists, though the reflecting mirrors make many appear and all different.[27]

The ultimate reality transcends all relativity, all conflict and all knowledge. It is, in other words, non-dual entity; and this is the reason why it cannot be known by the creature of the relative world:

The ultimate reality because neither one nor many, concord nor discord, is symbolized as a phaseless sphere, but as all things fall into a series of antinomies in human experience it becomes, the moment it is thought of, what I shall presently describe as the thirteenth cone. All things are present as an eternal instant to our Daimon (or Ghostly Self as it is called, when it inhabits the sphere), but that instant is of necessity unintelligible to all bound to the antinomies.[28]

The creature of this time-world can only see things antinomially and therefore cannot know the ultimate reality which transcends the world of antinomies. The unintelligibility of the ultimate reality is the key idea of Yeats and must be clearly understood and remembered in order to understand his thought. The confession of failure at the end of *A Vision* is not an artistic gesture nor an abandonment of Vedantic philosophical abstraction; it is a statement of his epistemological belief. This belief, of course, strengthened his position as an artist, for it justifies the artist's work that falls in the domain of symbols. Helen Vendler's equation of the *Thirteenth Cone* with Phase Fifteen is based on two misunderstandings of Yeats's concept of the ultimate reality. Yeats never placed, as she believes he did, the *Thirteenth Cone* in the *mind*, nor Phase Fifteen in a form of created art.[29]

The non-dual ultimate reality is not an abstract idea, but a dynamic energy which is free from causal and other relationships. Its relative and causal aspects are only in our human perception:

The *Thirteenth Cone* is a sphere sufficient to itself; but as seen by Man it is a cone. It becomes even conscious of itself as so seen, like some great dancer, the perfect flower of modern culture, dancing some primitive dance and conscious of his or her own life and the dance.[30]

The ultimate reality as a personal, dynamic entity assumes an antithetical position to the antinomies of the phenomenal world. It is the spiritual destination of all creatures of the phenomenal world, for whom entering into the 'sphere' means to attain freedom, a deliverance from the cycle of birth and death:

It is that cycle which may deliver us from the twelve cycles of time and space. The cone which intersects ours is a cone in so far as we think of it as the antithesis to our thesis, but if the time has come for our deliverance it is the phaseless sphere, sometimes the Thirteenth Sphere, for every lesser cycle contains within itself a sphere that is, as it were, the reflection or messenger of the final deliverance. Within it live all souls that have been set free and every *Daimon* and *Ghostly Self*; our expanding cone seems to cut through its gyre; spiritual influx is from its circumference, animate life from its centre.[31]

This brief passage, which touches on the meaning of the ultimate reality in connection with the soul's freedom, brings in ideas from three different sources that are conspicuous among others in the making of *A Vision*. The idea of nonduality of the ultimate reality comes from the Vedantic sources, which emphasise the all-inclusive and all-pervasive and attributeless (phaseless in Yeats's language) Brahman as the sole reality. However, this phaseless sphere is the antithesis to the antinomies of the phenomenal world — an idea which Yeats obviously borrowed from Heraclitus, to whom life was a continuous flow in which death meant only a renewal of life and in which life and death were in complementary relationship. Yeats borrowed the idea of the interlocking gyres from Heraclitus. Explaining his fundamental symbol, Yeats said in *A Vision*: 'Here the thought of Heraclitus dominates all: "Dying each other's life, living each other's death".'[32] Heraclitus used the expression to explain the relationship of the mortal world and the immortal: 'Immortals become mortals, mortals become immortals; they live in each other's death and die in each other's life.[33] Yeats takes the phrase out of its original context to explain his own idea of the ultimate reality and the phenomenal world. Heraclitus, however, condemned plurality of the ultimate reality. There was for him one continuous Being and therefore one *logos*: 'We should let ourselves be guided by what is common to all. Yet, although the Logos is common to all, most men live as if each of them had a private intelligence of his own.'[34] Thus, it is not right, according to Heraclitus, to distinguish modes of life: 'It is one and same thing to be living or dead, awake or asleep, young or old. The former aspect in each case becomes the latter, and the latter again the former, by sudden unexpected reversal.'[35] According to Yeats, the souls have their antithetical daimons in the *Thirteenth Cone*:

Our actions, lived in life, or remembered in death, are the food and drink of the Spirits of the *Thirteenth Cone*, that which gives them separation and solidity.[36]

The *Thirteenth Cone*, in other words, has gyric relations with the cones of the *Faculties* and *Principles*, the two systems that control the spirits in life and between lives. It has a corresponding phase to each phase of the gyre. When we are in the twelfth month of our expanding gyre, we are in the first of the *Thirteenth Cone*, so that the contrary Cone serves us as the other half of the antinomy. Which simply means that the *Thirteenth Cone* as a whole is the 'spiritual objective' of the souls in the gyre. Individual spirits of the *Thirteenth Cone* have their control over the souls in the relative world, and the individual souls of the relative cycles are, upon death, put through six purgatorial stages before they are reborn or delivered from the cycles of birth and death; during the round of incarnations the souls in the lesser gyres are controlled by the whirling of greater gyres:

All the involuntary acts and facts of life are the effect of the whirring and interlocking of the gyres; but gyres may be interrupted or twisted by greater gyres, divide into two lesser gyres or multiply into four and so on. The uniformity of nature depends upon the constant return of gyres to the same point.[37]

The souls whirl round in the gyres until they are absorbed into the *Thirteenth Cone*, when the whirling of gyres comes to an end:

When all sequence comes to an end, and the soul puts on the rhythmic or spiritual body or luminous body and contemplates all the events of its memory and every possible impulse in an eternal possession of itself in one single moment. That condition is alone animate, all the rest is phantasy. . . .[38]

This combination of the individuality of souls and the macro-microcosmic periodicity of life is not Heraclitian nor Vedantic in origin. It is most likely derived from the Orphic doctrine of reincarnation. In the words of F. M. Cornford:

Orphism is focussed on the individual soul, its heavenly origin and immutable nature, and its persistence, as an individual, throughout the round of incarnations. It is 'an exile from God and a wanderer'; and it is reunited with God, and with other souls, only after its final escape at the end of the Great Year. Hence, the Orphic is preoccupied with the salvation, by purifying rites, of his individual soul.[39]

The idea of the *Thirteenth Cone*, then, has non-Vedantic substrata which make Yeats's concept extremely complex and, in a sense, self-contradictory, for what are we to make of the Sphere which is 'neither one nor many' and yet inhabited by the 'teaching spirits'? What saves Yeats from a hopeless confusion is the concept of maya that he borrowed from the Upanishads. As Brahman manifests itself as the Creator and Destroyer to man through its magic power of illusion, so the *Thirteenth Cone* appears as a cone to man who, forced by the antinomies, cannot find it otherwise.

Yeats, however, could not accept the concept of maya wholly. He adapted the concept to his system only in the epistemological sense. He totally disregarded its metaphysical implication. By condemning the phenomenal world as illusory, the Vedantic philosophy denied it reality, which belongs solely to non-dual Brahman. It follows from this that the soul, in order to attain the ultimate reality, its freedom, must discard all vestiges of duality and unite itself with Brahman. As long as it inhabits the illusory world of duality, it is not free. In order to be free, the soul must know that the only reality is Brahman with which it is united; that knowledge constitutes the experience of freedom. The Vedantic philosophy is thus monistic-experiential in its perspective.

The experience of freedom is gained, according to the Upanishads, by a fusion of Brahman and Atman, the Self in the individual soul. The individual Self is truly the same as Brahman itself, although it is not aware of it as long as it is enthralled in the illusory world. In the conversation between Svetaketu and his father in *Khandogya Upanishad* (VI, ix, 1–4), the father explains to the son the meaning of the Brahman-Atman relationship:

1. 'As the bees, my son, make honey by collecting the juices of distant trees, and reduce the juice into one form,

2. 'And as these juices have no discrimination, so that they might say, I am the juice of this tree or that, in the same manner, my son, all these creatures, when they have become merged in the True (either in deep sleep or in death), know not that they are merged in the True.

3. 'Whatever these creatures are here, whether a lion, or a wolf, or a boar, or a worm, or a midge, or a gnat, or a mosquito, that they become again and again.

4. 'Now that which is that subtle essence, in it all that exists has its self. It is the True. It is the Self, and thou, O Svetaketu, art it.'[40]

The famous phrase, 'Tat tvam asi' (Thou art it) defines the individual Self as one and the same as Brahman. The concept of the oneness of Brahman and Atman (Brahma-atma-aikyam) is expressed in another well-known phrase found in *Brihadaranyaka Upanishad* (I, iv, 10): 'Aham Brahma asmi' (I am Brahman).[41]

The liberation of the soul is achieved by knowing Brahman, by uniting the individual Self with the Supreme Self. *Svetasvatara Upanishad* (I, 10–12) has the following to say on the subject:

10. That which is perishable is the Pradhana (the first), the immortal and imperishable is Hara. The one god rules the perishable (the pradhana) and the (living) self. From meditating on him, from joining him, from becoming one with him there is further cessation of all illusion in the end.

11. When that god is known, all fetters fall off, sufferings are destroyed, and birth and death cease. From meditating on him, there arises, on the dissolution of the body, the third state, that of universal lordship; but he only who is alone, is satisfied.

12. This, which rests eternally within the self, should be known; and beyond this not anything has to be known. By knowing the enjoyer, the enjoyed, and the ruler everything has been declared to be three-fold, and this is Brahman.[42]

In another place the same Upanishad has this:

7. Those who know beyond the High Brahman, the vast, hidden in the bodies of all creatures, and alone enveloping everything, as the Lord, they become immortal.[43]

It is clear, then, that the knowledge of Brahman means the knowledge of the identity of Brahman and the individual Self, Atman, and the knowledge constitutes the experience, which in turn means immortality. The idea is singularly monistic and experiential in its world-view.

To Yeats, whose thinking was dualistically oriented and to whom the earthly realm of particulars mattered so much, this thoroughly transcendental perspective was hardly congenial. Although he conceded to the Vedanta in the idea of the unintelligibility of the ultimate reality and even adapted, though half-heartedly, the Braham-Atman relationship to his system, in which the *Thirteenth Cone* is 'in every man and called by every man his freedom',[44] Yeats found Heraclitus's idea of continuity of life more congenial to him. After all, to be steeped in a Brahmanic vision meant to lose sight of the world of conflict, which was as real to him as the world of unity, for unity arose out of conflict. Thus Heraclitus's dictum,

'Opposition brings concord. Out of discord comes the fairest harmony'[45] was more easily accepted than the Vedantic concept, 'Brahma-atma-aikyam'.

Thus, *A Vision* gives us little or nothing on the subject of the soul's freedom; instead, it speaks about the transmigration of individual souls. The book mentions, however, the Hindu idea of the states of the soul in Book Three, in which four states of the soul that the Upanishads describe are briefly explained. Yeats fails, however, to relate those states of the soul to his concept of the *Thirteenth Cone*.

Elsewhere, however, Yeats vaguely tries to relate the Hindu concept of the soul's states to his system. In the series of essays and introductions which he produced as a result of his association with Shri Purohit Swami, Yeats discusses the question of the freedom of the soul. The essays are informative but offer very little of Yeats's own idea on the subject. From scattered passages and incomplete statements, however, we gather that Yeats connected the Hindu concept of *sushupti* (dreamless sleep) with his Phase One, the phase of the dark moon, and *turiya* (the fourth, transcendental state) with his Phase Fifteen, the phase of the full moon:

I find my imagination setting in one line *Turiya* — full moon, mirror-like bright water, Mount Meru; and in the other *Sushupti*, moonless night, 'dazzling darkness' — Mount Ginár.[46]

Mount Meru stands for the perfect freedom that Bhagwan Shri Hamsa attained; Mount Ginár, on the other hand, stands for *Sushupti* which Shri Purohit Swami attained.

Yeats, then, had presumably two ideas about the meaning of freedom, although he held one superior to the other. Freedom, on the one hand, means a state resulting from a free choice, where the effort and the aim are indistinguishable. On the other hand, it means that state of bliss where the self is completely absorbed into its anti-self. The former is a positive kind of freedom which is attained through positive choosing; the latter is a negative kind which is attained because there is no choice, no desire.

The positive freedom is attained at Phase Fifteen of Yeats's lunar cycle, where the antithetical man gains his fullest expression. There the *Will* completely absorbs the *Creative Mind*, and the *Mask* desired by the *Will* submerges the *Body of Fate*. This is the state of perfect beauty, so much so that it is not possible in human life:

Its own body possesses the greatest possible beauty, being indeed that body which the soul will permanently inhabit, when all its phases have been repeated according to the number alloted: that which we call the clarified or Celestial Body.[47]

This is the state in which the dancer is indistinguishable from the dance, for 'all thought has become image'.[48] This state is related to *turiya*.

The negative freedom is attained at Phase One. There the *Will* is completely absorbed into the *Creative Mind* and the *Mask* into the *Body of Fate*. This is the state of complete objectivity, 'complete passivity, complete plasticity'.[49] Here the being is completely absorbed into its supernatural environment and the mind and the body have become 'the instrument of supernatural manifestation'.[50] The nearest that man can come to this phase is the Phase of the Fool, that is Phase 28. This is the dreamy state in which a person cares about nothing and lives according to the way his environment shapes him, with 'no act but nameless drifting and turning'.[51] A person in this state lives in perfect harmony with nature; birds and beasts are his friends. A passage from the poem, 'Two Songs of a Fool'[52] is illuminating at this point.

> I slept on my three-legged stool by the fire,
> The speckled cat slept on my knee;
> We never thought to enquire
> Where the brown hare might be,
> And whether the door were shut.
> Who knows how she drank the wind
> Stretched up on two legs from the mat,
> Before she had settled her mind
> To drum with her heel and leap?
> Had I but awakened from sleep
> And called her name, she had heard,
> It may be, and had not stirred,
> That now, it may be, has found
> The horn's sweet note and the tooth of the hound.

There certainly is a note of peacefulness and calm acceptance of the grim realities of the world. The phase of perfect objectivity is a step further than this phase of the Fool. There a person will shake off the last link he has with the worldly self and melt into the *Body of Fate*. He attains his freedom by obliterating his identity:

When man identifies himself with his Fate, when he is able to say, 'Thy Will is our freedom' or when he is perfectly natural, that is to say, perfectly a portion of his surroundings, he is free even though all his actions can be foreseen, even though every action is a logical deduction from all that went before it. He is all Fate but has no Destiny.[53]

In relating Phase One to *sushupti* and Phase Fifteen to *turiya* Yeats sought support for his ideas in the moon image that the Upanishads use to explain the soul's reincarnation and its escape. The Upanishads explain that the soul that goes to the bright half of the moon is met by 'a person not human'[54] and is led by him to 'Brahman (the conditioned Brahman)';[55] and the soul that goes to the dark half of the moon is, when it reaches the moon, 'loved (eaten) by the Devas'.[56] Yeats noticed a tremendous possibility that the image offered in supporting his own system:

A European would . . . call the increasing moon man's personality, as it fills into the round and becomes perfect, overthrowing the black night of oblivion. Am I not justified in discovering there the conflict between subjectivity and objectivity, between Self and Not-Self, between waking life and dreamless sleep?[57]

The Heraclitian mode of thinking which inspired him to conceive the interlocking gyres is basic here. Thus, Phase One, the phase of the dark moon, is related to *sushupti*; and Phase Fifteen, the phase of the full moon, is related to *turiya*, the final escape:

The bright fortnight's escape is *Turiyá*, and in the dark fortnight, the ascetic who, unlike the common people, asks nothing of God or Ghost, may, though unworthy of *Turiyá*, find *Sushupti* and absorption in God, as if the Soul were His food or fuel.[58]

Turiya, then, meant for Yeats a freedom gained in the subjective phase and *sushupti* was that gained in the objective phase.

What distinguishes Yeats's ideas of freedom from the Vedantic concept is perhaps their extrovert nature. For Yeats freedom is necessarily associated with the soul's environment. While Phase One means a complete absorption of the soul into its environment, Phase Fifteen means a complete absorption of the environment by the soul. This is how Yeats interprets the Hindu concept of *turiya* and *sushupti*. Whether it occurs in Phase One or Phase Fifteen, freedom means a vision of unity, a unity arising out of antinomy. This vision of unity is basically different from the Vedantic knowledge of Brahman, which emphasises introspection.[59] According to the Upanishads the soul is not expected to go outside it. It is expected to divest itself of all temporal attributes and intensely meditate upon itself, for there is no ultimate reality outside it: 'Sa va ayam atma Brahma' ('That Self is indeed Brahman').[60]

According to the Upanishads, Atman (the Self) is the witness of the experiences of three states: the states of waking, dreaming, and dreamless sleep. The third, dreamless state is called *sushupti* and is the closest that the soul can come to the knowledge of Brahman in the relative world. Atman completely detached from the three states is one and the same as the transcendental Brahman; and the knowledge of Brahman is the experience of freedom, which is called *turiya*. The method of attaining that experience described in the Upanishads is characteristically monistic and experiential in that it negates all relative attributes of the Self, which it calls unreal, and brings one to pure and undifferentiated consciousness. *Katha Upanishad* (II, vi, 10–15) explains how Brahman is attained as follows.[61]

10. When the five instruments of knowledge stand still together with the mind, and when the intellect does not move, that is called the highest state.
11. This, the firm holding back of the senses, is what is called Yoga. He must be free from thoughtlessness then, for Yoga comes and goes.
12. He (the Self) cannot be reached by speech, by mind, or by the eye. How can it be apprehended except by him who says: 'He is?'
13. By the words 'He is,' is he to be apprehended, and by (admitting) the reality of both (the invisible Brahman and the visible world, as coming from Brahman). When he has been apprehended by the words 'He is,' then his reality becomes immortal, and obtains Brahman.
14. When all desires that dwell in his heart cease, then the mortal becomes immortal, and obtains Brahman.
15. When all the ties of the heart are severed here on earth, then the mortal becomes immortal — here ends the teaching.

Mundaka Upanishad (III, i, 7–8) has the following:[62]

7. That (true Brahman) shines forth grand, divine, inconceivable, smaller than small; it is far beyond what is far and yet near here, it is hidden in the cave (of the heart) among those who see it even here.
8. He is not apprehended by the eye, nor by speech, nor by the other senses, not by penance or good works. When a man's nature has become purified by the serene light of knowledge, then he sees him, meditating on him as without parts.

The experience of Brahman, then, is essentially introspective. This aspect of Vedanta which denies the world of particular forms was hardly congenial to Yeats. He could not let the world of conflict go, even though his ultimate aim was the world of unity. His unity was to arise out of conflict.

The method of non-dualistic Vedanta, however, sets the goal of the ultimate experience too high for ordinary people to attain. In order to attain oneness with Brahman, one must cleanse his soul of all the dross of the relative world and bring it to a mirror-like clarity. This makes the goal next to an impossibility for most people. It must be difficult especially for those to whom the world of the senses appears so real that the cognitive perspective seems to be a valid way to true knowledge. It was, at any rate, difficult for Yeats, to whom knowledge meant something 'flowing, concrete, phenomenal'. It was natural, therefore, that he should have felt sympathetic towards the Tantric philosophy.

Unlike Vedanta, Tantra does not dismiss the relative world as illusive. Non-dualistic Vedanta insists that Brahman is attained only by divesting the soul of all its phenomenal attributes. Tantra, on the other hand, looks upon the world of duality as a manifestation of the ultimate reality which can be transformed back into its original form. Maya, according to Tantra, creates the world of relativity in which various elements are polarised. This process of polarisation is called the 'outgoing current' and it reveals reality in the state of evolution; a reversal of this current, called the 'return current', reveals reality in its original state of infinitude. Based on this concept, the Tantric way of realisation is to transform the outgoing current into the return current. Hence, it emphasises the sublimation of conflict into liberation. The ultimate reality is not to be realised by negating phenomenal attributes of the soul, but by positively affirming them, bringing together the poles of antinomy. The physical union of man and woman is thus one way to sublimate the polarity into the cosmic principle of Siva-Sakti. We find here Yeats's familiar idea of unity arising out of conflict.

In Section VII of his essay 'The Mandukya Upanishad' (1935), Yeats comments on the Tantric way of realisation:

An Indian devotee may recognise that he approaches the Self through a transfiguration of sexual desire; he repeats thousands of times a day words of adoration, calls before his eyes a thousand times the divine image. He is not always solitary, there is another method, that of the Tantric philosophy, where a man and woman, when in sexual union, transfigure each other's image into the masculine and feminine characters of God. . . .[63]

Whether the idea of the consummated physical love as a resolution of conflict was derived directly from the Tantric philosophy or not, the idea expressed in this passage is the theme of much of Yeats's later poetry. Yeats could not, however, wholeheartedly accept the

Tantric concept of sexual union as the way of realisation. Constantly haunted with a sense of failure, Yeats maintained a sceptical attitude to any claim of attainment of perfect knowledge. In 'Solomon and the Witch' there is no true consummation of love: when the sexual act is over, both Solomon and Sheba are thrown back into the cyclical process of life. In 'Three Bushes', the lady, the chambermaid and the lover are not united until after death. Cuchulain of *The Only Jealousy of Emer* renounces his only chance of being united with the supernatural Fand, and is brought back to the natural world, where he returns not to his wife, who retrieved him from Fand, but to his mistress, who herself realises that her lover's heart is subject to change.

To the Tantric philosophy, therefore, Yeats held an ambivalent attitude, just as he maintained the same attitude to Vedanta. On the one hand, he accepted the affirmative attitude of Tantra to the world of duality; on the other hand, he was sceptical over Tantra's claim that the perfect knowledge of reality can be attained by reversing the outgoing current of maya. To Yeats, any symbolic forms of action were capable and incapable of revealing the ultimate reality. The sexual union was no exception:

The present Pope has said in his last Encyclical that the natural union of man and woman has a kind of sacredness. He thought doubtless of the marriage of Christ and the Church, whereas I see in it a symbol of that eternal instant where the antinomy is resolved. It is not the resolution itself.[64]

Yeats's schooling in Indian philosophy is thus characterised by an absence of experience, of Brahmanic vision. In turning to the Upanishads he fell into the very Vedantic abstraction which he disliked so much; with Tantra he could not go all the way in the belief in sublimating antinomy into pure consciousness. The monistic-experiential wisdom of Hindu philosophers was an elixir he coveted, but the dosage they offered proved to be too strong for him to swallow at once. Thus he wrote to Sturge Moore in 1929:

My dreams and much psychic phenomena force me into a certain little-trodden way but I must not go too far from the main European track, which means in practice that I turn away from all attempts to make philosophy support science by starting with some form of 'fact' or 'datum': that way lie those deep-sea fish Taylor objects to in the extract and all the obscurantism of the Ratcatchers.[65]

5. THE FLOWER OR THE GYRE

I

Yeats was introduced to the Noh drama of Japan by Ezra Pound, who served him as a secretary during the winters of 1913–14, 1914–15, and 1915–16. Pound, while acting as Yeats's secretary, had a project of his own, which was to edit and publish Ernest Fenollosa's notes on the Noh. The discovery of the Noh meant for Yeats a confirmation of the aesthetic principles he was groping for since the publication of the book, *Ideas of Good and Evil*.[1] In the Noh he thought he found an ideal form of drama, an entirely new form for the West — the kind of drama that has for theme not so much the clash of characters as lyrical intensity. His infatuation with the Noh, however, did not wholly result from his reaction against the realistic school of Ibsen, nor from disbelief in the systematic tragedy of the Aristotelian or the Elizabethan type. It is true that Yeats reacted against the Aristotelian clash of characters on the stage and against Ibsenite realism, but such an unfavourable reaction stemmed from his basic dualistic doctrine of aesthetics, from which his theory and practice of the Noh sprang. The Noh theory of Yeats is a culmination of the years of his effort to formulate an adequate aesthetic doctrine that parallels his antinomial view of the universe. His essay, 'Certain Noble Plays of Japan', which he wrote for Pound's 1916 edition of Fenollosa's work on the Noh and which he included as the opening article in the 1919 edition of *The Cutting of an Agate*, embodies the theories that he had been working out when he discovered the Noh. This essay, therefore, which throws considerable light on the meaning of his earlier essays, can be better understood if it is not read in isolation but related to these earlier essays.

Pound completed his project and the book was published in 1916 with Yeats's introduction. In it Yeats exultingly wrote:

I have invented a form of drama, distinguished, indirect, and symbolic, and having no need of mob or Press to pay its way — an aristocratic form.[2]

This 'aristocratic form' of drama which Yeats declares himself to have invented has two basic elements, intimacy and distance. These seemingly contradicting terms represent the two sides of the same coin. By intimacy is meant ridding the stage of all superfluous ornaments and bringing the stage close to the audience so that the natural speech of the common people may be clearly heard in its simplest way. It has much to do with stagecraft. Distance means to keep all superficial, realistic representations from the stage and bring the audience into 'a deep of the mind'. Drama must deal with the essence of things, not ever-changing phenomena. We already see Yeats's dualistic theory in this intimacy-distance principle. The dualism is not irreconcilable but complementary. Intimacy is achieved only when distance is doggedly kept from the pushing world of realism, while distance is possible only when the actors and the audience commingle in close intimacy and pass together into 'a deep of the mind'. Neither is possible without the other. The dramatic principle expressed by the seemingly contradictory set of rules is the aesthetic counterpart of Yeats's cosmological belief similar to the Heraclitian continuity of concord and discord or the Blakean idea of contrary. The relationship between the opposite rules is not one of negation but of complementarity.

In the first four sections of the essay, 'Certain Noble Plays of Japan', Yeats elaborates on these two basic rules of good art. Intimacy, Yeats explains, comes from a simplification of the stage. The theatre since the Renaissance has grown less and less expressive because it has tended to be elaborate; and that elaboration destroys intimacy.

The stage-opening, the powerful light and shade, the number of feet between myself and the players have destroyed intimacy. I have found myself thinking of players who needed perhaps but to unroll a mat in some Eastern garden.[3]

The kind of drama that can create intimacy is of a drawing-room type that needs no more than a few players and a few people of good taste for an audience. It is an 'aristocratic form', being free from the mob and the press.

What effects would this type of drama bring about on the audience through the intimacy it creates? There are two. To begin with, because it has rid itself of the physical distance of a large commercial theatre, with a consequent need for certain ways of acting, it can now make the natural speech of the common people live. On a big stage in a large theatre the player must shout in order to be heard; besides, he has a loud orchestra to compete with. He must cease to speak like a camel-driver or a sailor, because his voice 'can only become louder by becoming less articulate, by discovering some new musical sort of roar or scream'.[4] By ridding itself of this difficulty the new drama can restore dignity to natural speech and song: 'It should be again possible for a few poets to write as all did once, not for the printed page but to be sung.'[5] Yeats was a firm believer in the life and speech of the common people. In this respect he was far from being aristocratic in the ordinary sense of the term. In his letter to Dorothy Wellesley, dated December 19, 1935, he wrote:

You have the best language among us because you most completely follow Aristotle's advice and write 'like the common people.' You have the animation of spoken words and spoken syntax.[6]

He believed that the essence of a culture is found in the folk tales and songs handed down the generations by the people. In order to grasp the essence one must go directly to common people. This belief of Yeats had remained constant since the days of the Celtic Twilight and had prompted him to study the songs and tales of the Irish country folk; and it was in the same spirit that he advised Synge, when he met him in Paris, to go to the Aran Islands and live among the islanders. The aristocratic form of drama is thus deeply rooted in the life of the common people. This explains the meaning of the remark that Yeats is reported to have made to a Japanese poet, Yonejiro Noguchi, in an interview. Yeats, commenting on the project Pound was carrying on at the time, said to Noguchi:

In my opinion, the racial element alone is the most valuable in any kind of poetry; and true literature must be the literature of the folk strengthened, not weakened, by discipline. For this reason I was delighted to read the Japanese Noh plays which the late Mr. Fenollosa translated and my friend Pound is editing. I was impressed with the Noh.[7] (my translation from Noguchi's Japanese)

The remark is illuminating, for it not only reveals Yeats's motive for adapting the medieval dramatic genre of Japan to his work, but also explains one of the aesthetic principles he had worked out at the time of his meeting with the Noh. True, the aristocratic form of drama is intended for a small audience of good taste, but that form will not impress the audience or satisfy Yeats unless the spirit of the race or culture is animated in it.

Thus the aristocratic drama brings home to the audience the spirit that runs in the life of the common people without the artificiality of oration and stage manners of a big theatre. In the essay on the Noh Yeats writes:

I love all the arts that can still remind me of their origin among the common people, and my ears are only comfortable when the singer sings as if mere speech had taken fire, when he appears to have passed into song almost imperceptibly.[8]

What Yeats is upholding here is naturalness, the kind of naturalness that animates the ordinary life of the common people. He is against all artificiality in the theatre that creates on the stage an illusion, realistic or otherwise.

The drawing-room type of drama has another effect tied in with the naturalness of its speech. Because it has rid itself of all artificiality that stands between the players and the audience, thereby creating naturalness in acting, it has now made it possible for the audience to take part in the aesthetic experience with the players. In the essay on the Noh Yeats tells of a group of Spanish professional dancers whom he saw dance in a drawing-room.

Doubtless their training had been long, laborious, and wearisome; but now one could not be deceived, their movement was full of joy. They were among friends, and it all seemed but the play of children; how powerful it seemed, how passionate, while an even more miraculous art, separated from us by the footlights, appeared in the comparison laborious and professional. It is well to be close enough to an artist to feel for him a personal liking, close enough perhaps to feel that our liking is returned.[9]

In such an intimate atmosphere the player seems to 'recede' into 'the deeps of the mind', and the spectator's imagination is stirred. In such an atmosphere alone is it possible for the audience to share the moment of the subjective experience of beauty with the players. Yeats reached this realisation when he saw a Japanese dancer, Michio Ito, dance in a drawing-room. In a most intimate atmosphere with no artificial lights to glare in the eyes, the Japanese dancer seemed to Yeats to dwell in the world of beauty and pure imagination.

In the studio and in the drawing-room alone, where the lighting was the light we are most accustomed to, did I see him as the tragic image that has stirred my imagination. There, where no studied lighting, no stage-picture made an artificial world, he was able, as he rose from the floor, where he had been sitting cross-legged, or as he threw out an arm, to recede from us into some more powerful life. Because that separation was achieved by human means alone, he receded but to inhabit as it were the deeps of the mind. One realised anew, at every separating strangeness, that the measure of all arts' greatness can be but in their intimacy.[10]

Such, then, is what Yeats means by 'intimacy'. What is of special interest to us is the dualistic nature of the principle. The type of drama that aims at intimacy is necessarily aristocratic, for it is intended only for a small audience of initiates. But the speech and the atmosphere it needs have their origin in the life of the common people. What it assumes is physical ease and naturalness, while what it achieves is spiritual intensity.

The second principle that sustains good art is distance. 'All imaginative art remains,' says Yeats in his essay on the Noh, 'at a distance and this distance, once chosen, must be firmly held against a pushing world. Verse, ritual, music, and dance in association with action require that gesture, costume, facial expression, stage arrangement must help in keeping the door.'[11] For a moment it might seem that this concept of distance is in direct contradiction with the previous concept of intimacy. True, in one respect it removes from a play that which is emphasised in the concept of intimacy; that is, it denies to a play an interest in familiarity. However, this seeming contradiction is not a contradiction of logic but of perspective. While the principle of intimacy, by concentrating on such formalistic aspects of drama as stage, audience, speech, controls the cognitive aspect of drama, the principle of distance has to do with the experiential side of drama. A play must be performed in a very intimate atmosphere with the audience and must take its stuff from the familiar life of the common people, but its effect is of a highly sophisticated sort, felt only by the initiates. The latter point — the aesthetic effect of a play — is what is emphasised in the principle of distance.

In contrast to the 'imaginative art' that remains at a distance, away from the pushing world, the 'unimaginative arts' represent the world as it appears to our senses as such and for its own sake. Yeats was against this sort of art because it denies one a reverie in the subjective world:

Our unimaginative arts are content to set a piece of the world as we know it in a place by itself, to put their photographs as it were in a plush or plain frame, but the art which interests me, while seeming to separate from the world and us a group of figures, images, symbols, enables us to pass for a few moments into a deep of the mind that had hitherto been too subtle for our habitation.[12]

Yeats felt a strong aversion to the realistic drama of Ibsen and his followers because it was too preoccupied with the surface detail of life. The Ibsenite drama, priding itself in giving the audience a real picture of life, *une tranche de vie*, failed to fathom the deeps of the mind. It gave a picture to the eyes, but not an intensity of experience to the mind. His kind of drama, Yeats believed, would enable the audience to forget themselves for a few moments and dwell in the subjective world of passionate reverie.

There are two ways whereby distance is maintained in drama. One is to exclude all artificiality from stagecraft, and the other is to appeal, not to the physical reality of life, but to the tradition, the tribal memory of beauty.

In order to achieve distance in drama, everything that is not human must be removed, for lyrical intensity is attained only through human elements.

As a deep of the mind can only be approached through what is most human, most delicate, we should distrust bodily distance, mechanism, and loud noise.[13]

Yeats's use of masks also originated in his distrust of surface detail. Realistic facial expressions only obstruct lyrical intensity. In fact, Yeats's distrust of physical vitality was so great that he seemed to put more faith in the state of being dead:

It is even possible that being is only possessed completely by the dead, and that it is some knowledge of this that makes us gaze with so much emotion upon the face of the Sphinx or of Buddha.[14]

Here again we see Yeats's double perspective. A deep feeling of life can be best expressed by a state resembling death.

Realism is only for less refined minds, not for the subtle. Even the humorous realism of the Elizabethan tragedy, which heightens the tragic effect, was originally intended for the common citizens in the pit. Even today, realism 'is the delight . . . of all those whose minds, educated by schoolmasters and newspapers, are without the memory of beauty and emotional subtlety'.[15]

What appeals, then, to the subtler minds? Yeats's answer is tradition. All great art appeals to the collective memory of beauty.

A poetical passage cannot be understood without a rich memory, and like the older school of painting appeals to a tradition, and that not merely when it speaks of 'Lethe wharf' or 'Dido on the wild sea banks' but in rhythm, in vocabulary. . . .[16]

The position Yeats takes here is essentially the position he took in 1901, when he wrote in his essay, 'Magic', that

what we call romance, poetry, intellectual beauty, is the only signal that the supreme Enchanter, or some one in His councils, is speaking of what has been, and shall be again, in the consummation of time.[17]

The principle of distance means, then, an appeal to the tradition, the tribal memory of beauty, from which a lyrical intensity in art is gained. Such an appeal, Yeats believed, is an Asiatic habit. The West, ever preoccupied with the idea of progress and a belief in physical reality, has all but lost the habit; it has barely kept it in lyrical poetry. This is the reason why Yeats went to the Noh drama of Japan for a model in dramatic form.

Europe is very old and has seen many arts run through the circle and has learned the fruit of every flower and known what this fruit sends up, and it is now time to copy the East and live deliberately.[18]

II

The dualistic principle of intimacy and distance that Yeats discusses in the four sections of the essay, 'Certain Noble Plays of Japan', was not a new discovery for him. It was something he had been developing for quite some time before he was introduced to the Noh. The dualistic principle already exists in the essays contained in *Ideas of Good and Evil* (1896–1903), although in those essays the principle of distance is emphasised.

It is convenient to divide the development of Yeats's aesthetic theory into two periods: the one before and about the time of the publication of *Ideas of Good and Evil* and the other immediately following it — roughly after 1903. In the earlier period Yeats's experiential perspective is predominant while in the latter period it is definitely on the wane, though never abandoned. On the other hand, the cognitive perspective is considerably played down in the earlier period, while in the latter period it assumes the predominant role in Yeats's mind. He never lost sight, however, of the experiential

perspective throughout both periods; indeed it constantly points to
the ideal state of art, for he always believed that art embodied
spiritual realities. He is strongly against the kind of art that delights
in descriptions of external things. Writing in 1899 to the editor of
the *Daily Chronicle*, Yeats argued:

The literature and painting of our time, when they come out of a deep life,
are labouring to awaken again our interests in the moral and spiritual realities
which were once the foundation of the arts; and the theatre, if it would cease
to be but the amusement of idleness, must cast off that interest in external
and accidental things which has marred all modern arts, and dramatic art
more than any.[19]

Yeats's reaction against the realistic drama of Ibsen stemmed from
his disbelief in nature *per se*. In the essay, 'The Tragic Generation',
he recalls his unfavourable reaction to Ibsen's *A Doll's House*, the
first Ibsen play to be performed in England:

I resented being invited to admire dialogue so close to modern educated
speech that music and style were impossible.
   'Art is art because it is not nature,' I kept repeating to myself. . . .[20]

Yeats frequently expresses his peculiar distrust of modern educated
speech. It contrasts sharply with his belief in the common speech
of the common people. The reason, of course, is that he believed
that ordinary people, particularly the uneducated, were the carriers
of archetypal ideas, which they handed from generation to generation
in folk songs and tales. Realistic drama was undesirable because it
neglected the folk tradition, while concentrating on modern city life.
Furthermore, it described the details of modern life for their own
sake. These ideas were rooted also, no doubt, in his preference of
the Romantic Irish peasantry to modern middle-class city-dwellers,
whom he detested.
   The type of drama that Yeats endorsed was subjective; it
represented man's inner feeling, not externality nor character. He
wrote to Fiona Macleod in 1897:

My own theory of poetical or legendary drama is that it should have no
realistic, or elaborate, but only a symbolic and decorative setting. . . . The
acting should have an equivalent distance to that of the play from common
realities. The play might be almost, in some cases, modern mystery plays.[21]

The modern mystery play was what Yeats wanted in the theatre.

In one sense Yeats was a reactionary. He would even carry his drama further back — perhaps to the original myth from which Nietzsche said tragedy derives its birth. His essay, 'The Autumn of the Body' (1898), indeed, makes a parallelism in theory to Nietzsche's 'The Birth of Tragedy' — a parallelism which Yeats confirmed later when he retracted the position. In that essay he says that the literature of Europe is struggling against the 'externality' which the scientific age has brought into literature. European literature once looked upon the world as 'a dictionary of types and symbols', but it has increasingly assumed a critical and interpretive position towards life. It has become weary of its form-consciousness and has begun to seek, in the Nietzschean term, a Dionysian ecstasy.

I see, indeed, in the arts of every country those faint lights and faint colours and faint outlines and faint energies which many call 'the decadence' and which I, because I believe that the arts lie dreaming of things to come, prefer to call the autumn of the body. An Irish poet whose rhythms are like the cry of a sea-bird in autumn twilight has told its meaning in the line, 'The very sunlight's weary, and it's time to quit the plough.'[22]

The time is about to come when the literature of Europe will enter upon a new era, a Dionysian era, which is characterised by a Dionysian urge to transcend the Apollonian form, a return to the essences of things, a reversal of the process in which the literature of Europe became Apollonian.

We are, it may be, at a crowning crisis of the world, at the moment when man is about to ascend, with the wealth he has been so long gathering upon his shoulders, the stairway he has been descending from the first days.[23]

And, Yeats thought, the artist will take the lead in the ascending movement:

The arts are, I believe, about to take upon their shoulders the burdens that have fallen from the shoulders of priests, and to lead us back upon our journey by filling our thoughts with the essences of things, and not with things. We are about to substitute once more the distillation of alchemy for the analyses of chemistry and for some other sciences; and certain of us are looking everywhere for the perfect alembic that no silver or golden drop may escape.[24]

Yeats was first introduced to Nietzsche by John Quinn and was absorbed in reading his work for a while. In a letter, probably written in September 1902, he tells Lady Gregory how excited he is about Nietzsche.

Dear friend, I have written to you little badly of late I am afraid, for the truth is you have a rival in Nietzsche, that strong enchanter. I have read him so much that I have made my eyes bad again. . . . Nietzsche completes Blake and has the same roots — I have not read anything with so much excitement since I got to love Morris's stories which have the same curious astringent joy.[25]

Nietzsche saw two opposing art impulses in nature, represented respectively by Dionysus and Apollo, from which music and tragedy developed in the culture of the Aryan race. Dionysus represents the impulse of ecstatic art through which the individual is drowned in an experience of oneness with 'the mysterious Primordial Unity'.[26] On the other hand, Apollo represents the impulse of plastic art which leads to individuation and 'the pictorial world of dreams'.[27] Music and tragedy, Nietzsche believed, originated in the Dionysian impulse, which was later reconciled by its contrary impulse, the Apollonian:

Music and tragic myth are equally the expression of the Dionysian capacity of a people, and are inseparable from each other. Both originate in a sphere of art lying beneath and beyond the Apollonian;. . . . Here the Dionysian, as compared with the Apollonian, exhibits itself as the eternal and original artistic force, which in general calls into existence the entire world of phenomena; in the midst of which a new transfiguring appearance becomes necessary, in order to keep alive the animated world of individuation.[28]

In Yeats's essay, 'The Autumn of the Body', these two art impulses are discussed. Although he does not give them Nietzschean terms and though he suggests in his letter to John Quinn that he arrived at these concepts independent of Nietzsche, the parallelism between the essay and Nietzsche's 'Birth of Tragedy' is striking. What interests us most, however, is not the parallelism itself. It is rather the fact that the order of the impulses in Nietzsche's essay is reversed in Yeats's. Nietzsche regarded the development of tragic drama as a reconciliation between the Dionysian impulse and the Apollonian, or the Apollonian imposition of the dream world on the Dionysian drunken ecstasy. Yeats, on the other hand, saw an art-impulse pervading Europe that tried to transcend the forms, and firmly believed that art would carry man back to the primordial myth. At the time he wrote 'The Autumn of the Body', then, he laid more emphasis on the Dionysian art-impulse than on the Apollonian. His main interest was, in our terms, in the experiential aspect of art rather than in the cognitive.

   Yeats, however, reverses the emphasis shortly after his excitement over Nietzsche's theory cools. When *Ideas of Good and Evil*, which contains 'The Autumn of the Body', was published in 1903, Yeats's enthusiasm for Dionysus had waned. He wrote to John Quinn in May 1903 and told him of the change of heart:

Tomorrow I shall send you my new book, *Ideas of Good and Evil*. I feel that much of it is out of my present mood; that it is true, but no longer true for me. . . . The book is too lyrical, too full of aspirations after remote things, too full of desires. Whatever I do from this out will, I think, be more creative. I will express myself, so far as I express myself in criticism at all, by that sort of craft. I have always felt that the soul has two movements primarily: one to transcend forms, and the other to create forms. Nietzsche, to whom you have been the first to introduce me, calls these the Dionisiac and the Apollonic, respectively. I think I have to some extent got weary of that wild God Dionysus, and I am hoping that the Far-Darter will come in his place.[29]

And he wrote in the same vein to George Russell (AE) around the same time:

I am no longer in much sympathy with an essay like 'The Autumn of the Body,' not that I think that essay untrue. But I think I mistook for a permanent phase of the world what was only preparation. The close of the last century was full of strange desire to get out of form, to get some kind of disembodied beauty, and now it seems to me the contrary impulse has come. I feel about me and in me an impulse to create form, to carry the realization of beauty as far as possible.[30]

It is difficult to say whether or not Yeats's change of attitude was influenced by Nietzsche. His aesthetic principles, however, have a close affinity to the theory of Nietzsche developed in 'The Birth of Tragedy'; and after the publication of *Ideas of Good and Evil*, his sympathy lies with the Apollonian perspective.

   It would be a mistake, however, to conclude that the cognitive perspective of Apollo won Yeats from the hands of Dionysus. The two perspectives are related to each other in such a way (reminscent of Yeats's interlocking gyres) that a predominance of one does not mean a defeat of the other. They are in reconciliatory conflict like Empedocles's concord and discord, or Heraclitus's mortals and immortals, 'dying each other's life, living each other's death', as Yeats says in *A Vision*.

Even after the publication of *Ideas of Good and Evil* Yeats's basic concept of art remains changeless. He still believes that art is essentially affective. In the essay, 'J. M. Synge and the Ireland of his Time' (1911), he praises Synge for finding his art 'where those monks found God, in the depths of the mind'.[31] And he goes on to say:

Only that which does not teach, which does not cry out, which does not persuade, which does not condescend, which does not explain, is irresistible. It is made by men who expressed themselves to the full, and it works through the best minds. . . .[32]

Any art that is declamatory and explanatory does not stir imagination. All good art, in Yeats's view, demands emotional participation; it does not ask for understanding, for, Yeats believed, 'literature is a child of experience, of knowledge never'.[33] 'We should not', he wrote in a letter to Brinsley MacNamara in 1919, 'as a rule have to say things for their own sake in a play but for the sake of emotion.'[34] Art, therefore, in Yeats's view, is ultimately Dionysian rather than Apollonian:

All art is dream, and what the day is done with is dreaming-ripe and what art has moulded religion accepts, and in the end all is in the wine-cup, all is the drunken fantasy, and the grapes begin to stammer.[35]

Ecstasy as the end of art and the aim of the artist is doggedly kept in view. At the same time, Yeats still keeps his belief in the dualistic nature of art and the artist.

This dualistic concept of art and the artist is essentially the same as that maintained before the publication of the *Ideas of Good and Evil*, although his emphasis shifts. In one of the essays titled 'Discoveries' (1906) Yeats writes:

The end of art is the ecstasy awakened by the presence before an ever-changing mind of what is permanent in the world, or by the arousing of that mind itself into the very delicate and fastidious mood habitual with it when it is seeking those permanent and recurring things.[36]

What the artist aims at is eternity, but it is approached through the things in this world. The aim of art is to arouse in our minds an experience of that eternity, but that aim is achieved only by presenting to the mind 'what is permanent in the world', or recurring images. If art keeps its house between time and eternity, so the artist finds his place between the saint and the common world. In other words, the artist must have a double perspective — experiential and cognitive. His true concern is a vision of eternity, but his job is to give expression to what he sees.

After the publication of *Ideas of Good and Evil*, the Apollonian cognitive perspective comes to seem to Yeats increasingly vital. He had earlier believed that Europe was entering upon a phase in which it felt quickening of the Dionysian art-impulse, an impulse to get out of form in art. He now believes that the contrary impulse has come in him and around him. In his aesthetic he shows his interest in the form and content of art than in its aim, more in the creative function of the artist rather than in his visionary experience. He had earlier believed that the poet was to take upon himself the task that fell from the shoulders of the priest. But he now believes that the artist's proper domain is here in this world. He had earlier maintained in such essays as 'The Autumn of the Body' and 'The Moods' that the artist should have the Dionysian experiential perspective — 'the mysterious instinct' as he calls it in the essay 'The Moods'. Now he believes that Apollo should take the place of Dionysus. The artist's job is not to transcend form but to order it so as to achieve the desired effect. He writes in 'Discoveries' (1906):

All art is sensuous, but when a man puts only his contemplative nature and his more vague desires into his art, the sensuous images through which it speaks become broken, fleeting, uncertain, or are chosen for their distance from general experience, and all grows unsubstantial and fantastic.[37]

This is quite a switch of emphasis compared to what he envisaged as the artist's 'only restraint' in the essay 'The Moods'. The artist should not be content with presenting a dim world of vague desires, which will only tire imagination.

If we are to sojourn there that world must grow consistent with itself, emotion must be related to emotion by a system of ordered images, as in the *Divine Comedy*. It must grow to be symbolic, that is, for the soul can only achieve a distinct separated life where many related objects at once distinguish and arouse its energies in their fullness.[38]

And this symbolic art must 'arise out of a real belief' and take its stuff from the procession of images sanctioned by 'a crowd of believers who could put into all those strange sights the strength of their belief and the rare testimony of their vision'.[39] Thus the artist is not allowed to forget himself in his personal ecstasy, but must

give expression to what he feels; and his manner needs discipline
and a sanction by tradition.

Yeats's shift of emphasis to the cognitive perspective now makes
it mandatory to make a clear distinction between the artist and the
saint. The artist, whose main concern is how to perpetuate in art
what is eternal, is essentially different from the saint, whose interest
is his own eternity. In one essay in 'Discoveries' Yeats discusses two
types of asceticism: one is the type followed by the saint who goes
straight to eternity, and the other is the type followed by the artist
who evokes eternity by critically arranging images:

The imaginative writer differs from the saint in that he identifies himself
— to the neglect of his own soul, alas! — with the soul of the world, and
frees himself from all that is impermanent in that soul, an ascetic not of
women and wine, but of the newspapers. Those things that are permanent
in the soul of the world, the great passions that trouble all and have but
a brief recurring life of flower and seed in any man, are indeed renounced
by the saint, who seeks not an eternal art, but his own eternity. The artist
stands between the saint and the world of impermanent things, and just in
so far as his mind dwells on what is impermanent in his sense, on all that
'modern experience and the discussion of our interests,' that is to say, on
what never recurs, as desire and hope, terror and weariness, spring and
autumn, recur, will his mind losing rhythm grow critical, as distinguished
from creative, and his emotions wither. He will think less of what he sees
and more of his own attitude towards it, and will express his attitude by
an essentially critical selection and emphasis.[40]

In another essay in 'Discoveries' Yeats places the saint and the artist
on the turning wheel of God, where the former goes to the centre
while the latter remains on the ring. The saint longs for calm and
fixity while the artist yearns for life. The artist tries to eternalise what
is perpetually returning, to grasp eternity in recurring images. His
job is to animate what he sees around him and put into it the divine
essence. If he sought for what is fixed and still, then 'his style would
become cold and monotonous, and his sense of beauty faint and
sickly. . . .'[41] The artist must be 'content to find his pleasure in all
that is for ever passing away that it may come again, in the beauty
of woman, in the fragile flowers of spring, in momentary heroic
passion, in whatever is most fleeting, most impassioned, as it were,
for its own perfection, most eager to return in its glory'.[42]

Yeats's wheel image is much the same as T. S. Eliot's, which also
has a centre where all the opposites of the 'turning world' are
reconciled. Like Yeats, Eliot recognises the significance of the world
of time in attaining a vision of eternity. Though the eternal moment

gained at the 'still point of the turning world' is out of time, it can
be remembered and made significant only in time. Thus, for Eliot,
'Only through time time is conquered'.[43] Yeats, however, is not so
positive about the vision of eternity that the recurring images of the
turning wheel promise. The artist may, after all, be seeing dreams
in images that never completely recur:

Yet [the artist] must endure the impermanent a little, for these things return,
but not wholly, for no two faces are alike, and, it may be, had we more
learned eyes, no two flowers.[44]

Of course, Eliot, too, recognized the limitations of art. Art is in time;
as such, it is not eternal:

> Words move, music moves
> Only in time; but that which is only living
> Can only die. Words, after speech, reach
> Into the silence.[45]

Eliot, however, believed that art can reach eternity by its form, which
is a resolution of movement and stillness:

> Only by the form, the pattern,
> Can words or music reach
> The stillness, as a Chinese jar still
> Moves in its stillness.[46]

Played music and written words pass away, but the inherent form
remains eternal. There is no beginning nor end in the form, which
exists before and after the music is played: 'And all is always
now'.[47] Yeats did not share this belief. For him, art had only an
evocative function; if it did not evoke a vision of eternity, it was
forever lost in the dark void of time. If art had an eternal value,
therefore, it must prove itself serviceable in its evocative function.

Perhaps it is in the theory of tragedy that we find a consummation
of Yeats's aesthetic. Yeats's tragic theory developed in the essays of
The Cutting of an Agate may be reduced to the following points:
(1) Tragedy is the noblest of the arts. (2) Tragedy aims at trance.
(3) Tragedy arises out of conflict. (4) Tragedy is poetical. These points
are closely interdependent, but the second and the third points are
of particular interest to us.

Yeats thought that tragedy was the noblest of the arts because it
embodied vast emotions to the neglect of the trivial sentiments of

daily life. The vast emotions of tragedy are not confined to particular individuals nor to particular ages; they belong to the Great Memory, from which the individual draws emotions that are of universal and eternal value. Any art that fails to draw upon the Great Memory cannot be called truly great. Spenser's art, Yeats thought, was mostly of this kind. Spenser was the poet of his times and 'his morality is official and impersonal — a system of life which it was his duty to support',[48] which makes him a lesser artist than Dante. A poet should not be state-oriented, like Spenser. He must work with vast emotions that spring from the eternal element of his race, not from the daily life that passes with time. The art that embodies vast emotions is tragic art, for

in mainly tragic art one distinguishes devices to exclude or lessen character, to diminish the power of that daily mood, to cheat or blind its too clear perception. If the real world is not altogether rejected, it is but touched here and there, and into the places we have left empty we summon rhythm, balance, pattern, images that remind us of vast emotions, the vagueness of past times, all the chimeras that haunt the edge of trance. . . .[49]

The vast emotions that tragic art embodies lead to trance. Yeats's idea of trance as the aim of tragic art is a natural outcome of his general theory of the Great Memory. It stems from his monistic-experiential view of reality. Tragic art helps man to obliterate his individual consciousness and allows him to sojourn in the world of the Great Memory in a Dionysian ecstasy:

Tragic art, passionate art, the drowner of dykes, the confounder of understanding, moves us by setting us to reverie, by alluring us almost to the intensity of trance. The persons upon the stage, let us say, greaten till they are humanity itself. We feel our minds expand convulsively or spread out slowly like some moon-brightened image-crowded sea. That which is before our eyes perpetually vanishes and returns again in the midst of the excitement it creates, and the more enthralling it is, the more do we forget it.[50]

And this tragic art was, for Yeats, the supreme art, for 'tragic ecstasy . . . is the best that art — perhaps life — can give'.[51]

This ecstatic view of tragic art, however, is qualified by Yeats's dualistic-cognitive perspective. The aim of tragic art is trance. That is fine; but what constitutes tragic art? Yeats's dualistic mode of thinking asserts itself strongly in his emphasis on conflict as the essential element of the tragic and in his recognition of art as an embodiment of ideas.

Yeats thought that unity arose out of conflict; he grows increasingly emphatic about this process after the publication of *Ideas of Good and Evil*. The antinomial view of life was never abandoned till the end of his life; indeed, it is given increasingly violent expressions in his last poems. Before the publication of *Ideas of Good and Evil* Yeats realised that perfection in art stemmed from imperfection, but he was full of 'vague desires' for perfection. After the publication of the book, he turns his artist's eye to 'the foul rag-and-bone shop of the heart' from which that perfection is supposed to proceed. He now sees conflict not only in art but also in all human activities:

I think that all noble things are the result of warfare; great nations and classes, of warfare in the visible world, great poetry and philosophy, of invisible warfare, the division of a mind within itself, a victory, the sacrifice of a man to himself.[52]

Art, in particular, arises out of such warfare in the artist's mind. Dante and Villon were two examples in whom the antinomial process took place. The earthly Beatrice led Dante to the yellow rose of *Paradiso*.

If tragic art is created by a mind in which conflict is a real crisis, tragic feeling has a strong hold on the minds of the people in an age of conflict. People are held together by a tragic sense of life when there is no security in their lives, but comic spirit becomes more appealing, Yeats thought, as life grows safe. Yeats believed that this is what happened in Ireland:

Poetical tragedy, and indeed all the more intense forms of literature, had lost their hold on the general mass of men in other countries as life grew safe, and the sense of comedy which is the social bond in times of peace as tragic feeling is in times of war, had become the inspiration of popular art. I always knew this, but I believed that the memory of danger, and the reality of it seemed near enough sometimes, would last long enough to give Ireland her imaginative opportunity. I could not foresee that a new class, which had begun to rise into power under the shadow of Parnell, would change the nature of the Irish movement, which, needing no longer great sacrifices, nor bringing any great risk to individuals, could do without exceptional men, and those activities of the mind that are founded on the exceptional moment.[53]

The tragic, then, is equated with the heroic. The tragic spirit is an inclination of the mind toward some sort of synthesis of conflicting elements. It is an impulse toward a successful resolution of all antinomies. Its starting point is the world of turbulency, war, multiplicity; its destination is the world of peace and unity. It embraces no static vision, but enhances a spiritual progress from despair to ecstasy. Its corpus is made of warring elements, but its soul is of pure material. It mingles contraries, but it aims at a resolution of those contraries. This idea of tragic process was never abandoned throughout his life. As late as 1935 he wrote to Dorothy Wellesley:

I think that the true poetic movement of our time is toward some heroic discipline. People much occupied with morality always lose heroic ecstasy. Those who have it most often are those Dowson described (I cannot find the poem but the lines run like this or something like this)

> Wine and women and song
> To us they belong
> To us the bitter and gay.

'Bitter and gay,' that is the heroic mood. When there is despair, public or private, when settled order seems lost, people look for strength within or without. Auden, Spender, all that seem the new movement look for strength in Marxian socialism, or in Major Douglas; they want marching feet. The lasting expression of our time is not this obvious choice but in a sense of something steellike and cold within the will, something passionate and cold.

The spiritual movement toward the heroic mood is what is enhanced by tragic spirit. Its aim is 'an act of faith and reason to make one rejoice in the midst of tragedy'.

The tragic art, then, proceeds from despair to ecstasy; it has a vision of both eternity and time; it embodies both joy and sorrow. The more conflicting the antinomial elements, the nobler the art,

for the nobleness of the arts is in the mingling of contraries, the extremity of sorrow, the extremity of joy, perfection of personality, the perfection of its surrender, overflowing turbulent energy, and marmorean stillness; and its red rose opens at the meeting of the two beams of the cross, and at the trysting-place of mortal and immortal, time and eternity.[56]

Another indication of the predominance of the cognitive perspective after the publication of *Ideas of Good and Evil* is Yeats's growing interest in the role of ideas in art. Yeats's attitude toward ideas, of course, was always ambivalent. He had earlier minimised their importance in art, though he could not eliminate them entirely. His association with the Rhymers, French symbolists, and 'the

Aesthetic School' of Arthur Hallam had made him sceptical about ideas, but he was, at the same time, strongly attracted to the popular beliefs of the Irish countryfolk. He notes this early contradiction of his aesthetic principle in the essay 'Art and Ideas' (1913):

Yet all the while envious of the centuries before the Renaissance, before the coming of our intellectual class with its separate interests, I filled my imagination with the popular beliefs of Ireland, gathering them up among forgotten novelists in the British Museum or in Sligo cottages. I sought some symbolic language reaching far into the past and associated with familiar names and conspicuous hills that I might not be alone amid the obscure impressions of the senses. . . .[57]

Although he alone among the Rhymers consciously followed Arthur Hallam's criticism, Yeats was left discontented with the 'delighted senses'. Yet his distrust of ideas was so great that he wrote against them in rather strong terms in a letter to George Russell (AE) in 1900:

I do not understand what you mean when you distinguish between the word that gives your idea and the more beautiful word. Unless you merely mean that beauty of detail must be subordinate to general effect, it seems to me just as if one should say 'I don't mind whether my sonata is musical or not so long as it conveys my idea.' Beauty is the end and law of poetry. It exists to find the beauty in all things, philosophy, nature, passion, — in what you will, and in so far as it rejects beauty it destroys its own right to exist. If you want to give ideas for their own sake write prose. In verse they are subordinate to beauty which is their soul. Isn't this obvious?[58]

By 1909, however, the situation was completely reversed. He now believed that ideas not only had their proper place in art but also gave strength to it. In his book on Eastern Painting Laurence Binyon showed Yeats that Whistler was wrong about Japanese painting, which, Whistler said 'in the confidence of his American naivete',[59] had no literary ideas. Hallam and his aesthetic school dissatisfied him, for they tried to sever the individual talent from tradition. Art, he came to believe, embodied the archetypal ideas handed down the generations. In his diary of 1909 he wrote:

Hallam argued that poetry was the impression on the senses of certain very sensitive men. It was such with the pure artists, Keats and Shelley, but not so with the impure artists who, like Wordsworth, mixed up popular morality with their work. I now see that the literary element in painting, the moral element in poetry, are the means whereby the two arts are accepted into the social order and become a part of life and not things of the study and exhibition. Supreme art is a traditional statement of certain heroic and religious truths, passed on from age to age, modified by individual genius, but never abandoned.[60]

Art is something more than the sensuous and individual in nature. It is deeply rooted in the tradition, which gives art its sanction for genuine feeling and archetypal ideas. In 'Art and Ideas' (1913) he wrote:

The old images, the old emotions, awakened again to overwhelming life, like the gods Heine tells of, by the belief and passion of some new soul, are the only masterpiece.[61]

The exclusion of ideas from poetry and the infatuation with momentary sensation, which were a canon that Yeats and the Rhymers obeyed, 'had deprived [them] of the power to mould vast material into a single image'.[62] Archetypal ideas give art its life and power. One should not be afraid to use them. 'Why,' asks Yeats in 'Art and Ideas,'

should a man cease to be a scholar, a believer, a ritualist before he begins to paint or rhyme or to compose music, or why if he have a strong head should he put away any means of power?[63]

It would be a mistake, however, to conclude that Yeats valued ideas for their own sake. Ideas were good insofar as they gave poetry its life and power sanctioned by tradition. Meanwhile, the true aim of art remains ecstasy. Arts are not mere containers of ideas; they have their own life: 'vast worlds moulded by their own weight like drops of water'.[64] While emphasising the importance of ideas in art, Yeats never abandoned the experiential view of art. In the same diary of 1909, in which he discredited Whistler and Hallam, he states his experiential view of tragedy:

Tragedy is passion alone, and rejecting character, it gets form from motives, from the wandering of passion; while comedy is the clash of character. . . . A poet creates tragedy from his own soul, that soul which is alike in all men. It has not joy, as we understand that word, but ecstasy, which is from the contemplation of things vaster than the individual and imperfectly seen, perhaps, by all those that still live. . . . is not ecstasy some fulfilment of the soul in itself, some slow or sudden expansion of it like an overflowing well? Is not this what is meant by beauty?[65]

Yeats's ambivalent attitude towards ideas in art is best expressed in a letter he wrote to his father in 1914. His double perspective is most evident in the following words:

What you say is true about abstract ideas. They are one's curse and one has sometimes to work for months before they are eliminated, or till the map has become a country. Yet, in some curious way, they are connected with poetry or rather with passion, one half its life and yet its enemy.[66]

At the base of Yeats's tragic spirit, then, we find real dualism. It follows from this that the tragic art for Yeats is also dualistic. On the one hand, it consists of conflicting elements: joy and sorrow, stasis and motion, the eternal and the temporal, and so on. On the other hand, it aims at a resolution of all these conflicts. Again, on the one hand, it embodies ideas; while, on the other hand, it aims at ecstasy. The dualism was rooted in Yeats's conflicting claims for art, with the cognitive perspective on the one hand and the experiential on the other. The polarities of emphasis, as always, had a relation with each other like that of the interlocking gyres. The experiential emphasis was predominant before the publication of *Ideas of Good and Evil*, while the cognitive emphasis became stronger afterwards. Neither emphasis completely negated the other.

So far, what has been traced is the vacillating movement of the conflicting perspectives in Yeats's aesthetic; it remains to see what significance this movement has to his meeting with the Noh.

III

The Noh drama of Japan developed from an earlier dramatic form called the *Sarugaku*, which flourished as a mimetic comedy in Japan in the middle of the Heian period (794–1185). The *Sarugaku* originated in China as a theatrical art of the lower type and was imported into Japan together with the *Gagaku*, a more refined type. The *Sarugaku* developed in Japan into a sort of a musical comedy in which the main features were humorous songs and dance. The *Sarugaku* players were usually of the lower class, who made their living solely out of the use of their talent. Their performance was a part of the entertainment for the aristocratic audience at religious festivals. Their performance was characterised by humorous realism whereby the popular manners were imitated. They were not concerned with dramatisation of historical events nor with literary or philosophical ideas. Indeed, their performance was not genuinely 'dramatic,' for it did not involve a clash of characters that makes plot possible. The performance was done mainly by a single character and only occasionally by two.

During the Kamakura period (1192–1333), the *Sarugaku* took a definite theatrical form. The performance was sustained by a plot involving two or more characters. The theatrical development along this line produced what was later called the *Kyogen*. In parallel with this another line of development took place. The mimetic element of the *Sarugaku* divested itself of humorous realism and adopted dance and music, which were becoming increasingly popular, for its medium of expression. It moved away from light humour and satire and tended toward gravity and refinement. This line of development found its fulfilment in the highly sophisticated form of theatrical art known as the Noh.

In the Muromachi period (1392–1573) the Noh theatre enjoyed its heyday under the patronage of the *Shogun*, whose financial support made it possible for the Noh players to concentrate on perfecting their art. In its technical aspect the Noh art reached its supreme refinement through the efforts of Kannami and his son Zeami*, who left behind them a unique Noh theory to which later Noh players were to turn for their artistic authority. Kannami and Zeami brought about a revolution in the art of the Noh by adapting to their performance the *kusemai***, a type of dance accompanied by singing which had become popular since the end of the Kamakura period. The adoption of the *kusemai* caused the Noh to take quite a different direction from the original genre of the *Sarugaku*, of which the basic elements were humour and mimesis. Instead of realistic representations and mockery of popular manners, the graceful presentation of the essences of things in dancing became the main concern of the Noh players. Kannami and Zeami perfected the new genre and postulated a theory of it.

Of the founders of the Noh drama, Zeami made outstanding contributions to the development of the genre in his multifarious capacities, as a player, stage director, playwright, as well as theorist. One Japanese Noh scholar looks upon Zeami's genius as a combination of Sophocles' and Aristotle's.[67] Although such an estimation hardly does justice either to Zeami or to the Greek dramatist and the philosopher, we do find in Zeami an extraordinary combination of the genius of an artist and that of a systematic thinker. Trained directly and closely by his father, Zeami's art was brought to perfection early in his life and was high in favour of Shogun Yoshimitsu. Part of the Noh theory was secretly taught

*Pronounced 'zay-ah-mee'. **Pronounced 'koo-say-mai'.

him by his father, but he is generally credited with its systematisation.

Zeami is known to have written twenty-three books, of which eighteen are extant. The books were meant to be secret, were jealously guarded as a secret tradition by generations of Noh players, and were not made public until after the Meiji Revolution (1868). Out of the eighteen extant books the most important one is perhaps the *Kadensho*, which was written by Zeami at the age of thirty-eight and is in the form of a record of his father Kannami's secret instruction.[68] Since it would require a book to discuss the whole book, let alone the other writings of Zeami, the three basic elements in the art that are expounded in the book will be treated here: the element of mimesis, the element of *yugen*, and the element of *hana* (flower). In the book Zeami has explanations of the form and content of the Noh plays and detailed instructions as to the training of players and actual performance on the stage. Such explanations and instructions on artistry are closely related to the general theory of the Noh art; therefore, they will be dealt with as need arises in the discussion of the three basic elements mentioned above.

Mimesis is a major element of art that the Noh inherited from the *Sarugaku*. In the older genre it meant realistic and humorous representations of manners, which were often exaggerated in order to heighten the humorous and satirical effect. When it was inherited by the Noh it underwent a considerable transformation.

In the first place, humour and satire disappear from Zeami's idea of imitation. Instead, we find beauty and elegance as the end of the mimetic art. Secondly, the superficial imitation of manners is replaced by the imitation of the essences of human types. Thirdly, the concept of imitation is raised to the transcendental level of 'no imitation': a perfect union of the imitator and the imitated.

In the prologue of the second essay of the *Kadensho*, Zeami explains how important imitation is in the art of the Noh:

The objects of imitation are so numerous that they cannot be described adequately. However, since imitation is extremely important, the objects [of imitation] must be studied closely. Now, the true aim of imitation is faithfully to represent whatever is imitated.[69]

The principle laid down here is not far from the modern concept of verisimilitude. It is generally understood that Zeami's true aim was to counterbalance the exaggerated practice of the earlier Sarugaku players. Zeami, however, went further, for he hastens to qualify the statement quoted above:

It is necessary, however, to know that there are different degrees of imitation.[70]

Zeami distinguishes two general classes: nobility and peasantry. Of the two the former is more desirable as the object of imitation and should be imitated closely, for noble persons have grace and beauty in their manners. Zeami admits that it is impossible for the ungraceful Noh players to imitate noble persons perfectly, but he says that they should do their best 'to imitate as faithfully as possible the persons of the higher stations of life and such manners as have grace and beauty.'[71] Of peasants Zeami had an extremely low estimation as the object of imitation. They should not be imitated at all unless their manners are graceful and beautiful. Thus it is plain that Zeami's idea of imitation is strongly coloured with aestheticism.

This aestheticism of Zeami was derived from the concept of *yugen* which was highly appreciated in poetry and dance by the aristocracy and warriors of medieval Japan. Zeami evidently tried to please his aristocratic audience. Ungraceful manners of peasants, Zeami advises, should not be presented to the noble audience, for 'if they are presented, they are so vulgar that they will not be appreciated'.[72] Even the imitation of an old man should be beautiful and pleasing to the eye. It should be 'as if a flower bloomed upon an old tree'.[73]

Zeami's mimetic theory was thus characterised by aestheticism; it was further characterised by the concept of essence ('hon-i'). Zeami contributed to the development of the Noh drama by purging it of vulgar realism. Imitation for Zeami did not mean surface realism; it meant grasping the essence of what is to be imitated and presenting it in such a manner as will give the audience a truth-like impression. We can deduce from Zeami's second essay two ways whereby imitation may be accomplished effectively. One way is to grasp some outstanding traits of the object of imitation. The following suggestion on the imitation of the Chinese character is illuminating:

No matter how one may try to be like a Chinaman in singing and acting, one would not impress the audience; it is therefore advisable to contrive one point of resemblance. This seeming anti-realism is universally applicable in the act of imitation. Anti-realism is not at all desirable; but since it is impossible to imitate the Chinaman perfectly, a strange manner will impress the audience.[74]

It is clear that Zeami was not at all concerned with the surface detail of the object of imitation. His interest was the effect of imitation on the audience. Even the objects of imitation are reduced into three main human types: the woman, the aged person, and the warrior. This alone is enough to prove Zeami's disinclination to surface realism.

The other way to accomplish imitation effectively is to grasp what makes things appear the way they do; not the appearance itself, but the cause of it; not human behaviour itself, but the motive. Zeami refers to it as the 'hon-i' (or the heart) of things in his essays. He warns against the tendency of inexperienced Noh players to imitate the appearance and behaviour of a character to the neglect of what really makes the character appear and behave the way he does. Concerning the imitation of madness he writes:

Even players with considerable experience simply act like a mad man without knowing what made him mad with the result that the audience is not moved. When madness caused by mental suffering is to be imitated, one would certainly move and interest the audience if one should endeavour to act madness mindful of the mental suffering as the heart and the act of madness as the flower (corpus) of his acting.[75]

We may say that what Zeami means by 'hon-i' is the essence of things. He believed that unless the essence of what is to be imitated is expressed it will not appear real. Simple feigning of the appearance of an old man, for instance, would not make an actor look like an old man; it is essential for the actor to grasp the old man's hidden mind: an old man wishes to look young but his physical strength fails him. In the last essay of the *Kadensho* Zeami gives the cue:

It is essential not to act like an old man. Dancing and acting mean tapping the feet and waving the hands to the rhythm and music. An old man's behaviour is such that he would be slightly behind the rhythm of the drum and songs. This gives us the principle of imitation of an old man. As long as this principle is firmly held in mind, other things should be done as gaily as possible. For, an old man is wont to act young; however, since he is slow of motion and hard of hearing due to his old age, his physical strength betrays his wishes. To know this principle is essential to the imitation of an old man. Thus, one should act young as an old man wishes to act, which, after all, means to imitate the mind and behaviour of an old man envious of the young. However, an old man could not help lagging behind the rhythm and music, no matter how he tried to act like a young man. This 'youngish behaviour' of an old man is what creates novelty: a flower blooms upon an old tree.[76]

The Noh since Zeami strictly adhered to this unique idea of 'hon-i'. In consequence, it tended toward symbolism and patternisation of movements. It sacrificed surface realism to artistic expression of the essence of things in the way that might impress the audience. Thus, according to a modern Noh commentator, the ghost is more real than the living man, for 'the living man has individual traits and they are disturbing to the Noh. When such superfluity is completely removed, there emerges what constitutes the core of a character.'[77] The commentator ascribes the reason why the Noh generally prefers the ghost as the main character (the *shite*)* to this belief in essence.

The theory of imitation assumes dualism for artistic expression and creation as long as the act of imitation remains as such. That is, mimetic art is impossible without the dualistic framework of the imitator and the imitated. Zeami's theory, however, ultimately transcends this dualistic framework. In the essay on imitation in the *Kadensho* he started with 'the true aim of imitation is faithfully to represent whatever is imitated'; in the final essay in the same book he reveals the ultimate aim of imitation in the following words:

In the act of imitation there is the level of no imitation. When the act of imitation is perfectly carried out and the actor becomes the thing itself, the actor will no longer have the desire to imitate.[78]

This is echoed in another book, the *Kakyo*: 'In the imitation of all human types, the actor should first learn to become the thing itself, and then act.'[79] Thus in Zeami's theory the immediate aim of faithful imitation is relinquished for the sake of the ultimate aim of no imitation. The dualistic world of cognition, where imitation is possible, is sublimated to the monistic world of experience, where the imitator is fused with the imitated.

Another basic element of the Noh in the theory of Zeami is *yugen*. The meaning of *yugen* has been subject to various interpretations. Differences of opinion arise mainly from the historical consideration of the term. Some interpreters of the term derive its meaning from the *Kokinshu*,[80] in which the earliest use of the word is found; some trace the development of the meaning of the word in the poetic tradition of medieval Japan; some try to find the use of the word in the intellectual milieu of Zeami. Although it is admitted that such historical considerations do throw much light on the meaning of the word, our present discussion needs to concentrate on its meaning as it is used by Zeami in his writing, for Zeami defines the term quite clearly and uses it in that sense consistently in his theory of the Noh.[81]

*Pronounced 'shee-tay'.

Zeami's concept of *yugen* is sensuous. He attached to the meaning of the word no more than beauty and elegance as perceived by the human senses. We see clearly what he means in the following definition found in the *Kakyo*:

Now then, what constitutes yugen? Firstly, surveying various stations of life that exist in our society, we may perhaps say that the noble manners and the distinguished appearance of the peers represent the state of yugen. Yugen, then, lies in what is simply beautiful and gentle. Gentleness of manners constitutes the yugen of personality. Elegance of speech modelled after the noble persons, which is constantly maintained even in careless speech, constitutes the yugen of speech. And in music, when the tune is of beautiful and flowing kind, gentle and elegant to the ear, it constitutes the yugen of music. Dance, when, after a thorough practice, it pleases the eye by producing a beautiful and quiet effect in the movement of the body, represents the yugen of dance. And in the imitation of the three human types, when the appearance is beautiful in each type, it represents yugen.[82]

According to this definition there is nothing mysterious or transcendental about the concept of *yugen*. Zeami meant by it that which pleases the senses. It was an aesthetic device to check the danger of vulgarity into which the mimetic art was apt to fall.

The sensuous nature of *yugen* is also emphasised in numerous references throughout the *Kadensho*. In the sixth essay in the book, for instance, we find:

The two [yugen and that which is strong] are found in the nature of the things themselves. For instance, in human types, the noble lady, the elegant lady, the beautiful lady, the handsome man, and in plants, various kinds of flowers, are of yugen in form. And, the warrior, the violent man, the demon, the god, the pine tree, the cedar, etc. are strong things.[83]

Elsewhere in the *Kadensho* Kannami says in reply to Zeami's question:[84] 'The main actor who appears beautiful, no matter how you look at him, represents yugen.'[85] And concerning the training of a child in the art of the Noh, Zeami says that the child of twelve or thirteen 'is yugen itself no matter how he acts, because he wears children's costume'.[86]

Thus, in Zeami's theory, *yugen* is an aesthetic quality which is sensuous in nature. When Zeami defined *yugen* as that which 'is simply beautiful and gentle,' he must have had in mind no more than the actor's appearance on the stage. He repeatedly emphasises the importance of beautiful appearance throughout his essays. He thought, in fact, that the act of imitation loses its purpose if the beautiful appearance of the actor is lost sight of in his acting. He strongly urges the actor to 'learn the various aspects of yugen that have hitherto been enumerated, absorb them into [his] system, and never leave [them] no matter what is to be imitated'.[87] It should also be remembered, Zeami urges, that 'although various things may be imitated, what creates yugen is an appearance that is beautiful'.[88] For Zeami *yugen* meant 'all the beautiful things that are seen and heard'.[89]

The relationship of the concept of *yugen* to that of imitation is close, indeed. In one sense, of course, *yugen* was an aesthetic check upon the vulgarity of imitation practised in the earlier *Sarugaku*. Zeami's immediate aim as an innovator of the *Sarugaku* was to transform the mimetic art into a more refined genre. His ultimate aim, however, was to orient the basically mimetic art of the Noh to the ideal of aesthetic experience. The human types are not imitated *per se*. They are imitated for the sake of the beauty that they produce. The ultimate aim of imitation therefore is to create *yugen*. Thus in Zeami's theory the supreme level of imitation — the level of no imitation — is equated with the supreme attainment of *yugen*:

Know that all the beautiful things that are seen and heard represent yugen. One that enters the realm of yugen is he who makes this principle his own working principle and becomes that which embodies yugen. He who only wishes to attain yugen while neglecting to study these aspects of it or to become the thing [of yugen] itself will never attain yugen.[90]

The supreme level of imitation, for Zeami, was the level of no imitation. The actor was expected to attain the level at which he no longer wishes to imitate but becomes the thing itself. Likewise, a true attainment of *yugen* is to become the thing of *yugen* itself. The actor that *wishes* to imitate or to attain *yugen* has not reached the supreme level of art.

The concept of imitation and the concept of *yugen* find their synthesis in the third basic element of the Noh — the concept of flower. That is, when the act of imitation attains its supreme level, it enters the realm of *yugen*, which produces an artistic effect that Zeami calls *hana*, or flower. When an accomplished actor does his best, his performance is like the blooming of a flower, the sum total of his artistic effort which is unique and interesting. Whether his performance is a flower or not, of course, depends on the audience. If the audience is duly impressed and attracted by it, then it may be called a flower. In order to impress the audience, however, his imitative act must have reached its supreme level and have created *yugen*. In other words, the actor must create beauty on the stage as naturally as the thing he is imitating.

There are two crucial factors that make an actor's performance bloom into a flower. To begin with, his performance must be interesting to the audience. Unless the audience is impressed with the actor's performance, the whole purpose of art is lost. Zeami is keenly conscious of the audience as the sole judge of his art. It is not too much to say that the purpose of putting his Noh theory into writing was to let his posterity know how to impress the audience. His Noh theory is thus characteristically audience-oriented. In the fifth essay of the *Kadensho* he writes:

There are many ways to win fame in the art of the Noh. The accomplished artist finds it difficult to be appreciated by men of no taste, while the unaccomplished artist is never appreciated by men of taste. . . . However, a truly accomplished artist who is ingenious enough would act in the way that would impress even men of no taste. An actor with such ingenuity and accomplishment may be called the one who has attained the flower. An actor who has attained this level of art will never be overwhelmed by a young actor no matter how old he becomes. Such an actor would be universally recognised as an accomplished actor and would be appreciated even by remote country folk. . . . The purpose of writing this *Kadensho* is to reveal the true meaning of this accomplishment of art.[91]

What Zeami aimed at, then, was a universal acceptance. In order for his art to be accepted, he realised, his art must be universally interesting, as a flower is.

The second factor that makes an actor's performance a flower is uniqueness. If an actor is like any other actor and if his performance is always the same, he will tire the audience. He must be different from other actors and he must always have a fresh charm. A flower is universally appreciated because it blooms at a particular time and is unique. If it was like any other flower and bloomed all the year round, Zeami maintained, it would not attract us. The Noh actor must have this uniqueness in his art.

In order to understand the meaning of flower in this secret instruction, one should first observe how a flower of nature blooms and thereby understand how all [art] came to be likened to a flower. Now, people appreciate flowers because they are all seasonal and have their own time to bloom. In the Noh, too, the uniqueness with which it impresses the audience makes the art interesting. Thus, 'flower,' 'unique' and 'interesting' mean the same thing.[92]

The unique charm of a flower of nature, then, is something that an actor must have in his art.

The meaning of flower in Zeami's theory of Noh is the sum total of an actor's artistic effort. It subsumes an act of imitation on the part of the actor and the aesthetic quality of *yugen* on the part of the imitated. The flower is the synthesis of the two. It emerges when the act of imitation reaches its supreme level, and constitutes an aesthetic experience of the actor as well as of the audience.

The Noh, therefore, is essentially an experiential art. It is not interested in story nor in ideas; its sole interest is how to create an aesthetic experience — the blooming of a flower. The whole artistic endeavour — of acting and writing Noh texts — is guided by this interest. In the way of acting, a major part of the action is devoted to the main actor's dance, and action consists of little or no conflict of forces.

The *shite* is all-important in the Noh. An entire piece must be oriented toward the role and performance of the main actor. Zeami even goes so far as to suggest that the personality of the main actor should determine the nature of the whole piece. In the *Nosakusho* he cautions:

It is most important, therefore, to suit the material to the personality of the *shite* in writing a Noh piece. A Noh writer should be able to discriminate [the type of] the Noh that is becoming to the character of the *shite*.[93]

Minutest care must be taken even in the choice of words to be spoken by the *shite*. Zeami cautions that rhetorical emphases must be placed in the *shite's* speech. In the same book he writes: 'Beautiful words and well-known phrases must be used for the *shite's* speech'.[94] Conversely, he warns against using important words in speeches not spoken by the *shite*. In the *Kadensho* we find the following words: 'Do not use important words in places that have nothing to do with the *shite's* speech or action.'[95] The reason for this, Zeami says, is that 'the audience is wont to be impressed with the interesting speech and action of none other than the main actor.'[96] The whole piece in the Noh, in other words, is constructed so as to make the bud of *yugen* that the *shite* has in him open into a beautiful flower. Of course, there is the *waki* (the side character), but his role is far less significant in comparison to the *shite's* and his part is to help the *shite*, and not to oppose him. During the main part of action, he situates himself by the *waki-bashira* (the pole of the *waki*) one of the four poles supporting the ceiling of the Noh stage, quietly watching the *shite's* performance. In one sense, the *waki* is the point of view in the play through which the audience sees the action. The absence of conflict between the *shite* and the *waki* has led a Noh scholar to the conclusion that the *shite* is the sole 'actor' in the Noh while the *waki* represents the audience.[97] The *waki's* subservient role is also manifest in the delicate, almost unnoticed movement which he makes, while crouching by the *waki-bashira*, in conjunction with the *shite's* movement: He shifts his posture slowly as the *shite* moves, always turning his front to the *shite*. In most Noh plays the *waki* is an itinerant priest who serves as no more than an interlocutor drawing a story out of the *shite*, who tells the story — usually his own story — in dance and song; and as soon as his part is done he goes to the *waki-bashira* where he remains while the story goes on.

It must be remembered, however, that the narrative interest is minimised in the Noh. The story is not told for its own sake, but is used as a device whereby the beauty of *yugen* is effectively brought about on stage. Using an original story in a Noh play is therefore discouraged. The measure of excellence of the Noh does not lie in originality but in whether or not a 'flower' has bloomed. A Noh writer, instead of boasting of his originality, is expected to work on 'authentic' material, as Zeami calls it, which has been tested by tradition for the quality of *yugen*; and such material may be obtained most appropriately from the classical Chinese and Japanese literature. In other words, the writer's craftsmanship is far more important than his genius. In the sixth essay of the *Kadensho* we find: 'Writing of the Noh text is of vital importance in this art. A good Noh piece requires only craftsmanship, not profound learning or genius.'[98] The Noh playwright's interest lies solely in producing an aesthetic effect to the neglect of all other creative efforts. From the audience's viewpoint, a Noh piece must be divested of all literary elements save those conducive to experiencing that aesthetic effect which the Noh aims to produce, the beauty of *yugen*. Thus, such elements as plot complications, surprise, suspense, and so on, that play vital part in successful narrative literature must be dispensed with.

It is clear, then, that the Noh is a theatrical art centring around the main actor, the *shite*, who appears before the audience as an incarnation of *yugen*, a blooming flower. Its aesthetic is singularly monistic and its ideal experiential.

IV

The kind of drama that Zeami and his father, Kannami, tried to found was thus monistic-experiential in its outlook. It is

understandable, therefore, that Yeats was strongly attracted to the
Noh. Yeats was opposed, after all, to the traditional stage of the
West where characters clashed with each other and to the modern
realistic school which denied the audience passionate reverie. The
Noh holds the position antithetical to the drama of the West in theory
and practice.

Generally speaking, what characterises Western drama is its
dualistic-cognitive nature. It assumes the world of duality in which
conflict of forces occurs. It also assumes the world of cognition in
which recounting a history of a conflict of forces is not only possible
but delightful. Its interest is in an exploration of human action, and
its finding is perhaps what we might call 'human nature'. In the words
of a modern student of drama: 'Drama is one, and perhaps the major,
instrument invented by human beings for the exploration and
explanation of the nature of man.'[99]

The mimetic theory of Aristotle is also rooted in the dualistic-
cognitive perspective. The idea of imitation is based on the dualistic
relation of the imitator and the imitated, and Aristotle let the two
remain separated. A human action, which is the object of imitation,
consists of a series of events. Thus, the history of a human action,
or the plot, gets the primary emphasis in Aristotle's theory. Of the
six parts of tragedy, according to Aristotle, the plot is the most
important of all. In the *Poetics* we find:

But the most important of all is the structure of the incidents. For Tragedy
is an imitation, not of men, but of an action and of life, and life consists
in action, and its end is a mode of action, not a quality. Now character
determines men's qualities, but it is by their actions that they are happy
or the reverse. Dramatic action, therefore, is not with a view to the
representation of character: character comes in as subsidiary to the actions.
Hence the incidents and the plot are the end of a tragedy; and the end is
the chief thing of all.[100]

The least significant of all, by contrast, is the spectacle:

The spectacle has, indeed, an emotional attraction of its own, but, of all
the parts, it is the least artistic, and connected least with the art of poetry.
For the power of Tragedy, we may be sure, is felt even apart from
representation and actors.[101]

We find a number of antitheses between Aristotle and Zeami. For
Aristotle the plot is 'the soul of a tragedy',[102] while, for Zeami, it
is a device whereby *yugen* is created. While Aristotle insists that an
action is to be imitated, Zeami is mainly interested in three human

types: aged person, woman, and warrior. The spectacle, which matters least in Aristotle's theory, matters most in Zeami's. The list of antitheses does not end here. They all come to this — that the two dramatic theorists of the East and the West had perspectives antithetical to each other: Zeami had the monistic-experiential perspective, which aimed at a resolution of duality and the creation of a purely aesthetic experience in the realm of art; Aristotle, on the other hand, had the dualistic-cognitive perspective, which affirmed the world of duality where it was possible for the imitator to create a sense of pleasure by a miming act, and which believed in the ability of the mind to perceive the original action being imitated.

The dramatic theory of Renaissance theorists is also dualistic-cognitive in nature. Combining the Aristotelian mimetic theory with the typically Renaissance love of didacticism and the Horatian teleology, it assumed the dualistic world of the imitator and the imitated, and emphasised the learning process rather than pleasure itself. Thus, tragedy, says Sidney,

openeth the greatest wounds, and showeth forth the ulcers that are covered with tissue, that maketh kings fear to be tyrants, and tyrants manifest their tyrannical humours; that with stirring the effects of admiration and commiseration teacheth the uncertainty of this world, and upon how weak foundations gilden roofs are builded.[103]

The didactic purpose is achieved by showing an illustrious example. Here again the dramatic interest is in an exploration of human action, which is antithetical to Zeami's interest in *yugen*.

The modern realistic drama, which antagonised Yeats so much, is based, beyond doubt, on the dualistic-cognitive perspective. Although Ibsen and his followers are admittedly different from their Greek and Elizabethan predecessors in their concept of drama and its significance to life, they nevertheless maintain a similar perspective by assuming a critical position to the social conventions of their time and taking pathological interest in human action. The only significant difference between the modern realists and the ancients perhaps lies in the fact that the modern realists have brought their perspective to play in the immediate, commonplace milieu.

Risking an over-simplification, it may be possible to say that the main current of Western drama represents a school of aesthetic that takes an active interest in an exploration of human action and in reconstructing that action into a coherent whole. The work involves dualistic thinking and a cognitive process of the mind. Whether this formula is an over-simplification or not, it was this tendency to which

Yeats responded unfavourably. He was consistently against 'all art that is . . . mere story-telling' and declared 'unimaginative' all arts that 'are content to set a piece of the world as we know it in a place by itself, to put their photographs as it were in a plush or a plain frame.'[104] He could not tolerate the kind of art that derived its life from the bifurcated world of subject and object, and he was so obsessed with an experiential view of art that he could not be completely at home with the aesthetic tradition of the West that turned art into an object of knowledge. Conversely, it was this obsession that caused Yeats to respond favourably to the Noh. Although there is no denying the fact that lack of information led Yeats to some outrageous misconceptions, such as confusing the Noh dance with the *Joruri*,[105] his understanding of the Noh is accurate in some respects. Insofar as the Noh tended away from exploration and portraiture, Yeats found it quite congenial.

It would be jumping to a conclusion, however, to infer from the above discussion that Yeats, repelled by the traditional dramatic theory and practice of the West, completely baptised himself into the Eastern school of Zeami. Yeats's perspective was neither completely Eastern nor, of course, completely Western: his was a double perspective. He had, so to speak, one foot in the East and the other in the West. He gained from this anomalous position something which earned his dramas 'a sphere by themselves'[106] in the history and development of the Western theatrical art. However, he lost as much as he gained from either side. His dramatic theory and practice consequently became characteristically his own. His schooling in the Noh aesthetic and his Noh-like dramas must be considered in this light.

In Sections V, VI, and VII of 'Certain Noble Plays of Japan', Yeats explains the Noh drama of Japan. In these sections he points out the qualities of 'intimacy' and 'distance' that he finds in the Noh. He emphasises its tendency away from *surface realism. 'No "naturalistic" effect is sought', he observes.[107] The use of masks, the interest in the rhythm, and the simple and suggestive stage-setting characterise the Noh. These characteristics help to simplify the Noh.

Earlier in the essay Yeats said that the stage must be simplified in order to achieve intimacy. The use of the mask helps in this, because it has a stilling effect which helps to produce deep feeling. The mask will also suppress the realistic facial expressions of the actor. Explaining the use of a mask in his own play, he writes:

A mask will enable me to substitute for the face of some common-place player, or for that face repainted to suit his own vulgar fancy, the fine invention of a sculptor, and to bring the audience close enough to the play to hear every inflection of the voice. A mask never seems but a dirty face, and no matter how close you go is yet a work of art; nor shall we lose by stilling the movement of the features, for deep feeling is expressed by a movement of the whole body. In poetical painting and in sculpture the face seems the nobler for lacking curiosity, alert attention, all that we sum up under the famous word of the realists, 'vitality.'[108]

Yeats's use of a mask definitely has a disciplinary purpose. The mask is expected to check surface realism and direct the attention of the audience to perceiving the inner truth. The disciplinary function of the mask is generally acknowledged in the Noh. Zeami has very little to say about the function of the mask, but his remark about the *hitamen** (the unmasked face) is helpful:

It [the hitamen] imitates a living person and therefore should not be difficult. Strangely enough, however, it is hardly worth seeing unless the [actor's] art is superior. As for the manner of imitation, it depends, of course, on individual cases. Some try to make facial expressions different from their usual faces, although there is no reason why they should counterfeit facial expressions. It is unbearable to see such [an act of imitation]. One should imitate only the behaviour and the general impression of what he is imitating, and keep his face as it usually is.[109]

Zeami abhorred the realistic expressions some of his contemporary Noh players liked to make when they acted living persons without using masks. Noh players today are still expected to keep a straight face when they appear on stage without a mask on. A high standard of art is required to create a deep feeling without resorting to facial expressions. Thus in the Noh, facial expressions are subject to discipline. In an imitation of a masked figure the mask does the disciplinary function; in the case of an unmasked figure, an internal discipline is necessary.

Like Yeats, Zeami also realised the artistic quality of masks. In the *Sarugaku-dangi* he gives a list of masterpieces that were available for his use at the time. One of them even inspired him in his dream. For Zeami, however, a mask was an instrument as well as a work of art. He even advised that the top of a mask be cut off if it got in the way of the head gear. He also advised that a player should be careful about the choice of a mask and 'should choose one that suits the level of art he has attained'.[110] For Zeami, therefore, a mask was more than a disciplinary device or a work of art: it was

---

*   Pronounced *'hit-a-men'*.

an instrument that was to be actively used for creating *yugen*. In other words, a mask was a component of the flower that bloomed on the stage. For Yeats it was a device to create intimacy.

Yeats also found an interest in rhythm characteristic of the Noh. His enthusiasm was particularly stirred by (1) the fact that a dance, 'instead of the disordered passion of nature,' marked the climax, (2) seeming indifference to the human form, and (3) an intensity of rhythm. These features cause the Noh to tend away from a 'naturalistic' effect. The rhythmical elements form, of course, the vital part of the Noh. Zeami stipulated two rhythmical parts and three human types as the essential elements of the Noh. The two rhythmical parts were song and dance. The three human types included the aged person, the woman and the warrior. A mimetic act of the three human types performed in a dance accompanied by singing was to produce an effect of *yugen*.

Yeats was particularly impressed with the fact that the Noh was interested not in the human form but the rhythm to which it moved:

The interest is not in the human form but in the rhythm to which it moves, and the triumph of their art is to express the rhythm in its intensity.[111]

The human form, however, is an indispensable element of the Noh. *Yugen*, Zeami said, was derived from the human form itself. Even an aged person was a flower blooming upon an old tree. That Yeats should have overlooked the importance that the Noh gave to the human form clearly shows the distance that lies between Yeats and Zeami in their artistic ideals. Yeats had little faith in the human form for a number of reasons. For one thing, he believed that drama began in ritual in the form of a chanted ode, in which the magical power of words was of prime importance. 'We have forgotten,' Yeats wrote to the editor of the *Daily Chronicle*, 'that the Drama began in the chanted ode, and that whenever it has been great it has been written to delight our eyes, but to delight our ears more than our eyes.'[112] In ritual, Yeats believed, song had priority over action, and the theatre 'cannot come to its greatness again without recalling words to their sovereignty'.[113] Yeats's enthusiasm for the two rhythmical parts of the Noh comes from his belief that words and music are the archetypal media of the theatrical art. The principle of intimacy was born of this faith in words. Intimacy creates a natural atmosphere in which words can fully exert their power.

A song, too, means for Yeats a series of words that have 'taken fire'. In order to be artistically effective, words must move imperceptibly into chanting, and no artificiality must be allowed in the process:

What was the good of writing a love-song if the singer pronounced love 'lo-o-o-o-o-ve,' or even if he said 'love,' but did not give it its exact place and weight in the rhythm? Like every other poet, I spoke verses in a kind of chant when I was making them; and sometimes, when I was alone on a country road, I would speak them in a loud chanting voice, and feel that if I dared I would speak them in that way to other people.[114]

The relationship between music and speech is thus close. In 'Poems for the Psaltery' (1907), a section added to 'Speaking to the Psaltery', Yeats suggests that music developed from speech:

The relation between music and speech will yet become the subject of science, not less than the occasion of artistic discovery. I suggest that we will discover in this relation a very early stage in the development of music, with its own great beauty, and that those who love lyric poetry but cannot tell one tune from another repeat a state of mind which created music and yet was incapable of the emotional abstraction which delights in patterns of sound separated from words.[115]

And in a letter to the editor of the *Academy*, June 7, 1902, he makes the same suggestion in simpler terms:

I imagine men spoke their verses first to a regulated pitch without a tune, and then, eager for variety, spoke to tunes which gradually became themselves the chief preoccupation until speech died out in music.[116]

The relationship between words and music was a theme which never left Yeats's mind throughout his life. Sometimes he tended to separate the two by emphasising one or the other; but mostly he tried to fuse the two. Toward the end of life he wrote many poems to old Irish tunes in an 'attempt to unite literature and music.'[117]

It was in restoring speech to its original importance that the task of the modern theatre lay. Yeats loathed the tendency of the traditional theatre of the West in which action had become more and more important, speech lost its original simplicity and naturalness, and the stage-setting had become elaborate and artificial, destroying the intimacy of art. In order for the theatre to recover the greatness it once enjoyed, speech must be restored to its former position:

Racine and Shakespeare wrote for a little stage where very little could be done with movement, but they were as we know careful to get a great range of expression out of the voice. Our art, like theirs, without despising movement, must restore the voice to its importance, for all our playwrights, Synge just as much as myself, get their finest effects out of style, out of the expressiveness of speech itself.[118]

In an ideal drama, which means a tragic drama for Yeats, the human form must be obliterated to find itself in the world of a passionate reverie. A celebration of the human form tends, on the one hand, toward elaboration and artificiality, and therefore away from intimacy; on the other hand, it tends toward individuation and therefore away from the passionate reverie. This is the tendency that comedy and the modern realistic school of drama have taken.

By finding in the Noh the intensity of rhythm, therefore, Yeats found a tragic art in the Noh. By suppressing the interest in the human form for the sake of the rhythm to which it moved, the Noh succeeded, Yeats thought, in creating a passionate reverie. It succeeded, in other words, in gaining distance by maintaining intimacy. Yeats missed, however, a crucial element in Zeami's theory. The Noh, as Zeami stipulated, consisted of two rhythmical parts and three human types, and the formula, of course, is still kept today. The human form, which is represented by three general types, holds a position equal in its importance to the rhythmical parts. The five parts collaborate to bring about the blooming of a flower, the beauty of which is *yugen*; and no part is sacrificed for the sake of any other. What Yeats missed, then, was the fact that Zeami aimed at the fusion of the rhythm and the form, a purely monistic-experiential level of art.

Yeats also found that suggestiveness characterised the Noh. It is quite understandable that this element should have appealed to Yeats, for it was his belief that what destroyed intimacy in the drama of the West was elaborate artificial stage-setting. By pushing the stage to extreme simplicity, leaving only such details as may be suggestive, the Noh succeeded, Yeats believed, in creating intimacy. Zeami's main interest was not, of course, in simplicity for its own sake, but in the effectiveness of impression. He advised, for instance, sacrificing truth to effectiveness, as we have seen in the case of imitating a Chinese figure. His concern was rather with an effective creation of the beauty of *yugen*. Thus the dress worn by the Noh players is far from being simple or suggestive, but is quite colourful and elaborate. On the whole, however, Yeats came close to Zeami in de-emphasising the elaborate surface details and substituting in their place 'a child's game become noble poetry,' that sets before the audience 'all those things which we feel and imagine in silence'.[119]

Such, then, was Yeats's understanding of the Noh from the viewpoint of the principle of intimacy. Along with intimacy, Yeats also found distance, the other one of the twin aesthetic principles, attained in the Noh. Art attains distance from the pushing world of business, Yeats believed, by finding its source of life in tradition. Yeats traced the beauty of the Noh to its three-fold origin. From the courtly life of the medieval Japanese, Yeats thought, came the nobility of the love sorrows that one finds in so many Noh dramas. In the Buddhist doctrine he found the source of the intellectual subtlety. And finally, in the Shinto legends and beliefs he found the sources of the narrative proper of the Noh dramas.

Of the three origins what interested Yeats most was the Shinto tradition, which he thought paralleled the Irish folk tradition. The Noh dramatists, Yeats found, were keenly aware of the historical places which were closely associated with the myths and legends of the Shinto religion, and they expressed their emotion to the holy places in much the same manner as the Gaelic-speaking country people of Ireland. With these dramatists Yeats felt a close affinity:

The men who created this convention were more like ourselves than were the Greeks and Romans, more like us even than are Shakespeare and Corneille.[120]

That Yeats should have felt a closer affinity to the Japanese Noh dramatists than to the classical authors of the West, of course, is no surprising matter in the light of his belief in the archetypal myths as the true sources of all good arts. Yeats put more faith in the popular tradition than in the written. The archetypal beliefs of a given culture are handed down the generations by the common people, in whose life the beliefs are constantly animated and kept alive. The archetypal beliefs are not mere abstractions, but are something that has an emotional foundation in the flesh and blood of the people's lives. There is a definite anti-intellectual element in Yeats's principle of distance, as there is a similar tendency in his symbolism, as Frank Kermode has commented.[121] The idea of the 'thinking body' has parallel in Yeats's general view of an ideal culture — that a culture must have a unity that finds its expression in every piece of art and furniture around a single image as if it has been wrought by a single mind. Conversely, any art that attains distance, Yeats believed, appeals to the archetypal beliefs so unified and to the tribal memory of beauty so enhanced, whereby a lyrical intensity is achieved.

Yeats thought that the Noh dramatists found their material in the popular tradition of Japan. In some sense, he was right, for Zeami de-emphasised the value of originality on the part of the Noh writer and emphasised instead the 'authenticity' of the material; and it is true that a lot of materials of the Noh are drawn from folk tradition. However, Zeami's idea of 'authenticity' was not restricted to the materials of folk origin. On the contrary, he favoured the materials drawn from the written tradition of the classical literature. He advised that the Noh dramatist should draw heavily on the classical literature not only for the narrative but also for poetry and specific passages that had become clichés. He advised especially the use of *renga*, a genre of poetry which was popular among the aristocrats at Zeami's time. What Zeami aimed to achieve, after all, was not a mysterious art, but an art which had a beauty of universal appeal, drawing upon the material tested and refined by the literary tradition. His interest was neither in the narrative quality of the material *per se* nor in its philosophical or intellectual subtlety, but in the beauty it could help create. The mysterious and difficult part fell on the actor himself in his art of creating beauty of *yugen*. Contrary to Zeami's ideal, Yeats's aim was to create 'an unpopular theatre and an audience like a secret society where admission is by favour and never to many,'[122] but an art that could still remind us of its 'origin among the common people'.[123] The 'Noh plays' Yeats wrote were meant to fit this formula. Their materials were drawn from the popular legends and myths, but they were highly sophisticated dramas intended for a small select audience of initiates. It is easy to imagine how Yeats felt when *At the Hawk's Well* was performed in a theatre in New York without his permission. He wrote to John Quinn:

Fate has been against me. I meant these 'Noh' plays never to be played in a theatre, and now one has been done without leave; and circumstances have arisen which would make it ungracious to forbid Ito to play *The Hawk* as he will. I had thought to escape the press, and people digesting their dinners, and to write for my friends.[124]

Thus, Yeats tried to fit the Noh into his twin principles of intimacy and distance. He partly succeeded in the attempt, but he failed, at the same time, to realise the purely monistic-experiential nature of the Noh which is crystalised in the concept of the flower.

This failure is aggravated by branding the Noh as a tragic art in the Yeatsian sense. The age in which the Noh was perfected interested Yeats unduly and led him to the false conclusion that the spiritual milieu which fostered the Noh sought a heroic discipline and that the Noh was its literary product. The misunderstanding is based on another misunderstanding that the founder of the Noh was 'a small *daimio* or feudal lord of the ancient capital Nara, a contemporary of Chaucer.'[125] The Japanese warriors of the feudal age, Yeats believed, combined in their minds the masculine worship of power and the feminine sense of beauty. The Noh was a product of such a mind:

These plays arose in an age of continual war and became a part of the education of soldiers. These soldiers, whose nature had as much of Walter Pater as of Achilles, combined with Buddhist priests and women to elaborate life in a ceremony, the playing of football, the drinking of tea, and all great events of State, becoming a ritual.[126]

Thus Yeats believed that the Noh was a product of a heroic age, developed and perfected by the artistic warriors whose spiritual thirst was eased by drinking out of the fountain of beauty and archetypal beliefs they uncovered in the art. It was a veritable example of a tragic art of the Yeatsian brand that arose in an age of uncertainty which made the people's minds incline towards some sort of synthesis of conflicting elements, toward some spiritual unity.

Yeats's meeting with the Noh, then, was only a part of the whole cycle in which his warring aesthetic perspectives 'gyred' and 'perned' for an ideal form of art. Yeats found in the Noh what he wanted to find. He interpreted the Noh in a way that might reinforce his own theory. In some respects he came quite close to the ideals set forth by Zeami; and, of course, he assimilated some of the Noh conventions into his dramaturgy, such as dance, chorus (which does not take part in the action), simple and suggestive stage-setting, etc. On the other hand, either intentionally or unintentionally, he overlooked some of the vital elements of the Noh and imposed his own ideas on it. The Noh did not cause any change in his double perspective. Furthermore, it gave him very little as the source of his plays. The Noh actually helps us very little in understanding his plays and his dramatic theory. It is more helpful to look for discrepancies, rather than similarities, that exist between the Noh and Yeats's dramatic theory and practice.

6. THE FLOWER THAT NEVER BLOOMED

The double perspective with which Yeats viewed the Noh is also carried into his 'Noh' plays themselves. This chapter will concentrate on the structural significance that the double perspective has in the plays. The discussion of Yeats's obvious borrowings from the Noh, such as dance, chorus, and musicians will be dispensed with. Also, his obvious deviations from the Noh convention, such as the rhythmical pattern of *jo-ha-kyu*, the form of dancing (not the *joruri* dance that Yeats obviously had in mind), and the types of costumes, will be excluded from the present discussion.

Of the five plays written under the Japanese influence, four are modelled after the Noh and one after the Kyogen.* Since what Yeats calls 'noble plays of Japan' are the Noh plays, we should concentrate our discussion on the relationship between the Noh and his plays; but some comment on the Kyogen is also needed before we plunge into our main discussion. Yeats seems to have known very little about the Kyogen, but it is surprising that the distinction Yeats makes between tragedy and comedy is actually quite similar to the kind of distinction that the Noh and the Kyogen came to assume in the course of time.[1] Although some scholars of Japanese literature argue that the Kyogen and the Noh have independent origins, there is a general agreement that the two genres had a common origin and that the Kyogen developed as a mimetic art of a lower type while the Noh took a more refined and sophisticated line of development. What distinguishes the Kyogen from the Noh is that its main interest is in the comic, not beauty and elegance.

The earliest authoritative reference to the nature of the Kyogen is found in Zeami's *Shudosho* (1430), in which Zeami says: 'It is generally known that in the Kyogen the actor's performance consists in improvisation or adaptation of an old tale or some interesting story to his comical purposes'.[2] The reference is only preamble to what

* Pronounced with a hard 'g'.

143

Zeami really wanted to say, i.e., that the Kyogen actor should refrain from vulgarism and aim at a refined type of laughter that is not incompatible with *yugen* of the Noh. There is no denying that Zeami's warning against vulgarism contributed to the development of the Kyogen into a refined comedy rather than slapstick, but we can just as easily take the warning as an evidence that the Kyogen was a genre which essentially did not fit the Noh scheme.

The personal element is quite strong in the Kyogen, as Yeats perceived it also in the comedy of the West. Laughter is largely derived from ludicrous speech and behaviour of the actors or from the comical situation in which the characters find their interests conflicting. In fact, the Kyogen shows very little interest in non-human elements, natural or supernatural, as a Japanese critic has remarked.[3] Characters are clearly defined and in some Kyogen pieces they are fully developed. Action or narrative is not *shite*-centered, and in many Kyogen pieces the comical effect depends on the dramatisation of the conflict between the characters, resulting in the pain of one.

Yeats had in mind two antithetical types of poetical drama, tragedy and comedy. What distinguished comedy from tragedy was that it was interested mainly in character and the clash of character, from which tragedy tends away concentrating instead on lyric feeling. In great tragedies of the past, he believed, character had an insignificant place; while in comedies it received a main emphasis. When character is present in such great dramatic works of Shakespeare, it is defined only in the moments of comedy; and such works are for Yeats tragi-comedy: 'Shakespeare is always a writer of tragi-comedy'.[4]

Yeats's idea of comedy is clearly based on his idea of conflict and the cognitive bias in his theory of art. Comedy takes interest in character, which means to Yeats the creation of individuality, a state similar in essence to the Nietzschean condition of individuation. (It should be remembered that Yeats defined tragedy as 'a drowner of dykes that separate man from man.') Individuality means 'a display of energy', which results in action. The joy of comedy is derived from that action:

Comedy is joyous because all assumption of a part, of a personal mask, whether of the individualized face of comedy or of the grotesque face of farce, is a display of energy, and all energy is joyous.[5]

And joy has to do with the active will: 'Joy is of the will which labours, which overcomes obstacles, which knows triumph'.[6] On the other hand, tragedy has to do with vision, a state of the soul, not with the will or the display of energy:

> The masks of tragedy contain neither character nor personal energy. They are allied to decoration and to the abstract figures of Egyptian temples. Before the mind can look out of their eyes the active will perishes, hence their sorrowful calm. . . . The soul knows its changes of state alone, and I think the motives of tragedy are not related to action but to changes of state.[7]

Character and energy, action and will — these are essentially the materials of comedy. In order to take form, they must be put through a process, and that process, when it is complete, gives us a sensation of joy. Yeats, of course, was not so certain about his idea of comedy. He could not separate tragedy from comedy and keep them separate, placing one on the ecstatic end and the other on the cognitive end of his perspective. In Yeats one end always interfered with and qualified the other. Thus he says at the end of Section XXIV of 'Estrangement', which we have been following:

> I feel all this [that the motives of tragedy are related to changes of state] but do not see clearly, for I am hunting truth into its thicket and it is my business to keep close to the impressions of sense, to common daily life. Yet is not ecstasy some fulfilment of the soul in itself, some slow or sudden expansion of it like an overflowing well? Is not this what is meant by beauty?[8]

In Zeami and Yeats, then, we see contrary processes of art. Zeami tried to qualify the cognitive art (the Kyogen) with the experiential scheme (the Noh), while Yeats let his cognitive perspective interfere with the experiential. The interference is evident also in his 'Noh' plays. As we shall see presently, character and action, comic materials according to Yeats's dramatic theory, are carried into the plays.

There is no denying that in the four dance plays Yeats practises his own principles of intimacy and distance. The plays have a relatively small number of characters in them and need only a drawing room with no elaborate stage-setting for performance. The simplicity of the plays is 'no mere economy' but necessary in order to produce the desired effect, a lyrical feeling. Distance is successfully maintained by removing surface realism and taking the materials not from modern life but from popular myths and legends.

When we compare the plays with the Noh plays of Japan, we cannot but notice a wide gap between them. Yeats's plays are strongly characterised by his dualism and cognitive perspective, which is revealed in his total disregard of Zeami's concept of flower and in his introduction into the plays of his own tragic concept of conflict and of literary ideas. It is not certain that Yeats ever knew about Zeami's concept of flower. Even if he had, the concept would have been hardly palatable for him. At any rate, he completely disregarded it in his 'Noh' plays. Zeami's concept of flower subsumed two basic concepts, that is, the concept of *yugen* and the concept of imitation. The concept of *yugen* rendered the Noh a singularly aesthetic and non-literary art, which is not dissimilar to the sort of art envisaged in the 'aesthetic school' of Arthur Hallam, which Yeats had outgrown long since. The concept of imitation was elevated by Zeami to 'the level of no imitation', a purely experiential level of art. This concept would have been more congenial to Yeats, but it would have necessitated a radical qualification of his concepts of conflict.

Zeami made it clear that the sole aim of the Noh was to create the beauty of *yugen*. The narrative element and the literary or philosophical ideas were therefore unimportant or subservient to the supreme aim. Instead, the two rhythmical parts of dance and song and the three human forms constituted the vital part of the Noh; and as to speech, rich allusion was valued instead of character-revealed words. Zeami emphasised that extreme care must be taken in the choice of material, keeping in mind the ultimate aim of *yugen*. He even advised that beautiful words or poetical passages from the classical literature be given to the *shite*. In Yeats's plays we do not notice such an aesthetic consideration. His plays, also, cannot be said to be richly allusive. Nor do we find the characters to be conducive to the creation of sensuous beauty. The speeches, too, are not particularly poetical or lyrical but character-revealing. Above all, the plays are not free from ideas. At least, *Calvary*, as Wilson has pointed out, is one example which is based on an idea.

Anyone who is familiar with the Japanese Noh will immediately notice, when reading Yeats's 'Noh' plays, his heavy dependence on speech. The Noh heavily relies on dance and song for its aesthetic effect. Even the *shite's* role consists mainly in the rhythmical parts and his speech is reinforced with beautiful words and phrases chosen from the classical sources in order to bring about a desired aesthetic effect. The Noh, in other words, aims at a total aesthetic effect of *yugen* through a fusion of words and music, and of form and rhythmical movement. In Yeats's 'Noh' plays, words have their own *raison d'être* by their communicative ability. The difference is clearly seen in the case of Yeats's *The Dreaming of the Bones* and its Japanese model, *Nishikigi*. In Yeats's play the narrative part, the legend of Diarmuid and Dervorgilla, forms the major part of the play and is presented in the speech of the Stranger and the Young Girl, the dead lovers in the mortal form. In *Nishikigi*, the prosaic background of the play, the legend of unrequited love spun around the wand and the cloth, is taken out of the context of the play and recounted in what is called the *ai-kyogen*, a narrative interlude that takes place between the first act and the second. In the main part of the play, the two rhythmical parts of dance and song form the major part of the performance. The arrangement is universally applied to the two-act pieces of the Noh. The communicative and expressive function of words is thus curtailed in favour of their aesthetic quality. The situation is all the worse for the modern audience of the Noh, to whom the language of the *Noh* is frequently unintelligible due to its archaism and to the distorted pronunciation by the players, so much so that a modern Noh commentator advises to read the Noh text before going to the theatre.[9] Yeats would have abhorred such a failure of communication. To him words meant the life of drama. The principle of intimacy and his disbelief in surface realism stemmed from the conviction that words must be restored to their ancient dignity.

The same conviction made Yeats suspicious about formal music. Although it is true that he had a lifelong faith in the union of words and music and in fact wrote poems to old Irish tunes in his later life, he consistently maintained, at the same time, a sceptical attitude toward music in which the 'natural music [of words] was altered'.[10] In his experiments with speaking verse in collaboration with Florence Farr, he was frustrated by the interference of the rhythm of the music with that of the verse. Although he detested 'prosaic lifeless intonations' of ordinary speech, he abhorred as much the artificiality of music that killed the naturalness of the speech rhythm. Divining the future of the 'new art' of speaking verse, he wrote:

I am not certain that I shall not see some Order naming itself from the Golden Violet of the Troubadours or the like, and having among its members none but well-taught and well-mannered speakers who will keep the new art from disrepute. They will know how to keep from singing notes and from prosaic lifeless intonations, and they will always understand, however far they push their experiments, that poetry and not music is their object; and they will have by heart, like the Irish *File*, so many poems and notations that they will never have to bend their heads over the book, to the ruin of dramatic expression and of that wild air the bard had always about him in my boyish imagination.[11]

Music was necessary only in so far as it made poetry live; if it killed the vividness of words, it must not be applied to poetry. By 1906 Yeats's scepticism over pure music became so strong that he would allow only so much music as is inherent in the words:

Walter Pater says music is the type of all the arts, but somebody else, I forget now who, that oratory is their type. You will side with the one or the other according to the nature of your energy, and I in my present mood am all for the man who, with an average audience before him, uses all means of persuasion — stories, laughter, tears, and but so much music as he can discover on the wings of words. I would even avoid the conversation of the lovers of music, who would draw us into the impersonal land of sound and colour, and I would have no one write with a sonata in his memory.[12]

The importance of words he stressed till the end of his life. In 'An Introduction for My Plays', an essay he wrote for a complete edition of his works which was never produced, he writes about the two dominant desires in his theatrical activities:

I wanted to get rid of irrelevant movement — the stage must become still that words might keep all their vividness — and I wanted vivid words.[13]

Yet he firmly believed in the fusion of music and poetry, also. Writing in the same essay, he stressed that poetry was meant for the ear alone:

I wanted all my poetry to be spoken on a stage or sung and, because I did not understand my own instincts, gave half a dozen wrong or secondary reasons; but a month ago I understood my reasons. I have spent my life in clearing out of poetry every phrase written for the eye, and bringing all back to syntax that is for ear alone.[14]

Yeats's attitude to music was thus ambivalent. On the one hand, he believed in a fusion of music and poetry in which words passed imperceptibly into chanting, and on the other hand, he guarded the beauty of his poetry against the spoiling effect of pure music.

The ambivalent attitude is carried into his 'Noh' plays. The singing part is given to the chorus, which alternates the singing and the speaking depending on what function it performs. When the chorus is explaining the situation or making an editorial comment, it speaks; and it sings when it expresses the inner feeling of the protagonist or intensifies the lyrical feeling of the situation. Let us see how this is done in *At the Hawk's Well*.

In *At the Hawk's Well* two different attitudes to the supernatural are dealt with: One is represented by the Young Man, who heroically challenges the supernatural power in his own terms (and therefore

misses it), and the other by the Old Man, who shrinks away
unheroically from it. After the song for the unfolding of the cloth,
which calls 'to the eye of the mind' the setting and the two characters
to be involved in the play, the First Musician sings:

> The boughs of the hazel shake,
> The sun goes down in the west.

The second Musician continues the singing:

> The heart would be always awake,
> The heart would turn to its rest.

Then the First Musician *speaks* after the rolling up of the cloth:

> Night falls;
> The mountain-side grows dark;
> The withered leaves of the hazel
> Half choke the dry bed of the well;
> The guardian of the well is sitting
> Upon the old grey stone at its side,
> Worn out from raking its dry bed,
> Worn out from gathering up the leaves.
> Her heavy eyes
> Know nothing, or but look upon stone.
> The wind that blows out of the sea
> Turns over the heaped-up leaves at her side;
> They rustle and diminish.

The lyric that is sung by the First Musician and the Second Musician
emphasises the lyrical atmosphere of the play which is created around
the two states of the mind — the waking state, the heroic mind of
the Young Man, and the resting state, the unheroic mind of the Old
Man. The lyric describes not the physical circumstance but the inner
feelings of the characters. The First Musician's speech, by contrast,
describes the well, its surrounding and its guardian. The descriptive
or narrative element is strong in the speech, while the lyrical element
is strong in the song.

The alternating of the singing and the speaking is more skillfully
done in *The Dreaming of the Bones*. Here is the scene of the journey
to the summit of the mountain, where the young rebel seeks refuge
from the British troopers and where the dead lovers seek 'some one
of their race' to forgive their past crime so that 'Lip would be pressed
on lip':

First Musician [*speaking*]. They passed the shallow well and
the flat stone
Fouled by the drinking cattle, the narrow lane
Where mourners for five centuries have carried
Noble or peasant to his burial;
An owl is crying out above their heads.

[*Singing*]
Why should the heart take fright?
What sets it beating so?
The bitter sweetness of the night
Has made it but a lonely thing.
Red bird of March, begin to crow!
Up with the neck and clap the wing,
Red cock, and crow!

[*They go round the stage once. The First Musician speaks.*]
And now they have climbed through the long grassy field
And passed the ragged thorn-trees and the gap
In the ancient hedge; and the tomb-nested owl
At the foot's level beats with a vague wing.

[*Singing*]
My head is in a cloud;
I'd let the whole world go;
My rascal heart is proud
Remembering and remembering.
Red bird of March, begin to crow!
Up with the neck and clap the wing,
Red cock, and crow!

[*They go round the stage once. The First Musician speaks.*]
They are among the stones above the ash,
Above the briar and thorn and the scarce grass;
Hidden amid the shadow far below them
The cat-headed bird is crying out.

[*Singing*]
The dreaming bones cry out
Because the night winds blow
And heaven's a cloudy blot.
Calamity can have its fling.
Red bird of March, begin to crow!
Up with the neck and clap the wing,
Red cock, and crow!

The above rather lengthy quotation shows how the speaking and the singing part are alternated by the Musician. The speaking part is only descriptive or narrative, while the singing is lyrical. Different interpretations have been offered as to the meaning of the song. F. A. C. Wilson treats the three stanzas separately, giving an atmospheric meaning to the first, a political meaning to the second, and the synthesis of the two to the third.[15] Helen Vendler, on the other hand, takes the whole song to be a description of the Young Man's inner feeling.[16] Thus, to Wilson, the Young Man is reminiscing about the unsuccessful but heroic Easter rebellion during the ascent to the summit. To Helen Vendler, the Young Man is dreaming back with the ghosts. Although Wilson's interpretation is ingenious, the context of the play does not require such an interpretation; moreover, there is no reason why the Young Man should recall the Easter rebellion during the ascent. Vendler's reading is forced just as much, for the Young Man is a living person and is in a different gyre from the one the ghosts are in, and therefore cannot have 'joined the ranks of the "rogues" who wander the hills'.[17] That is why he does not know what the ghosts are and why they dance before they disappear:

> Why do you dance?
> Why do you gaze, and with so passionate eyes?
> One on the other; and then turn away,
> Covering your eyes, and weave it in a dance?
> Who are you? What are you? you are not natural.

It is false to ascribe the song to any one character in the play. The song and the speech of the Musician are about the ascent to the summit, and it is necessary to read them in that context. The speech is a physical description of the ascent and a foreboding of its outcome. The question is what the ascent means. At one level it means an ascent from the natural world to the supernatural, 'the haunted stones', as the setting (a mountain) appropriately shows. At another level it means an ascent of the dead lovers to the primary phase where they try in vain to find their masks through an absolving act of the Young Man. The crowing of a cock is longed for because the ghostly night is feared and also because a new cycle is about to begin, and is yet powerless to be born.

The speech of the Musician aptly describes the ascent by mentioning a cry of an owl in the last line of each paragraph, which indicates the progress of the ascent. At the outset the owl cries above the climbers' heads; then it beats its wing at the foot's level; and finally, after the second stanza of the song, it cries 'Hidden amid the shadow far below them'. At this time the climbers are almost at the summit.

The song, by contrast, shows no such progress, its aim being a lyrical intensity. The first stanza re-emphasises the atmospheric fear that the opening chorus set up and the tragic nature (bitter sweetness) of the night. The tragic sense is deepened by the loneliness of the heart which longs for the crowing of a cock, a daybreak. The tragic sense is emphasised because the ascent itself is tragic for the dead lovers, who seek their masks wrongly; that is, the dead lovers seek an absolution from one from whom it is least likely to come, an Easter Rising rebel in flight. Furthermore, the dead lovers' predicament shows that they are out of phase: they seek their masks in the objective phase, that is, the fulfilment of their desire is subject to the absolution of their past crime by one of their race. Thus they desire their own masks but their masks are entirely in the hands of another. In other words, the lovers' seeking is in the antithetical phase, but its fulfilment is possible only in the primary.

The dead lovers are presumably near Phase 15, which Yeats describes as 'a phase of complete beauty' where 'effort and attainment are indistinguishable';[18] and when their love is consummated they will be the 'creatures of the full' moon that Robartes describes in 'The Phases of the Moon'. Their fright and loneliness are akin to what Aherne and Robartes ascribe to the creatures of Phase 15:

> *Aherne.* It must be that the terror in their eyes
> Is memory or foreknowledge of the hour
> When all is fed with light and heaven is bare.
>
> *Robartes.* When the moon's full those creatures of the full
> Are on the waste hills by countrymen
> Who shudder and hurry by: body and soul
> Estranged amid the strangeness of themselves,
> Caught up in contemplation, the mind's eye
> Fixed upon images that once were thought;
> For separate, perfect, and immovable
> Images can break the solitude
> Of lovely, satisfied, indifferent eyes.

In the antithetical phase, the creature can 'let the whole world go', and can proudly seek its own image. In *The Dreaming of the Bones*, however, the dead lovers cannot seek their own images, because their union requires an absolution by one of their race. They have an antithetical will, but their lot is in the primary phase.[19] When

the Young Man declines to forgive their past crime, therefore, they
are swept away by the cloud — a negation of the attainment of the
phase of the full moon. The cloud of the second and the third stanza
means, then, the primary phase in which the moon is out of sight.
In that condition the 'dreaming bones cry out/ Because the night
winds blow/ And heaven's a cloudy blot.' Again in Robartes' words:

> Because all dark, like those that are all light,
> They are cast beyond the verge, and in a cloud,
> Crying to one another like the bats; . . . .

The dead lovers of the play, however, are not 'dough-like'
creatures. They are eager to get out of their phase. The refrain at
the end of each stanza signifies a longing for a new cycle. It is now
common knowledge that for Yeats a cock stood for a herald of a
new era. The red cock of March in the song is also expected to
perform the same function as that performed by a cock in 'Solomon
and the Witch'. The month of March is especially appropriate,
because in the Yeatsian system it is given Phase 15 and is the first
month of the year.[20] The refrain means, then, a longing for a new
era as well as for a daybreak. At the end of the play, however, it
is the cock of the natural world that crows 'from far below' telling
that 'now the night is gone', which means that for the ghost lovers
the chance for consummated love is lost and for the Young Man the
'sweet wandering snare' has lost its hold on him and he has returned
to the natural world.

'Calamity' in the third stanza must be taken as the end of a cycle
and the beginning of another. In Yeatsian terms the end of a cycle
is always calamitous. A breaking up of an old cycle prepares for
a new revelation: 'Things fall apart; the centre cannot hold;/ Mere
anarchy is loosed upon the world'.[21] According to *A Vision*:

The loss of control over thought comes towards the end; first a sinking in
upon the moral being, then the last surrender, the irrational cry, revelation
— the scream of Juno's peacock.[22]

Leda goes through the same process when attacked by Zeus in the
form of a swan:

> A sudden blow: the great wings beating still
> Above the staggering girl, her thighs caressed
> By the dark webs, her nape caught in his bill,
> He holds her helpless breast upon his breast.

> How can those terrified vague fingers push
> The feathered glory from her loosening thighs?
> And how can body, laid in that white rush,
> But feel the strange heart beating where it lies?

This violent act engenders the whole panorama of the history of the Trojan war:

> A shudder in the loins engenders there
> The broken wall, the burning roof and tower
> And Agamemnon dead.[23]

Whether the screaming of Juno's peacock occurred for Leda Yeats does not say explicitly, for the poem ends in an ambiguous question in a typically Yeatsian manner.

The foregoing discussion is meant to show how Yeats alternated speech and song in his dance plays and what functions he gave them. The use of speech and song reveals his double perspective of cognition and experience. The fact that he uses song only sparingly and depends largely on speech for communication indicates that he meant not to let himself be completely engulfed in the impersonality of music. 'Music is the most impersonal of things,' wrote Yeats in 'Discoveries' (1906), 'and that is why musicians do not like words.'[24] Conversely, he disliked pure music because it killed the personal and intimate effects of words. Music can be beautiful, however, as long as it retains personal quality:

When, however, the rhythm is more personal than it is in these simple verses, the tune will always be original and personal, alike in the poet and in the reader who has the right ear; and these tunes will now and again have great beauty.[25]

That was as much music as he allowed in his dance plays. He could not accept Zeami's formula of beauty nor the Paterian aestheticism of music. In his adaptation of the Noh to his drama, the cognitive perspective played a considerable role; to the extent that it checked him from being completely infatuated with the East, his plays remained cognitive in nature and Western in essence. On the other hand, it checked him also from attaining his own ideal form of art, that is, 'a mysterious art, . . . doing its work by suggestion, not by direct statement, a complexity of rhythm, colour, gesture, not space-pervading like the intellect but a memory and a prophecy'.[26]

Yeats's deviation from the Noh model is decisively shown in the structure of the dance plays. The dance plays actually do not depend much on dance and song but on words, and on the plot for their artistic effects. There is a decided dualistic interest on Yeats's part. What characterises the Noh is the meagreness of the plot; and as much plot as there is, the action is *shite*-centred, involving no antagonist in conflict with the *shite*. In contrast, Yeats's dance plays are characterised by plurality of characters and conflict-laden plot.[27] What is more, all of Yeats's dance plays end in a failure to resolve the conflict to which the characters have been subjected, while Japanese Noh plays usually end in a Nirvanic vision or a redemption of the spirit. There is a definite plot in all dance plays of Yeats, and the plot consists in a development of a spiritual conflict of the main character, or characters, with the opposing forces. No dance plays of Yeats can be appreciated apart from this plot, for they are not mere dancing and singing nor are they free of ideas. There is a definite exploratory interest in the plays. We are not supposed to be interested in the beauty of the dancing and singing alone, but in the words that express the conflict the characters go through; and that conflict is ultimately to bring us a tragic ecstasy.

In *At the Hawk's Well* the main characters are the Old Man and the Young Man, who have come to the remote shore with a common quest, the spring of eternal youth. The plurality of character is Yeats's significant deviation from the Noh convention. In watching the play the audience cannot focus their attention on a single character, as they would in a Noh play, but must follow two lines of action, the Young Man's and the Old Man's. Moreover, a key part of the performance is given to the Hawk-Woman, who is the opposing force to both seekers.

The Noh made a complete circle when *At the Hawk's Well*, translated with considerable modifications by Mario Yokomichi, was first performed at Somei Noh Theatre in Tokyo on October 20, 1949. The comparison between the Japanese version and Yeats's original play shows us essential differences that distinguish Yeats's dance plays from the Noh. In the Japanese version the Old Man becomes the *shite* (main actor) and the Young Man becomes the *waki* (interlocutor). The play begins with the Young Man's revelation of his identity followed by a journey to the remote island of the West Sea, where he is met by the Old Man, the wreck of a once youthful traveller, who takes the newcomer to the Hawk's well and tells him of its curse upon himself. The opening of the play, the journey and the conversation are done strictly in accordance with the Noh convention. The conversation is followed by the Hawk-Woman's dance accompanied by the alternated singing by the chorus and the Hawk-Woman herself. The dance concludes the first part of the play.

In the second part, the ghost of the Old Man appears before the Young Man and tells him that he is what has become of a young traveller who was enchanted by the well until he became a ghost. Then the ghost reveals to the Young Man his agony in a dance and fades into the dark of the mountain like a wind.

At the Hawk's Well, then, suffered considerable changes when it was added to the Noh repertory. The most significant change was that the role of the Young Man was reduced from a heroic character to a mere point of view. With this reduction the play lost the heroic thread of the Cuchulain legend and gained the singleness of aesthetic effect that is derived from the Old Man's ghostly affliction turned into a flower. The change was necessary in order to maintain the *shite*-centredness of the Noh scheme. And yet a Japanese Noh critic criticises the Japanese version for putting too much weight on the role of the *tsure** (Hawk-Woman).[28]

Yeats's original work is a play which develops the internal conflict of the protagonists whose spiritual quest for eternity is doomed to failure because of their weaknesses. The Old Man fails to drink of the well because of his cowardice and his petty, selfish motive. He recoils from the well when the Guardian of the Well starts dancing, and sleeps through the dance; when he awakes he discovers the stones of the well wet but finds no water there. The Young Man's quest is also thwarted by the Guardian of the Well, but unlike the Old Man he heroically goes after her:

> Run where you will,
> Grey bird, you shall be perched upon my wrist.
> Some were called queens and yet have been perched there.

But, of course, the Young Man is really enchanted by the bird and led away from the well as if he was in a trance, dropping his spear. When he returns to the well, the water has already plashed and gone again. The Young Man loses his quest because of his heroism and earthly desires. It is difficult to say which is the main character in the play, the Old Man or the Young Man. They have equal weight in terms of their quest and their failure. Perhaps they represent 'two moods of the heart', as Helen Vendler suggests.[29] If so, the play may be said to be a study in the conflict of two psychic patterns typified in the minds of the Young Man and the Old Man, which reveal to us not only the spiritual make-up of the two but the nature of their quest as well. The plot — the development of the conflict

---

* A third character in a Noh piece; pronounced 'tsu-ray'.

— is what sustains the play; without it the play would not exist. The audience, in turn, are expected to make explorations of the meaning of the conflict; the play, in this respect, is basically of cognitive nature. The cognitive interest is minimised in Yokomichi's Japanese version, which concentrates on the Old Man who expresses the agony of his spiritual thraldom in a dance according to the Noh convention, which is to say that the Japanese adaptation follows Zeami's formula for the Noh of the Spirit: 'a flower upon a rock'. It is difficult to see the Old Man of the original play as a flower of any sort; and the author's aim was not to make a flower out of the Old Man either: his aim was that we should see the conflict itself and its tragic outcome. That is the note the songs for the unfolding and folding of the cloth stress at the end of the play. The entire lyric is a vision of a disaster in a vain human quest for the supernatural. The first three stanzas, the song for the unfolding of the cloth, point out the tragic nature of the quest and stress a sense of total defeat. The first stanza contrasts the human and the supernatural and hails the return of the 'human faces,/ Familiar memories.' The second stanza expresses a total resignation to the cycle of birth and death of nature:

> Folly alone I cherish,
> I choose it for my share;
> Being but a mouthful of air,
> I am content to perish;
> I am but a mouthful of sweet air.

If the 'folly' is accepted in the second stanza, 'wisdom' is rejected in the third stanza:

> O lamentable shadows,
> Obscurity of strife!
> I choose a pleasant life
> Among indolent meadows;
> Wisdom must live a bitter life.

An easy life in the natural world is chosen instead of a tragic life of wisdom which 'must live a bitter life'. The life of wisdom is a life of conflict, an 'obscurity of strife', and is shunned by the weak mind. The song is associated by different critics with the Old Man and with the Young Man alternately, but such associations are without sufficient ground and are, in fact, unnecessary. The song describes lyrically a disaster that fell on the weak mind that attempted to grasp something beyond its power. The Old Man must be strong enough to face the terror of the supernatural in order to experience it; and the Young Man must forsake his earthly heroism. They must have the self that seeks what is most unlike itself, its mask.

The song for the folding of the cloth is a mockery of the weak mind by the supernatural presences. The empty well and the leafless tree, the withered images of eternity (cf. 'Among School Children') which the weak mind can grasp at best, ironically praise the kind of people who would not even attempt the supernatural quest, being content with their own lives:

> 'The man that I praise,'
> Cries out the empty well,
> 'Lives all his days
> Where a hand on the bell
> Can call the milch cows
> To the comfortable door of his house.
> Who but an idiot would praise
> Dry stones in a well?'

> 'The man that I praise,'
> Cries out the leafless tree,
> 'Has married and stays
> By an old hearth, and he
> On naught has set store
> But children and dogs on the floor.
> Who but an idiot would praise
> A withered tree?'

Notice the humorous and self-mocking tone of the song. The well and the tree are mocking themselves by saying that only an idiot would praise them, but are, in reality, deriding the weak mind that cannot grasp reality but its shadows. *At the Hawk's Well*, then, is a study in the conflict of the mind seeking the supernatural, which ends in failure. It exposes the 'vanity of human wishes'. It ends on the note it started with:

> What were his life soon done!
> Would he lose by that or win?
> A mother that saw her son
> Doubled over a speckeled shin,
> Cross-grained with ninety years,
> Would cry, 'how little worth
> Were all my hopes and fears
> And the hard pain of his birth!'

The Only Jealousy of Emer is also a study of conflict, and is characterised by the plurality of character. Structurally, Emer corresponds to the *waki*, but she is more than a mere point of view and is actually the main character whose distress (jealousy and love for her flirting husband) is dramatised. The play is complicated further by the sub-plot in which Cuchulain's temptation by the Woman of the Sidhe is dramatised. Thus, it is necessary for the audience to follow two threads of events in order to understand the meaning of Emer's problem. One thread is Emer's involving Cuchulain, and the other is the Woman of the Sidhe's also involving Cuchulain; the two threads are brought together to a conclusion, but not to a resolution, by uniting Cuchulain to his mistress, Eithne Inguba.

Emer is Cuchulain's wife, who has only 'two joyous thoughts', a memory of her happiness in her husband's love and a hope to regain that happiness, and who would not feel jealous of her husband's earthly loves but 'valued every slut above her'. Her only jealousy is directed towards the supernatural Woman of the Sidhe. She tries hard to retrieve her husband from her supernatural rival but is told by Bricriu, the Woman of the Sidhe's rival spirit from the court of Manannan, that Cuchulain's life can be retrieved only if she renounces all hope of reunion with him. By the supernatural sight given by Bricriu she sees her husband being tempted by the Woman of the Sidhe and about to yield, when she gathers up her courage and renounces her husband's love forever. Thereupon Cuchulain wakes and throws himself not into Emer's arms but Eithne Inguba's, which means a failure of love on Emer's part.

The Woman of the Sidhe's lot is just as bad as Emer's. She needs Cuchulain's kiss in order to attain a perfection of beauty and personality. But Cuchulain is hard to win because of his earthly ties that linger with him in memory of Emer. Thus when Emer pays her due price for Cuchulain's life, the Woman of the Sidhe has to free him.

The play is about failure of love on both the natural and the supernatural planes. The play begins with the opening lyric for the folding and unfolding of the cloth, which presents Yeats's familiar theme of feminine beauty. The first stanza envisages a woman's beauty as a frail sea-bird, a symbol of earthly beauty which has taken the human soul centuries of intellectual labour to exalt. As Helen Vendler has pointed out, the stanza anticipates 'The Statues', but it is also reminiscent of 'Adam's Curse', in which three parallel labours — the poet's, the woman's and the lover's — are dealt with in a tone of disillusionment. The 'beautiful mild woman' of the poem, presumably Maud Gonne's sister Kathleen, says that 'To be born

woman is to know −/ . . . That we must labour to be beautiful.'
Yeats replies: 'It's certain there is no fine thing/ Since Adam's fall
but needs much labouring.'

If the earthly beauty of a woman is like a frail sea-bird exalted
by the 'sedentary soul/ In toils of measurement', yet frail enough
to be dashed to the time-bound earth at any moment, it is also a
sea-shell rejected by the sea of eternity and stranded on the human
shore − a hollow image of eternal beauty. The stanza is again
reminiscent of 'Adam's Curse', which symbolises a profound sense
of failure of love by a hollow moon and a shell.

> We sat grown quiet at the name of love;
> We saw the last embers of daylight die,
> And in the trembling blue-green of the sky
> A moon, worn as if it had been a shell
> Washed by time's waters as they rose and fell
> About the stars and broke in days and years.
>
> I had a thought for no one's but your ears:
> That you were beautiful, and that I strove
> To love you in the old high way of love;
> That it had all seemed happy, and yet we'd grown
> As weary-hearted as that hollow moon.

An empty sea-shell is used in 'Ancestral Houses' as a symbol of the
vain glory of humanity that employs art to create an exalted image
of beauty which will in time be inherited only by a mouse.

> Mere dreams, mere dreams! Yet Homer had not sung
> Had he not found it certain beyond dreams
> That out of life's own self-delight had sprung
> The abounding glittering jet; though now it seems
> As if some marvellous empty sea-shell flung
> Out of the obscure dark of the rich streams,
> And not a fountain, were the symbol which
> Shadows the inherited glory of the rich.
>
> Some violent bitter man, some powerful man
> Called architect and artist in, that they,
> Bitter and violent men, might rear in stone
> The sweetness that all longed for night and day,
> The gentleness none there had ever known;
> But when the master's buried mice can play,
> And maybe the great-grandson of that house,
> For all its bronze and marble, 's but a mouse.

A sea-shell is also used in 'The Sad Shepherd' as a symbol of time's destruction of once noble words turned into 'inarticulate moan'.

The second stanza of the opening lyric of *Emer* has the sea-shell washed upon the strand by 'the vast troubled waters' in a storm that 'arose and suddenly fell' during the night. The shell, in other words, was rejected by the sea, that dispenser of time that rejected the shell of the 'Ancestral Houses' and destroyed the song of the Sad Shepherd. And thus it was through an act of violence and degradation that a feminine beauty was brought into existence on earth:

> What death? what discipline?
> What bonds no man could unbind,
> Being imagined within
> The labyrinth of the mind,
> What pursuing or fleeing,
> What wounds, what bloody press,
> Dragged into being
> This loveliness?

The opening lyric, then, emphasises the two-fold nature of the earthly beauty of a woman. Viewed from the mundane world of time, it is an exalted yet frail sea-bird which was made air-borne with much labour but is liable to fall to the ground. Viewed from the world of eternity, it is a hollow image of eternal beauty that takes an act of violence and degradation foreordained by the great sea of eternity in order to exist in the world of time. Both qualities are rejected by the sea, which cries outside the fisherman's hut where Cuchulain's body is laid:

> White shell, white wing!
> I will not choose for my friend
> A frail, unserviceable thing
> That drifts and dreams, and but knows
> That waters are without end
> And that wind blows.

The earthly beauty of a woman is represented in the play by Emer and Eithne Inguba. They are bound together against the forces of the supernatural. Emer does not feel jealous of Cuchulain's earthly lovers, including Eithne, but feels jealous of the Woman of the Sidhe alone. When Eithne comes into the fisherman's hut to see Cuchulain's body, Emer asks her help to get Cuchulain back to life by saying:

> We're but two women struggling with the sea.

Eithne on her part does not feel inimical to Emer. So, when Emer invites her to sit by Cuchulain's bed she says hesitantly:

> No, Madam,
> I have too deeply wronged you to sit there.

It is only after Emer's strong urging that she comes near Cuchulain's body and tries to wake his spirit.

Both Emer and Eithne are hollow images of consummate love, for they are both subject to time's devastation. Although they are assigned by the Woman of the Sidhe to Phase 14 for being women 'that did not reach beyond the human,/ Lacking a day to be complete', it is not certain that the context of the play requires them to be perfectly phasal.[30] As a matter of fact, they could belong either to Phase 14 or 16, according to *A Vision*, because in either phase 'the greatest human beauty becomes possible'. [31] It is sufficient to have them together as an incarnation of earthly beauty opposed to supernatural beauty. Their earthly and cyclical nature is recognised and confessed in their own words. Emer, her hour passed, lives with only two thoughts. When Bricriu urges her to renounce Cuchulain's love forever in order to save him from the hands of the Woman of the Sidhe, she replies:

> I have but two joyous thoughts, two things I prize.
> A hope, a memory, and now you claim that hope.

She ultimately renounces that hope in order to retrieve Cuchulain from the spirit of the sea, condemning her own love to eternal failure. Eithne Inguba, too, realises her earthly and cyclical nature when she speaks to Emer of her own status to Cuchulain:

> Women like me, the violent hour passed over,
> Are flung into some corner like old nut-shells.

Thus, for both Emer and Eithne there is no chance of eternal love. Their love is like Sheba's — momentary and cyclical in nature.

In contrast to the opening lyric, the closing lyric concerns itself with the supernatural beauty — the beauty of Phase 15. The stanzas, except the refrain, refer to an inhuman beauty that has almost attained Phase 15. The figure is a cold 'statue of solitude', but its heart is strangely beating fast. From such a cold figure, though it may attract the attention of the world,

> He that has loved the best
> May turn . . .
> His too human breast.

When it attains the zenith of its perfection, the figure becomes a pure image in which thought and body are fused:

> What makes your heart so beat?
> What man is at your side?
> When beauty is complete
> Your own thought will have died
> And danger not be diminished;
> Dimmed at three-quarter light,
> When moon's round is finished
> The stars are out of sight.

This is the attainment of Phase 15, which nullifies the meaning of the figure's craving for love. *A Vision* has this description:

Now contemplation and desire, united into one, inhabit a world where every beloved image has bodily form, and every bodily form is loved. This love knows nothing of desire, for desire implies effort, and though there is still separation from the loved object, love accepts the separation as necessary to its own existence.[32]

At Phase 15 thought has become an image and that image has a bodily form. Aherne in 'The Phases of the Moon' describes the condition, using Dante's analogy:

> All dreams of the soul
> End in a beautiful man's or woman's body.

Yeats envisages thought as a process of the mind toward its object, and all thought necessarily tends towards extinction because there will be no thought when it finds its object. Thought, thus, implies effort and strife in the antinomial world. When Phase 15 is attained all is resolved into a single incarnation of beauty, which is free from effort and thought:

As all effort has ceased, all thought has become image, because no thought could exist if it were not carried towards its own extinction.[33]

The attainment of Phase 15 means an end of process. In terms of the closing lyric:

Your own thought will have died
And danger not be diminished;

Which is to say that thought is fused into the body. The word 'danger'
has perplexed Yeatsian critics. Wilson's interpretation is as follows:

All beautiful women have the most absolute need for man's companionship;
it is their only escape from solitude. But beauty is no protection from loss;
even in the fifteenth rebirth, when physical loveliness is 'complete' and all
'thought' dies in self-absorption, the 'danger' of dereliction and loneliness
will remain; for man, loving the imperfect as he does, 'cannot bear very
much reality,' and will tend to turn away.[34]

Wilson looks upon the loneliness of a being at Phase 15 as a danger,
but solitude is the very mode of existence to such a being, as Robartes
says in 'The Phases of the Moon':

> All thought becomes an image and the soul
> Becomes a body: that body and that soul
> Too perfect at the full to lie in a cradle,
> Too lonely for the traffic of the world:
> Body and soul cast out and cast away
> Beyond the visible world.

Furthermore, Wilson seems to be oblivious of the fact that Yeats has
Phase 15 as a supernatural incarnation. Also, his interpretation
makes it necessary to read the conjunction 'And' in the line 'And
danger not be diminished' as 'But' or 'Nevertheless'. Helen Vendler,
who assigns the stanza from third line down to Fand speaking to
Emer, gives the following interpretation:

Though human beauty may have temporary victories, in reality these are
ephemeral, and the danger of losing Cuchulain to the other world is not
diminished by this temporary setback.[35]

This reading would have Emer a victor, which she is not. By
renouncing Cuchulain's love Emer lost him forever. Her loss of
Cuchulain is not a danger; it is a reality. Again, Vendler's
interpretation requires reading the third and the fourth lines as
contrary statements.

My own reading may be just as forced, but I believe that it makes
a smoother reading to have the third and the fourth lines hung
together syntactically as coordinate clauses. The ideas expressed in
these lines presumably refer to Yeats's concept of a Unity of Being

as a perfectly proportioned huaman body in which thought has reached its extinction, finding itself in the 'body which the soul will permanently inhabit'.[36] What is not diminished at Phase 15 is the importance of the body, which learned men such as mathematicians, theologians, and lawyers call 'danger'.

Although Yeats's earthly perspective tended to leave him to the 'toils of the sedentary soul', his saintly aspirations constantly gave him an incentive to free himself from his antinomial thinking. In such moments he would disparage the tendency of abstract thinking that 'those learned men who are a terror to children and ignominious sight in lovers' eyes'[37] are given to. These learned men

have followed some abstract reverie, which stirs the brain only and need that only, and have therefore stood before the looking-glass without pleasure and never known those thoughts that shape the lines of the body for beauty or animation, and wake a desire for praise or for display.[38]

Yeats had learned from Blake that eternity consisted in the concrete forms and not in abstractions of the Platonic or the empirical order. The 'learned men', by privileging abstract ideas, fell into the error of separating the body from the soul and thought from image — the error that the protagonist of 'Among School Children' and the old man of 'Sailing to Byzantium' loathe. The position of the 'learned men' is exactly the position taken by the dancer, possibly Iseult Gonne, in 'Michael Robartes and the Dancer', in which the dancer is determined to school herself in modern intellectual, abstractionist morality in spite of Michael Robartes' argument that the woman's beauty lies in 'uncomposite blessedness'. To Robartes' eulogy of the 'thinking body' the dancer replies:

> I have heard said
> There is great danger in the body.

To which Robartes makes a comment in a question:

> Did God in portioning wine and bread
> Give man His thought or His mere body?

Robartes' final say in the argument is:

> I have principles to prove me right.
> It follows from this Latin text
> That blest souls are not composite,
> And that all beautiful women may

Live in uncomposite blessedness,
And lead us to the like — if they
Will banish every thought, unless
The lineaments that please their view
When the long looking-glass is full,
Even from the foot-sole think it too.

The danger in the body that the dancer heard about should not be feared; it is actually the eternal form of beauty that every thought dies into. This, it seems to me, is what the word 'danger' in the final lyric of *Emer* means.

The final triplet of the stanza is a repetition of the same idea:

Dimmed at three-quarter light,
When moon's round is finished
The stars are out of sight.

When the moon reaches its fulfilment, that is, Phase 15, all else in the sky disappears, being absorbed into the light of the moon, as thought is absorbed into the body.

The closing lyric of the play means in the last analysis the futility of love between the supernatural and the natural. It takes two to love. In the supernatural realm, when the being reaches its perfect fulfilment its object is absorbed into it. From such a supernatural being, though it may be a form of absolute beauty, the natural man turns 'his too human breast', which finds it difficult to take a supernatural flight because of the weight of the memory of the earthly love.

The refrain is a choral comment on the unsuccessful meeting between the supernatural and the natural:

O bitter reward
Of many a tragic tomb!
And we though astonished are dumb
Or give but a sigh and a word,
A passing word.

This is a tragic vision of failure — the failure to achieve the Unity of Being at Phase 15. The failure falls on both Cuchulain and the Woman of the Sidhe. Why on the Woman of the Sidhe? In order to understand this, we must carefully read the description of the Woman of the Sidhe and the closing lyric. Although the closing lyric is about the beauty at Phase 15, it does not describe the absolute beauty itself. It describes a being that has nearly achieved a perfection at Phase 15. It pictures the 'statue of solitude' as walking in the hut with 'Its strange heart beating fast'. The last stanza except the refrain repeats the same emphasis on the beating heart, and pictures the figure with a man at its side, an object of love that has not yet been absorbed into love as it should be at Phase 15. Furthermore, the description of the perfected beauty is rendered in the future tense, which means that the figure is yet to reach Phase 15.

The description of the Woman of the Sidhe in the play proper also indicates that the Woman has not quite reached Phase 15. When she appears before Cuchulain she radiates with such beauty that Cuchulain asks:

> Who is it stands before me there
> Shedding such light from limb and hair
> As when the moon, complete at last
> With every labouring crescent past,
> And lonely with extreme light,
> Flings out upon the fifteenth night?

Cuchulain sees her as a being at Phase 15: she is beautiful and lonely like the full moon. The Woman of the Sidhe answers Cuchulain, however:

> Because I long I am not complete.

She needs Cuchulain's love in order to be complete. She then asks Cuchulain why he hides his face from her, and when Cuchulain answers that old memories are the cause, she says:

> Could you that have loved many a woman
> That did not reach beyond the human,
> Lacking a day to be complete,
> Love one that, though her heart can beat,
> Lacks it but by an hour or so?

The Woman of the Sidhe is not quite the being at Phase 15, as Wilson would have us believe; and her thread of action arises out of conflict and ends in failure due to the very imperfection. Wilson, who believes that *Hagoromo*, a Noh play, influenced Yeats's *Emer*, sees in the Tennin a prototype of the supernatural beauty:

Fand's symbol is the 'full moon' of 'perfect fulfilment,' to quote the passage from *Hagoromo* on which Yeats depends, and to which he will have attached one does not know what mystique. She belongs, consequently, to the fifteenth, supernatural incarnation. . . .[39]

Wilson takes not only the Tennin but also the bird symbolism, the fisherman and the whole sea-side atmosphere to have influenced Yeats's work. That is reading too much of *Hagoromo* into the play, for a parallelism of characters and their action, not to mention the plot itself, cannot be worked out satisfactorily: In *Hagoromo* the one who loses and recovers that which belongs to her is the Tennin, supernatural beauty; while in Yeats's play it is Emer who loses and retrieves what belongs to her. In *Hagoromo* the fisherman, the natural being, is the robber and the Tennin, the supernatural being, is the victim; but actually there is little conflict between them, for the fisherman returns the feather mantle to the Tennin readily and regrets his attempt to keep it. Besides, there is no real reason why the fisherman should hang on to the feather mantle. The rape of the feather mantle is nothing more than a device to draw a dance out of the Tennin. In *The Only Jealousy of Emer*, however, Fand, the supernatural being, is the usurper and Emer, the natural being, is the victim; and there is a real cause of conflict between them. The conflict is not a device but is the drama itself.

Wilson's interpretation of Yeats's play is based on further misunderstandings of *Hagoromo*. He takes the Tennin to be the moon-goddess who 'dances among her attendant nymphs, for "there are heavenly nymphs, Amaotome, one for each night of the month"; in the play fifteen of these nymphs wear the white and fifteen the black kimonoes'.[40] The play makes it clear that the Tennin is one of the thirty Amaotome, heavenly nymphs, each of whom performs a nightly service at the Katsura Palace of the Moon. Even Pound's frequently garbled translation makes this clear:

> Tennin: I also am heaven-born and a maid, Amaotome. Of
> them there are many.

The dance she dances for the fisherman is not 'a dance of pleasure', but is a ritual dance which, according to the Japanese tradition, was taught by a divine being who descended from heaven on the sands of Udo-hama in Suruga, and which was hence adopted by the Imperial Court as a ritual dance.[41] The dance of the full moon was considered to bring about abundance of heaven's grace which was shed universally upon earth like the moon's light.

Wilson also takes the bird-symbolism in *Hagoromo* as representing the souls of the dead that 'cross and recross above the"waves"

of the postmortem state'.[42] In *Hagoromo* the chorus refers to two
kinds of birds: One is the supernatural bird of Buddhist heaven, the
karyobinga, the other kind includes such birds of nature as geese
and plovers. The supernatural bird's voices, which the Tennin is
accustomed to hearing, become fainter and fainter, emphasising a
sense of separation that the helpless Tennin feels. The sight of the
natural birds that fly homeward with ease and freedom causes her
to grieve over her lost freedom. While it may be asking too much
of Wilson to have a correct understanding of the Noh play from
Pound's inadequate translation, we may, at the same time, rightly
say that he has taken some liberties with the meaning of the play
in connection with Yeats's *Emer*. Even if Wilson was right in
assuming that Yeats was inspired by *Hagoromo* in writing his *Emer*,
we must say that the poet drastically modified his model to suit his
purpose, for he dramatises the conflict which is all but meaningless
in the original and leaves that conflict unresolved, while the Noh
ends the play in a dance of the full moon, 'a shadow of the moon's
fulfilment and truth's eternity and perfection'.[43]

The Only Jealousy of Emer has been discussed at length because
its debt to *Hagoromo* and other Noh plays is overestimated and its
essential difference from the Noh drama is generally overlooked. The
case of *The Dreaming of the Bones* is a little different. It differs more
obviously from its Noh model than the previous one. The ending
of the play, which leaves the ghosts of Diarmuid and Dervorgilla
forever separated, makes a sharp contrast with that of *Nishikigi*, the
model, which redeems the dead lovers from their love sorrows and
consummates their love through the service of the journeying priest.
Even Wilson has to recognise this,[44] although he ignores its
significance. Shotaro Oshima ascribes the difference to the general
inferior quality of the Noh literature, and fails to account for Yeats's
departure from the Noh model.[45] The structural significance of
Yeats's deviation from the Noh convention calls for attention
especially in the case of *The Dreaming of the Bones*, for it not only
shows the fundamental difference between Yeats's drama and the
Noh but the whole meaning of the play depends on the structure
where Yeats departed from the Noh tradition.

In *Nishikigi* the *waki*, the itinerant priest, is a mere point of view
as far as the audience are concerned, and has no antagonistic interest
as far as the dead lovers are concerned. He is simply a functional
character, who keeps the show going. In *The Dreaming of the Bones*
the young Irish rebel corresponds to the *waki*, but he is not a mere
point of view through which we see the action of the play but a
definite character with his own thread of action; nor is he a neutral

travelling priest of the Noh play but a person who not only has a good reason to feel hostile to the dead lovers but also is involved in their action and actually interferes with their interests by denying them a forgiveness that is necessary for a consummation of their love. The young rebel's and his people's suffering was actually caused by the dead lovers, 'that most miserable, most accursed pair / Who sold their country into slavery'.[45a] The fulfilment of the dead lovers' wishes thus depends upon the will of the young rebel, one of their race, who ultimately refuses to grant their request. Thus, the plurality of characters and the conflict engendered between them constitute a significant difference between the play and its Noh model. The conflict is left unresolved at the end of the play and the ghosts of the dead lovers vanish in despair as the dawn descends on them. The tragic sense is heightened when we realise that the young compatriot is not aware of the true identity of the ghosts until they dance a dance of frustrated love, repeating 'Seven hundred years our lips have never met', and finally fade into the cloud that envelops the summit in a moment. As the play ends with the Young Man's

> I had almost yielded and forgiven all —
> Terrible the temptation and the place!

we descend the mountain and hear with the Young Man the cries of red cocks that come from the natural world far below:

> My heart ran wild when it heard
> The curlew cry before dawn
> And the eddying cat-headed bird;
> But now the night is gone.
> I have heard from far below
> The strong March birds a-crow.
> Stretch neck and clap the wing.
> Red cocks, and crow!

With whom are we to sympathise? Are we to feel pity and fear for the fate of the dead lovers? Or are we to feel justified in the Young Man's final decision? Yeats's intention is neither. A tragic sense is generated precisely from such a conflict. The play as a whole, however, presents the history of a conflict and its failure of resolution. At one level it represents the dead lovers' failure to achieve their Unity of Being. At another level it represents an unresolved conflict within a nation, an unreconciled quarrel between the ancient and the present generation of the Irish race.

The major point of difference between *The Dreaming of the Bones* and *Nishikigi* lies in this. In *Nishikigi*, as in other Noh plays of spirit, the main interest is in the beauty of the love sorrows of the dead lovers and of their consummated love, a beauty expressed in singing and dancing; while in *The Dreaming of the Bones* the major dramatic appeal stems from the character-revealing words and, as John Rees Moore and Richard Taylor have commented, from the immediacy of the action and the historicity of the subject matter.[46]

In *Calvary* we finally have a single action in which Christ is the actor. The play, however, is a curious work, in which the *shite*-centred action produces a single impression like a Noh play, but the relationship between the *shite* and other characters is inverted. In a Noh play the *shite** is the actor in the strict sense of the term: he is the one who *acts* and the *waki* is the 'side' character who serves as the point of view through which we see the *shite* act. In *Calvary* Christ, who corresponds to the *shite*, does not do much and is more like the *waki*, whose function is to officiate at the *shite*'s performance. Through his conversation with other characters — Judas, Lazarus, and the Roman Soldiers — we come to know their feelings. He is the point of view placed in the centre of action that whirls about him. He is so central in the play that he is almost a mere point, which we hardly notice without the light thrown upon him by other characters from the periphery. And yet he is more than a passive observer like the *waki* in the Noh; on the contrary, he is the observed, for everything happens to him and our interest is in what would become of him at the end; and he is the only person that changes in the play, though his change is not brought about by his own action. The singleness of action in *Calvary* is maintained, therefore, not by the active performer *shite* but by the passive character of Christ; not the subjectivity of the *shite* but by the objectivity of Christ, to use Yeatsian terms. The action is forwarded, therefore, by the antagonistic forces surrounding Christ. Once again we can throw much light upon the play by finding discrepancies that exist between the play and the Noh.

There are three major points at which Yeats deviates from the Noh convention. Like the other plays for dancers, the play is characterised by a plurality of characters, although it is free from a plurality of actions. Secondly, the play dramatises an idea.[47] Thirdly, the drama consists of a conflict that ends in irresolution.

The plurality of characters characterises Yeats's dance plays and makes it mandatory for the audience to pay attention to all the

---

* The Japanese word 'shite' literally means 'the one who does.'

characters that appear on stage. *Calvary* is no exception despite the fact that Christ is the main character who never absents himself throughout the play. Unlike the other plays, however, the play is unified by a single action that centres about Christ, who finds himself in conflict with the entire world surrounding him. At the exoteric level, at least, the conflict is not as complex as it is in the other dance plays. However, we must watch every character that comes in the way of Christ and see what sort of conflict develops between them.

The play, however, has a hidden conflict in the character of Christ, which does not reveal itself until the end when Christ cries out: 'My Father, why hast Thou forsaken Me?' The meaning of this cry is the theme of the play, and it reveals the nature of Christianity as Yeats understood it.

Various interpretations of the meaning of the play are offered by the critics of Yeats's drama. Critics generally agree that the play is about a relationship between the objective and the subjective cycles. They disagree widely, however, in assigning the cycles to the characters. Wilson, who believes, perhaps unfairly to Yeats, that Yeats condemned Christianity as 'a dark religion', turns the play into a thesis of comparative religion,[48] giving a superior status to the heron symbolising the subjective religion and stigmatising Christ's rule 'as something essentially sordid.'[49] To Wilson the characters that appear before Christ, insisting on their subjectivity, are the heroic figures who endeavour to keep their solitude and freedom amidst the dark tide of the inferior religion. Helen Vendler disagrees with Wilson, believing that Yeats's sympathies were divided.[50] Her main disagreement with Wilson, however, is that Christ comes from Phase 15 of the primary cycle, thus making the play's theme 'interaction of objective and subjective life, the double interlocking gyres'.[51] Regrettably, however, she does not satisfactorily relate this underlying pattern to the actual events that take place in the play. Nathan follows Wilson and Vendler in assigning Christ to the objective cycle and the other characters to the subjective. He differs from his predecessors, however, in seeing dual nature in Christ: 'though His divine nature is objective, His human nature, derived from the dying subjective cycle, experiences the agony of man out of phase and deprived of the possibility — in His isolated state — of completion.'[52] This seems to be an arbitrary view unwarranted by the text.[53] Peter Ure and John Rees Moore after him have presented a different view, assigning Christ to the same cycle as the other characters. Making much of the closing lyric, Ure argues that the conflict occurs between Christ and the other characters because the subjective God tries to make the subjective men into his objects:

God had not appeared to them, but this God is like them. . . . The stillness and loneliness of Christ are enhanced, and the songs are tied into the main antithesis of the play. As Yeats would have put it when writing in another mode, it is the subjective God who calls upon men to be his objects, who pours his own spirit into them.[54]

Ure's view is interesting, but it does not explain Christ's isolation from God.

These interpretations which have been discussed are useful, but the play can be seen differently — not as a thesis on impersonal cycles, but as a dramatisation of Christ's spiritual conflict and the failure to resolve it.

Christ's conflict and failure to resolve it is deeply rooted in his dual nature as the Son of God. As the Saviour, Christ is subjective in nature; and as the instrument of God, he is objective in nature. This dual nature of Christ caused Yeats to deviate considerably from the Noh convention. Christ indeed holds a curious position as a character in that he does very little to forward the action and yet is the leading character whose progress is the drama itself. He has the characteristics of both the *shite* and the *waki* of the Noh: He not only acts out his fate like the *shite* of the Noh, though passively, but also creates a dramatic situation for the other characters to act out their lives. Thus, in Yeatsian terms, he is both subjective and objective. This dual nature of Christ on the structural level of the play is closely related with its thematic level.

As Peter Ure and Leonard E. Nathan after him have pointed out,[55] the play is about 'a dreaming back' of Christ's passion. This is made clear by the chorus immediately after the opening lyric is sung:

> The road to Calvary, and I beside it
> Upon an ancient stone. Good Friday's come,
> The day whereon Christ dreams His passion through.

In 'the dreaming back' of his passion Christ is caught between his two opposing natures and falls into what Yeats in *A Vision* calls the *Victimage for the Ghostly Self*.[56]

The opening lyric stresses the note of conflict, indicating that daemonic relationship between the subjective white heron[57] and

God is impossible: 'God has not died for the white heron'. They cannot die each other's life. And they cannot live each other's death either; hence, the re-emphasis on the note of conflict in the closing lyric: 'God has not appeared to the birds'. Peter Ure is right about God being subjective, for He chooses himself and Christ. When a subjective creature is confronted with the subjective God, there can be only an irreconcilable conflict. Christ, however, has a dual nature. As an instrument of God, raising Lazarus from the dead and subduing Judas, he is subjective, but as God's choice he is completely objective in nature, willing nothing but God's will. This dual nature Christ makes clear in his exchange of words with Lazarus. When Lazarus complains that Christ is travelling to death he is denied, Christ says:

> But I have conquered death,
> And all the dead shall be raised up again.

But when Lazarus complains that his freedom and solitude (the subjective condition) are invaded, Christ says: 'I do my Father's will'. In defining humanity, Christ is as subjective as God himself, but in so doing he is not willing of himself but of God. His words to Judas aptly reveal his dual nature: 'My Father put all men into my hands'.

The dual nature of Christ has also the support of *A Vision*, in which Christ is said to have in him pity and love. Love is objective in nature and belongs to contemplation, while pity is subjective in nature and belongs to action. It was the latter, pity, in Christ that created Christendom:

We say of Him because His sacrifice was voluntary that He was love itself, and yet that part of Him which made Christendom was not love but pity, and not pity for intellectual despair, though the man in Him, being *antithetical* like His age, knew it in the Garden, but *primary* pity, that for the common lot, man's death, seeing that He raised Lazarus, sickness, seeing that He healed many, sin, seeing that He died.

Love is created and preserved by intellectual analysis, for we love only that which is unique, and it belongs to contemplation, not to action, for we would not change that which we love.[58]

What we see in *Calvary* is this pity for the *primary* (objective) creatures in open conflict with such subjective creatures as Lazarus and Judas. His sacrifice, of course, was love itself, because it meant for him to be chosen by God, to become an instrument of God. However, that love is not complete unless his pity has found its object; that is, unless God's will is fulfilled through him. Thus when he is repelled by Lazarus and Judas and is finally shown the meaning of the repulsion by the Roman Soldiers who dance a dance of God's chance, not choice, Christ cries out in despair: 'My Father why hast Thou forsaken Me?'

Christ's predicament is what Yeats calls the *Victimage for the Ghostly Self*. When the bond between an incarnate *Daimon* and a *Spirit of the Thirteenth Cone* is severed, the incarnate Daimon turns his natural craving into the supernatural; and this supernatural craving is a craving for a supernatural guide:

In the whirling of the gyres the incarnate *Daimon* is starved in its turn, but starved not of natural experience, but of supernatural; for compelled to take the place of the *Spirit*, it transforms its natural craving — *Eli! Eli! Lama Sabacthani!?* — and this state is called *Victimage for the Ghostly Self*, and is described as the sole means for acquiring a supernatural guide.[59]

In the relationship between a *Daimon* and a *Daimon* one is tyrant and the other is victim, living each other's death and dying each other's life: when one is subjective the other is objective. When some act prevents the union of two incarnate *Daimons*, the state is called *Victimage for the Dead*. Now, this *Victimage* sometimes coincides with *Victimage for the Ghostly Self*:

Sometimes, however, *Victimage for the Ghostly Self* and *Victimage for the Dead* coincide and produce lives tortured throughout by spirituality and passion.[60]

Christ's passion comes from this coincidence of *Victimages*. The subjective Christ is starved because he could not 'save' the world, which is totally subjective and seeks only solitude and freedom. He therefore turns to God, transforming his natural craving into a supernatural craving for divine guidance. In other words, when God's will does not seem to work through him, Christ feels abandoned by God. The loss of subjectivity towards the world means a loss of objectivity towards God. Such is Christ's problem, and it arises from his dual nature of subjectivity and objectivity.

This explains why Christ is such a curious character in the play. He does very little to forward the action and yet he is the main character around whom events take place and without whom events would never take place. He is the observed throughout the play and yet he is the actor in the true sense of the term, for he alone shows a significant change: from serene confidence to agonising despair. He is the window through which we get a glimpse of the world of God's Chance and yet it is his fate in which we are interested. In

Christ, in other words, Yeats combined the *shite* and the *waki* of the Noh. He gave Christ the subjectivity of the *shite* and the objectivity of the *waki*. The polarity, however, is deliberately left unresolved. The subjectivity in Christ fails to find its mask and the objectivity in him feels abandoned by its supernatural Self. This is the idea that Yeats dramatises in *Calvary*.

In all four plays for dancers Yeats's theme is a failure of experience. Yeats sees the world in eternal conflict and leaves it at that. The main interest of the plays lies in a study of action, human or supernatural, that takes place in the antinomial processes of the universe. The plays present singularly dualistic-cognitive perspective, though their monistic-experiential aspirations are quite apparent on both the thematic and the dramaturgic levels. The flower that Zeami fostered in the Noh never bloomed in Yeats, though the roots, one might say, were secured.

7. CONCLUSION

I

Yeats's imaginative process is characterised by a vacillation between the saint and the artist. Throughout his life he pursued these two objectives through philosophical contemplation, various types of psychic research and experiment, and creative activities. In pursuit of sainthood, Yeats ardently searched for a transcendental world and endeavoured to know that world immediately and concretely; in his artistic pursuit, he was keenly aware of the phenomenal world, from which he derived material and inspiration for his creative activities.

Yeats's life, however, was not a war fought between the saint and the artist. There certainly was a conflict between the saint and the artist, but the matter was not so simple as to be called a war in which one must emerge as the victor. The conflict was rather a complementary sort, in which 'one lived the other's death and died the other's life', to use the Heraclitian expression that Yeats borrowed from the ancient Greek philosopher. Neither the saint nor the artist could ultimately claim Yeats's soul, for Yeats was both and neither.

At the base of Yeats's vacillation there was an insoluble double perspective vis-à-vis reality and art. At one end of his perspective he envisaged the world of unity in which all conflict was resolved and in which only experience remained; at the other end he envisaged the bifurcated world of subject and object in which cognition took place. The double perspective operated in Yeats's mind throughout his life, though, at times, one pole was stronger than the other. When the monistic-experiential pole was stronger, Yeats aspired to sainthood. He was dominated by this perspective during his theosophist days, his Cabalistic infatuation and Hindu discipleship. However, when the dualistic-cognitive pole was predominant, he concentrated on his career as an artist. The Apollonic impulse (the term he borrowed from Nietzsche) set in when this perspective had a hold of Yeats's imagination. The first major change caused by this impulse came about 1903, when *Ideas of Good and Evil* was published. Yeats announces this change explicitly in his letters to John Quinn and George Russell (AE). Then, the reverse impulse of Dionysus set in when he was introduced to the Noh.

The double perspective, however, finds its microcosm in each of Yeats's pursuits. Yeats the saint was not free from the Apollonic impulse of the artist, and Yeats the artist always oriented his work in the direction that his saintly aspirations urged him to. Thus, we find his visionary documents charactersied by abstract symbolism and dualistic view of reality. *A Vision* is such a document. On the other hand, his creative theory and work are characterised by saintly aspirations and the monistic view of art. Thus his tragic theory and dramatic work are characteristically monistic in spirit, though always at their base is the dualistic-cognitive regard for the phenomenal world.

Yeats's dualism, which has been the subject of much discussion among the critics, should not be considered, in a simple two-dimensional fashion, as a war between two conflicting forces, such as: the self and the soul, as Bowra sees them; Easternism and Westernism, as Engelberg divides them; the mystic and the non-mystic, as Helen Vendler would have them. Yeats's dualism had a more complex mechanism than all these dichotomies. Generally speaking, his interest was divided into that of the saint and that of the artist. In each interest, however, there was a polarity of perspectives. Whichever interest was pursued, the polarised perspectives interestingly modified and complemented each other.

II

The Yeatsian aesthetic was based on the dualism delineated above. In it were conflicting claims for art, which regarded literature, on the one hand, as a valid vehicle of knowledge, and, on the other hand, as a sort of magic enticing people into a spiritual experience. The cognitive pole of this dualism was conducive to the formation of his antinomial view of art and symbolic theory, while the experiential pole generated his ecstatic view of art as represented by his tragic theory and his dramatic practice culminating in his Noh-like plays.

Yeats was not alone among Western artists and theorists of art in holding the polarised views of art. There is a tradition indeed in the history of Western theories of art that views literature as both cognitive and experiential. Platonic theory perhaps goes to the extreme of the cognitive view in its mimetic theory of art advanced in the *Republic* by completely severing art and the artist from reality. The neoclassical theory is a modification of the Platonic doctrine in that it recognises the ability of art to represent reality. Neither of these schools of aesthetic dualism, however, is free from the experiential view of art, for they both recognise the affective nature of art: Plato recognises the incantatory nature of poetry in *Meno*, *Ion*, and *Phaedrus*; while the neoclasssicists generally recognise pleasure as an essential aim of art.

Among the aesthetic monists, Plotinus perhaps goes to the extreme of the experiential view by identifying art and the artist with *nous*, the One from which all existence is derived and to which it returns. The Blakean monism is an inversion of the Plotinian in that it houses art and the artist in the world of 'Minute Particulars' which is nothing other than our ambient reality, which yet is the eternal world of Christ.

Yeats operated among these forces in order to work out an adequate aesthetic doctrine for himself. He endeavoured to reconcile the conflicting claims for art put forward by generations of artists and theorists. As a result, we have an unusual type of aesthetic theory and practice in Yeats, who set up the antipodal artistic ideals and tried to reconcile the two, and who, failing in this attempt, dramatised that failure in his poetry.

III

Yeats's relationship with the East has attracted the attention of many of his critics. The subject can be an interesting case study of East-West relationships; however, any such study must take into consideration the complex nature of Yeats's thought. Yeats's meeting with the East should not be considered an either-or case. He reacted to the East rather interestingly; he was not totally converted, nor did he flatly reject the East. This study has focussed on the way Yeats reacted to the East, which, as far as the poet was concerned, was largely represented by Hindu philosophy and the Noh drama of Japan. Yeats reacted to them with his double perspective, accepting so much of it as the perspective permitted him to. On the whole, however, the dualistic-cognitive pole of the perspective was the stronger, though Yeats did try to be free of its hold.

Schooling himself in the Eastern traditions, Yeats's main interest rested in the soul's emancipation, with which Hindu thought was concerned, and in the archetypal patterns and tragic vision of the

Japanese Noh drama as he saw it. Both traditions contained something that would satisfy his saintly aspirations. Hindu thought offered him the concept of non-dualistic Brahman, which is comparable to his *Thirteenth Sphere*, while the Japanese Noh offered him a concrete form of art which was characterised by the principles of intimacy and distance, the two principles that he thought were the measure of art's greatness.

Yeats, however, could not go all the way with the East. Yeats the Westerner always became sober before his enthusiasm for the East became too strong. Consequently, he missed what is most strongly emphasised in the Eastern school of thought: the experience that constitutes an emancipation from the dualistic world of names and forms. Yeats's failure to attain that experience was rooted in his basic mode of thinking. Like the being in his own system who finds itself between the *Self* and the *Mask*, between the warring forces of the *Will* and the *Creative Mind*, Yeats finds his own place between the wisdoms of definition and non-definition. The mask he seeks is the wisdom of non-definition, but his *Creative Mind* is always aware of the *Body of Fate*, which perpetually destroys this attainment, 'thereby leaving the Will to its own "dispersal" '.[1] Being at Phase Seventeen, Yeats cannot submerge the *Body of Fate* into the *Mask*, nor the *Creative Mind* into the *Will*, though his momentary vision corresponds to the image of 'Shelley's Venus Urania, Dante's Beatrice, or even the Great Yellow Rose of *Paradiso*'.[2]

The antinomy also shows itself in the way Yeats sees things. Yeats's approach is fundamentally rationalistic and cognitive, although his ideal is the experience of unity. Central in his thought is his awareness of conflict in human experience, and the world of unity and eternity is enclosed in the phaseless *Thirteenth Sphere*, which defies human understanding. While he does not deny the importance of the world of unity, Yeats insists that one should make what he can out of the world of duality:

The soul cannot have much knowledge till it has shaken off the habit of time and of place, but till that hour must fix its attention upon what is near, thinking of objects one after another as we run the eye or the finger over them.[3]

The world of objects is what the Eastern sages discard as mere shadows of reality.

In a sense Yeats is caught in his own trap. He has made an elaborate system of the universe, realising, when the labour was over, that his true business was to get out of the system; but it is too late, for the system entwines him like a living snake.

Yeats struggles to free himself from the antinomies of the world, and there are moments when he seems to resolve the conflict. In the poem called 'Demon and Beast', for instance, we have:

> For certain minutes at the least
> That crafty demon and that loud beast
> That plague me day and night
> Ran out of my sight;
> Though I had long perned in the gyre,
> Between my hatred and desire,
> I saw my freedom won
> And all laugh in the sun.

Though briefly, he enjoys the happiness of liberation, being out of the tension between the subjective and the objective. The freedom is presumably won in the primary phase, for 'all laugh in the sun'. Then the poet grows warm and intimate toward life around him:

> But soon a tear-drop started up,
> For aimless joy had made me stop
> Beside the little lake
> To which a white gull take
> A bit of bread thrown up into the air;
> Now gyring down and perning there
> He splashed where an absurd
> Portly green-pated bird
> Shook off the water from his back;
> Being no more demoniac
> A stupid happy creature
> Could rouse my whole nature.

Yet the happiness is not without this realisation:

> Yet I am certain as can be
> That every natural victory
> Belongs to beast or demon
> That never yet had freeman
> Right mastery of natural things,

and he only wishes that he

> may find out a way
> To make it linger half a day.

Yeats, then, being trapped in his own system of antinomies, violently tries to escape it, but he cannot quite escape the system, nor this world itself. As he acknowledges at the end of *A Vision* (1937), Yeats estranged himself from the final enlightenment by resorting to intellection and symbolism in his approach to the ultimate reality. His intellect labored for years but was not rewarded with a final vision, and he laments this fact. He did not lack 'the ideas of India' or of the final emancipation; he was, no doubt, given those ideas by his instructors,[4] but he lacked a personal experience. Yeats was never able to lift himself up to the realm where the sages of India, Christian mystics, or Existentialists[5] were able to ascend. Toward the end of his life Yeats still sees things in conflict. Indeed he seems to affirm the conflict more strongly than ever. In one of his last essays we find:

Opposites are everywhere face to face, dying each other's life, living each other's death. When a man loves a girl it should be because her face and character offer what he lacks, the more profound his nature the more should he realise his lack and the greater be the difference. It is as though he wanted to take his own death into his arms and beget a stronger life upon that death.[6]

Until death Yeats seems to have been unable to see life in any way other than in conflict. The idea of conflict is repeated in his letter to Ethel Mannin, dated about three months before his death:

To me all things are made of the conflict of two states of consciousness, beings or persons which die each other's life, live each other's death. That is true of life and death themselves. Two cones (or whirls), the apex of each in the other's base.[7]

Of course, Yeats tried to resolve the antinomy, but his mind was constantly made aware of it. He could not resolve it within himself. Instead, he came to accept the antinomy in a sort of tragic spirit:

> Cast a cold eye
> On life, on death.
> Horseman, pass by!

Yeats, in the last analysis, is a failure as a visionary poet; but as Hazard Adams says, his true greatness lies in that he turned his failure into creative energy.

NOTES

Preface

1 W. B. Yeats, *A Vision*, London: Macmillan, 1937, p. 25.
2 Letter to J. B. Yeats, Sept. 12 [1914]. Allan Wade, ed., *The Letters of W. B. Yeats*, New York: Macmillan, 1955, p. 588.

1: Introduction

1 For detailed discussion on this topic, see M. H. Abrams, *The Mirror and the Lamp: Romantic Theory and the Critical Tradition*, Oxford University Press, 1953.
2 The question as to the reality of image in connection with the problem of *eidolon*, the question of whether or not something that appears real without being real can exist, is a highly controversial question. For conflicting opinions on this question, see: John Burnett, *Greek Philosophy*, London: Macmillan, 1950, p. 286 and F. M. Cornford, *Plato's Theory of Knowledge*, New York: Liberal Arts Press, 1957, pp. 321f.
3 Edith Hamilton and Huntington Cairns, eds., *The Collected Dialogues of Plato*, Princeton University Press, 1961, p. 826. *The Republic*, Bk. X, 601 c.
4 *Ibid.*, p. 828. *The Republic*, Bk. X, 603 b.
5 Stephen MacKenna, tr., *Plotinus The Enneads*, London: Faber and Faber, 1969, p. 329.
6 *Ibid.*, p. 286.
7 *Ibid.*, pp. 422f.
8 *Ibid.*
9 *Ibid.*
10 *Ibid.*

2: Knowledge or Experience

1 Richard McKeon, ed., *Introduction to Aristotle*, New York: The Modern Library, 1947, p. 427 (*Nicomachean Ethics*, Bk. VI, Chapt. 4).
2 *Ibid.*, p. 428.
3 *Ibid.* p. 427.
4 S. H. Butcher, ed., *Aristotle's Theory of Poetry and Fine Art*, Dover Publications, 1951, p. 11 (*The Poetics*, II, 1).
5 *Ibid.*, p. 27 (*The Poetics*, VI, 9).
6 *Ibid.*
7 *Ibid.*, p. 35 (*The Poetics*, IX, 1).
8 *Ibid.* (*The Poetics*, IX, 3).
9 *Ibid.* (IX, 4).
10 *Ibid.*, pp. 105f. (*The Poetics*, XXV, 17).

11 *Ibid.*, p. 99 (*The Poetics*, XXV, 5).
12 *Ibid.*
13 John Locke, *An Essay Concerning Human Understanding*, Dover Publications, 1959, Vol. II, p. 431.
14 See Basil Willey, *The Eighteenth Century Background, Studies in the Ideas of Nature in the Thought of the Period*, London: Chatto Windus, 1940.
15 John Locke, *op. cit.*, II, p. 307.
16 Arthur Sherbo, ed., *Johnson on Shakespeare*, New Haven and London: Yale University Press, 1968 (*The Yale Edition of the Works of Samuel Johnson*, Vol. VII), pp. 89f.
17 W. P. Ker, ed., *Dryden's Essays*, Oxford, 1926, Vol. I, p. 183.
18 *Ibid.*, II, pp. 33f.
19 *Ibid.*, I, p. 123.
20 Sherbo, *op. cit.*, p. 77.
21 *Ibid.*, p. 96.
22 Ker, *op. cit.*, I, p. 123.
23 Edmund Gosse, ed., *Sir Joshua Reynolds's Discourses on Art*, London: Kegan Paul, French, 1884, p. 248.
24 Geoffrey Keynes, ed., *The Complete Writings of William Blake*, London: Oxford University Press, 1966, p. 465.
25 Gosse, *op. cit.*, p. 32.
26 They are enduring forms transcending the ephemeral world of particulars; yet they are reached through an empirical process. More of this later.
27 Gosse, *op. cit.*, p. 33.
28 *Ibid.*
29 *Ibid.*, p. 34.
30 *Ibid.*, p. 35.
31 *Ibid.*
32 *Ibid.*
33 Keynes, *op. cit.*, p. 459.
34 Gosse, *op. cit.*, p. 46.
35 *Ibid.*, p. 49.
36 *Ibid.*, p. 119.
37 *Ibid.*, p. 123.
38 *Ibid.*, p. 126.
39 *Ibid.*, p. 230.
40 *Ibid.*, p. 236.
41 *Ibid.*, p. 233.
42 *Ibid.*, p. 236.
43 *Ibid.*, p. 231.
44 *Ibid.*, p. 234.
45 *Ibid.*, p. 248.
46 Keynes, *op. cit.*, p. 246 ('Song of Los').
47 In his annotations to Swedenborg's *Divine Love and Divine Wisdom*, Blake puts an approving note to the following passage: ' . . . this thought [from the perception of Truth] is the Thought of Wisdom, but the other is Thought from the Memory by the Sight of the Natural Mind'. See Keynes, *op. cit.*, p. 95.
48 The analogy comes from 'All Religions Are One', Keynes, *op. cit.*, p. 98.
49 Keynes, *op. cit.*, p. 533 ('Milton', 41: 21–4).
50 *Ibid.*, p. 459 ('Annotations to Sir Joshua Reynolds's *Discourses*).
51 *Ibid.*, p. 774 ('Annotations to Bishop Berkeley's "Siris" ').

52   A. A. Luce and T. E. Jessop, eds., *The Works of George Berkeley, Bishop of Cloyne*, London: Nelson, 1964, Vol. V, p. 140.

53   Keynes, *op. cit.*, p. 605 ('A Vision of the Last Judgment').

54   *Ibid.*, p. 738 ('Jerusalem', 91: 30–31).

55   *Ibid.*, p. 98 ('All Religions Are One').

56   *Ibid.*, p. 672 ('Jerusalem', 43: 19–20).

57   *Ibid.*, p. 607 ('A Vision of the Last Judgment').

58   *Ibid.*, p. 459.

59   *Ibid.*, p. 605 ('A Vision of the Last Judgment').

60   *Ibid.*, p. 576 ('A Descriptive Catalogue', No. 5).

61   *Ibid.*, p. 605.

62   *Ibid.*, p. 567 ('A Descriptive Catalogue', No. 3).

63   *Ibid.*, p. 453.

64   *Ibid.*, p. 453.

65   *Ibid.*

66   *Ibid.*, pp. 576f.

67   *Ibid.*, p. 776 ('The Laocoön').

68   *Ibid.*, p. 455.

69   *Ibid.*, p. 454.

70   *Ibid.*, p. 778 ('On Homer's Poetry and On Virgil').

71   W. J. B. Owen and Jane Worthington Smyser, eds., *The Prose Works of William Wordsworth*, Oxford: Clarendon, 1974, Vol. I, p. 127 and p. 149 ('Preface of 1850').

72   *Ibid.*, p. 141.

73   Roger Ingpen and Walter E. Peck, eds., *The Complete Works of Percy Bysshe Shelley*, New York: Gordian Press, 1965, Vol. VII, pp. 111f.

74   Here I must disagree with the generally accepted conclusion, advanced particularly by M. H. Abrams, that the autonomous world of the artist's creation is immune from the cognitive claims of art. Whether on grounds of analogy or otherwise, the Romantics who advanced the aesthetical view of art were never oblivious of the relation of art with the real world.

75   'Mont Blanc', ll. 38–40.

76   Roger Ingpen and Walter E. Peck, *op. cit.*, V, p. 207.

77   *Ibid.*, VI, p. 56.

78   *Ibid.*, p. 194 ('On Life').

79   *Ibid.*, p. 197.

80   *Ibid.*, p. 196.

81   *Ibid.*, VII. p. 65.

82   *Ibid.*, p. 135.

83   *Ibid.*, p. 112 ('A Defence of Poetry').

84   Tilottama Rajan, *Dark Interpreter, The Discourse of Romanticism*, Ithaca and London: Cornell University Press, 1980, p. 179.

85   Earl R. Wasserman's argument that Shelley's epistemology restricts itself to the transaction 'between the self and its mental impressions' is not only unfair to Shelley but also obscures the significance of one of the basic problems confronting Shelley and other Romantics, i.e., how to reconcile the conflicting claims of the inner and outer realities on art. See Earl Wasserman, 'The English Romantics: The Grounds of Knowledge', *Romanticism, Points of View*, edited by Robert Gleckner and Gerald E. Enscoe, Detroit: Wayne State University Press, 1979, p. 344.

86   Roger Ingpen and Walter E. Peck, *op. cit.*, VII, p. 140 ('A Defence of Poetry').

87   Samuel Taylor Coleridge, *Shakespearean Criticism*, edited by Thomas Middleton Raysor, London: Dent, 1960, Vol. II, p. 41 ('The Second Lecture').
88   A. D. Snyder, ed., *S. T. Coleridge's Treatise on Method as Published in the Encyclopaedia Metropoliana*, London: Constable, 1934, 25, 35–6.
89   J. Shawcross, ed., *Biographia Literaria*, London: Oxford University Press, 1907, Vol. I p. 183.
90   'Intimations of Immortality,' 1. 105.
91   Owen and Smyser, *op. cit.*, I, p. 138 ('Preface of 1850).
92   *Ibid.*, III, p. 26 ('Preface of 1815').
93   *Ibid.*, I, p. 139 ('Preface of 1850').
94   McKeon, *op. cit.*, p. 427 (*Nicomachean Ethics*, Bk. VI, Chapt. 4).
95   For a contrary view see Wasserman, *op. cit.* and Clarence D. Thorpe, 'The Imagination: Coleridge versus Wordsworth,' *Philological Quarterly*, XVII, no.1 (January 1939): 1–18.
96   *The Collected Poems of W. B. Yeats*, New York: Macmillan, 1959, p. 159 ('Ego Dominus Tuus').
97   Allan Wade, ed., *The Letters of W. B. Yeats*, New York: Macmillan, 1955, p. 583 (Letter to J. B. Yeats, 5 August 1913).
98   *Ibid.*, p. 653 (Letter to J. B. Yeats, 17 Oct. [1918]).
99   H. Buxton Forman, ed., *The Poetical Works and Other Writings of John Keats*, New York: Phaeton Press, 1970, Vol. VI, p. 192 (Letter to John Taylor, 24 April 1818).
100 *Ibid.*, VII, p. 5 (Letter to John H. Reynolds, 3 May 1818).
101 *Ibid.*
102 *Ibid.*, VI, p. 154 (Letter to John Taylor, 27 Feb. 1818).
103 *Ibid.*, VII, p. 129 (Letter to Richard Woodhouse, 27 Oct. 1818).
104 See Chapter IV of *Theory of Criticism, A Tradition and Its System*, Baltimore and London: Johns Hopkins University Press, 1976.
105 Owen and Smyser, *op. cit.*, I, p. 139 ('Preface of 1850').
106 *The Prelude*, XIII, 11. 1–10.
107 Owen and Smyser, *op. cit.*, III, p. 26 ('Preface of 1815').
108 *Ibid.*, I, p. 141 ('Preface of 1850').
109 George Watson, *op. cit.*, p. 48.
110 E. L. Griggs, ed., *The Collected Letters of Samuel Taylor Coleridge*, London and New York: Oxford University Press, 1956–71, Vol. I, p. 279.
111 *Ibid.*, p. 709.
112 Immanuel Kant, *Critique of Judgement*, translated by J. H. Bernard, New York: Hafner Press, 1951, p. 54.
113 *Ibid.*, p. 53.
114 *Ibid.*, p. 49.
115 J. Shawcross, *op. cit.*, II, p. 242.
116 Kant, *op. cit.*, p. 73.
117 Shawcross, *op. cit.*, II, p. 243.
118 Kant, *op. cit.*, p. 63.
119 Forman, *op. cit.*, VI, p. 98 (Letter to Benjamin Bailey, 22 Nov. 1817).
120 Ingpen and Peck, *op. cit.*, VII, p. 137 ('A Defence of Poetry').
121 *Ibid.*
122 *Ibid.*, p. 53.
123 *Ibid.*, p. 118.
124 *Ibid.*, p. 128 ('Discourse on the Manners of the Ancients, Relative to the Subjects of Love').
125 *Ibid.*, VI, p. 210 ('On Love').

126   *Ibid.*, VII, p. 116 ('A Defence of Poetry').
127   *Ibid.*, VI, p. 195 ('On Life').
128   'Endymion', I, 1. 779.
129   Forman, *op. cit.*, VI, p. 160 (Letter to Benjamin Bailey, 13 March 1818).

3: The Saint or the Artist

1   For a contrary view see Helen Regueiro, *The Limits of Imagination, Wordsworth, Yeats, and Stevens*, Ithaca and London: Cornell University Press, 1976, pp. 142ff. I cannot side with this view, for gaiety is not the principle of synthesis for Yeats, nor is it the creative principle of poetry; it is only an element in the 'sad and gay' antithesis of the mythological world of such poems as 'The Dedication to a Book of Stories Selected from the Irish Novelists' and 'The Host of Air' or in the 'bitter and gay' antithesis out of which a heroic cry must be uttered 'in the midst of despair' (*Letters on Poetry from W. B. Yeats to Dorothy Wellesley*, London: Oxford University Press, 1964, p. 8).
1a *Collected Poems*, p. 175.
2   *Essays and Introductions*, New York: Macmillan, 1961, p. 422.
3   *Ibid.*, p. 421f.
4   See in particular Harold Bloom, *Yeats*, New York: Oxford University Press, 1970.
5   *Essays and Introductions*, p. 116.
6   *Ibid.*
7   *Ibid*, p. 117.
8   *A Vision* (1937), New York: Macmillan, 1961, p. 68.
9   See 'The Circus Animals' Desertion' in *The Collected Poems of W. B. Yeats*, New York: Macmillan, 1956, pp. 335f.
10 *Mythologies*, New York: Macmillan, 1959, p. 270.
11 *Essays and Introductions*, p. 429.
12 *Ibid.*, p. 428.
13 *Mythologies*, p. 337.
14 *Essays and Introductions*, p. 287.
15 *A Vision*, p. 302.
16 *Essays and Introductions*, p. 288.
17 *A Vision*, p. 301.
18 *Ibid.*, p. 214.
19 *Essays and Introductions*, p. 79.
20 *Autobiographies*, London: Macmillan, 1961, p. 269.
21 *A Vision*, p. 301.
22 *Autobiographies*, p. 269.
23 *Essays and Introductions*, p. 162.
24 *Autobiographies*, p. 269.
25 Allan Wade, ed., *The Letters of W. B. Yeats*, New York: Macmillan, 1955, p. 731.
26 *Autobiographies*, p. 272.
27 *Ibid.*
28 *Ibid.*, p. 273.
29 *A Vision*, p. 268.
30 *Autobiographies*, p. 482.
31 *Ibid.*, p. 295.
32 *A Vision*, p. 268.
33 *Ibid.*, p. 303.
34 *Ibid.*
35 *Autobiographies*, p. 115.

36   *Ibid.*, p. 254.
37   *Essays and Introductions*, pp. 156f.
38   *Letters*, p. 588.
39   In his letter to Ernest Boyd Yeats said: 'My chief mystical authorities have been Boehme, Blake and Swedenborg.' (*Letters*, p. 592).
40   *Essays and Introductions*, p. 149.
41   *Ibid.*
42   *Ibid.*, pp. 163f.
43   *Ibid.*, p. 195.
44   *Ibid.*, p. 150.
45   Yeats thought an intellect of Spinoza's type to be an important element of mysticism. In a letter he wrote to his father in June 1918 he said: 'Why do you call Bunyan a mystic? It is impossible to make a definition of mysticism to include him. The great mystics of that epoch are Spinoza and Pascal. Nearly all our popular mysticism derives indirectly from the first or from a movement he was first to explain.' (*Letters*, p. 650).
46   *Letters*, p. 262.
47   A. Norman Jeffares, *The Circus Animals, Essays on W. B. Yeats*, London: Macmillan, 1970, p. 33.
48   *The Collected Poems*, p. 456.
49   Edward Engelberg, *The Vast Design, Patterns in W. B. Yeats's Aesthetic*, Toronto: University of Toronto Press, 1964, p. 177.
50   Yeats has the following to say in the 1937 version of *A Vision* (p. 68): ' . . . I see that the gyre of "Concord" diminishes as that of "Discord" increases, and can imagine after that the gyre of "Concord" diminishes, and so on, one gyre within the other always. Here the thought of Heraclitus dominates all: "Dying each other's life, living each other's death".'
51   'The knowledge of reality', wrote Yeats in 1909, 'is always in some measure a secret knowledge. It is a kind of death.' (*Autobiographies*, p. 482).
52   This is precisely the meaning in which 'blood' is used in 'Oil and Blood'.
53   T. R. Henn, *The Lonely Tower, Studies in the Poetry of W. B. Yeats*, New York: Pellegrini and Cudahy, 1952, p. 13.
54   Joseph Hone, *W. B. Yeats, 1865–1939*, London: Macmillan, 1962, p. 319.
55   Daniel Albright, *The Myth Against Myth: A Study of W. B. Yeats's Imagination in Old Age*, London: Oxford University Press, 1972.
56   *Mythologies*, p. 329.
57   *Ibid.*
58   *Autobiographies*, p. 273.
59   *A Vision*, p. 214.
60   The Ledaean body is generally taken for Maud Gonne. Although the context does not require such an association, it can hardly be otherwise, since Maud Gonne is frequently associated with Helen of Troy in other poems. For a contrary view, see Cleanth Brooks, *The Well Wrought Urn*, p. 183.
61   *Letters*, p. 719.
62   *The Collected Plays of W. B. Yeats*, New York: Macmillan, 1961, p. 137.
63   John Unterecker, *A Reader's Guide to William Butler Yeats*, New York: The Noonday Press, 1961, p. 192. It is difficult for me to see how the poem *constructs* such a justification.
64   C. M. Bowra, *The Heritage of Symbolism*, London: Macmillan, 1962, p. 212. Professor Bowra's conclusion comes from the premise that in Yeats the struggle between Soul and Self was terminated in the triumph of the latter. But then, Yeats always associated Self with conflict; and Stanza VIII is about a resolution of conflict.

65   M. L. Rosenthal, *Sailing into the Unknown: Yeats, Pound, and Eliot*, New York: Oxford University Press, 1978, p. 149.
66   *A Vision.*, p. 268.
67   *Letters*, p. 343.
68   *Mythologies*, p. 331.
69   *Ibid.*, p. 340.

4: Brahman or Daimon

1   Naresh Guha, *W. B. Yeats, An Indian Approach* (an unpublished doctoral thesis, Northwestern University, 1962).
2   There is an excessive claim for the Tantric source of Yeats's ideas in this connection. Naresh Guha, for instance, believes that Yeats found the sources of his interlocking gyres and sexual mysticism of his later years in Tantra. As to the sources of the interlocking gyres, however, Yeats is silent about Tantra in *A Vision* while he mentions several other possible sources of inspiration. As to sexual mysticism, he may well have derived it from the Cabala among others.
3   *Autobiographies*, p. 89.
4   *Ibid.*, p. 90.
5   *Hellas*, 11. 135–136.
6   *Autobiographies*, p. 173.
7   *Ibid.*, p. 181.
8   *Ibid.*, p. 188.
9   *Ibid.*
10   *Letters*, p. 469.
11   Joseph Hone, *op. cit.*, pp. 458f.
12   *Letters*, p. 794 (Letter to Olivia Shakespear, postmarked 10 March 1932).
13   *Essays and Introductions*, p. 518.
14   *Ibid.*
15   *Ibid.*
16   *A Vision*, p. 23.
17   *Ibid.*, p. 193.
18   *Letters*, p. 690, p. 695.
19   *Ibid.*, p. 916.
20   Max Muller, *The Upanishads*, New York: Dover Publications, 1962, II, p. 107.
21   *Ibid.*, p. 185 (*Brihadaranyaka Upanishad*, IV, v, 15).
22   *Ibid.*, I, p. 311.
23   *Ibid.*, p. 237.
24   *Ibid.*, II, pp. 36f. (*Mundaka Upanishad*, II, ii, 1, 2, 9).
25   *Ibid.*, pp. 249, 251, 253, 254 (*Svetasvatara Upanishad*, IV, 1, 9, 10, 19, 20).
26   *Ibid.*, pp. 280f. (*Prasna Upanishad*, V, 7–9).
27   *A Vision*, p. 240.
28   *Ibid.*, p. 193.
29   Helen Vendler, *Yeats's VISION and the Later Plays*, Cambridge: Harvard University Press, 1963, p. 69.
30   *A Vision*, p. 241.
31   *Ibid.*, p. 210.
32   *Ibid.*, p. 68.
33   Philip Wheelwright, *Heraclitus*, New York: Atheneum, 1964, p. 68 (Fragment 66).
34   *Ibid.*, p. 19 (Fragment 2).

35 *Ibid.*, pp. 90f. (Fragment 113).
36 *A Vision*, p. 230.
37 *Ibid.*, p. 237.
38 *Mythologies*, p. 357.
39 F. M. Cornford, *From Religion to Philosophy, A Study in the Origins of Western Speculation*, New York: Harper & Row, 1957, p. 179.
40 Muller, *op. cit.*, I, p. 101.
41 *Ibid.*, II, p. 88.
42 *Ibid.*, pp. 235f.
43 *Ibid.*, p. 245.
44 *A Vision*, p. 302.
45 Wheelwright, *op. cit.*, p. 90 (Fragment 98).
46 *Essays and Introductions*, p. 472.
47 *A Vision*, p. 136.
48 *Ibid.*
49 *Ibid.*, p. 183.
50 *Ibid.*
51 *Ibid.*
52 *The Collected Poems*, pp. 166f.
53 *A Vision*, p. 112.
54 Muller, *op. cit.*, I, p. 80 (*Khandogya Upanishad*, V, x, 1).
55 *Ibid.*
56 *Ibid.*
57 *Essays and Introductions*, p. 470.
58 *Ibid.*, pp. 470f.
59 Rudolph Otto distinguishes two ways of mystical knowledge: 'the mysticism of introspection' and 'the mysticism of unifying vision'. The former is characterised by a 'withdrawal from all outward things into the ground of one's own soul', while the latter 'knows nothing of "inwardness" ' but is characterised by 'the emphasis on unity, and the struggle against all diversity'. See *Mysticism East and West, a Comparative Analysis of the Nature of Mysticism*, translated by Bertha L. Bracey and Richenda C. Payne, New York: Meridan Books, 1957, pp. 29–69.
60 Muller, *op. cit.*, II, p. 176 (*Brihadaranyaka Upanishad*, IV, iv, 5).
61 *Ibid.*, pp. 22f.
62 *Ibid.*, p. 39.
63 *Essays and Introductions*, p. 484.
64 *A Vision*, p. 214.
65 Ursula Bridge, ed., *W. B. Yeats and T. Sturge Moore, Their Correspondence 1901–1936*, London: Routledge & Kegan Paul, 1953, p. 149.

5: The Flower or the Gyre

1 I accept the theory, put forward by Engelberg, Helen Vendler and others, that the discovery of the Noh meant for Yeats a confirmation rather than a complete 'about face' in his aesthetic belief; however, it is important not to see the Noh through Yeats's eyes in appraising Yeats's principle in connection with the Noh: the discrepancies that exist between the Noh and Yeats throw more light on the subject than the similarities.
2 *Essays and Introductions*, p. 221.
3 *Ibid.*, pp. 222f.

4 *Ibid.*, p. 223.
5 *Ibid.*
6 *Letters*, p. 846.
7 Yonejiro Noguchi, *Airurando Jōchō*, 1925. Quoted by Hisashi Furukawa in *Obeijin no Noh-gaku Kenkyu* (Studies of the Noh by Western Hands), Tokyo: Tokyo Women's College, 1963, p. 15.
8 *Essays and Introduction*, p. 223.
9 *Ibid.*, pp. 223f.
10 *Ibid.*, p. 224.
11 *Ibid.*
12 *Ibid.*, pp. 224f.
13 *Ibid.*, p. 225.
14 *Ibid.*, p. 226.
15 *Ibid.*, p. 227.
16 *Ibid.*
17 *Ibid.*, p. 52.
18 *Ibid.*, p. 228.
19 *The Daily Chronicle*, 27 January 1899. *Letters*, p. 310.
20 *Autobiographies*, p. 279.
21 *Letters*, p. 280.
22 *Essays and Introductions*, p. 191.
23 *Ibid.*, p. 192.
24 *Ibid.*, p. 193.
25 *Letters*, p. 397.
26 Friedrich Nietzsche, 'The Birth of Tragedy' in *The Philosophy of Nietzsche* translated by Clifton P. Fadiman, New York: The Modern Library, 1954, p. 956.
27 *Ibid.*, p. 957.
28 *Ibid.*, p. 1087.
29 *Letters*, p. 403.
30 *Ibid.*, p. 402.
31 *Essays and Introductions*, p. 341.
32 *Ibid.*
33 *Ibid.*, p. 317.
34 *Letters*, p. 657.
35 *Essays and Introductions*, p. 285.
36 *Ibid.*, p. 287.
37 *Ibid.*, p. 293.
38 *Ibid.*
39 *Ibid.*, p. 294.
40 *Ibid.*, p. 286.
41 *Ibid.*, p. 287.
42 *Ibid.*, pp. 287f.
43 *The Complete Poems and Plays of T. S. Eliot*, London: Faber and Faber, 1969, p. 173 ('Burnt Norton', II, 1. 44).
44 *Essays and Introductions*, p. 288.
45 T. S. Eliot, *op. cit.*, p. 175 ('Burnt Norton', V, 11. 1–4).
46 *Ibid.*, ('Burnt Norton', V, 11. 4–8).
47 *Ibid.*, ('Burnt Norton', V, 1. 13).
48 'Edmund Spenser', *Essays and Introductions*, p. 369. The essay on Spenser was written in 1902 and first appeared as an introduction to *Poems of Spenser* (Edinburgh, 1906). It is noteworthy that Yeats included this essay in *The Cutting of an Agate* (1912), together with such essays as 'Discoveries' and 'Poetry and Tradition'.

49 *Ibid.*, p. 243.
50 *Ibid.*, p. 245.
51 *Ibid.*, p. 239.
52 *Ibid.*, p. 321.
53 *Ibid.*, p. 259.
54 *Letters*, pp. 836f.
55 *Ibid.*, p. 838.
56 *Essays and Introductions*, p. 255.
57 *Ibid.*, p. 349.
58 *Letters*, p. 343.
59 *Essays and Introductions*, p. 349.
60 *Autobiographies*, p. 490.
61 *Essays and Introductions*, pp. 352f.
62 *Ibid.*, p. 354.
63 *Ibid.*, p. 355.
64 *Ibid.*, p. 354.
65 *Autobiographies*, pp. 470f.
66 *Letters*, p. 588.
67 Toyoichiro Nogami, *Zeami Motokiyo*, Tokyo: Sogensha, 1942, p. 165.
68 It is generally agreed that the *Kadensho* is a faithful record of Kannami's instruction. However, since the book was written by Zeami who is credited with systematising the Noh theory, I shall hereafter refer to Zeami as the author of the book and the theory.
69 Asaji Nose, *Zeami Jurokubushu Hyoshaku* (An annotated edition of Zeami's sixteen books), Tokyo: Iwanami, 1949, I, p. 35. This and all subsequent English versions of the quotations from Zeami's work are my translation. I have consulted the modern Japanese versions by Asaji Nose and Kazuma Kawase when doubt arose in construing Zeami's original version.
70 *Ibid.*
71 *Ibid.*
72 *Ibid.*
73 *Ibid.*, p. 43.
74 *Ibid.*, pp. 66f.
75 *Ibid.*, p. 48.
76 *Ibid.*, p. 229.
77 Masako Shirasu, *O-Noh* (The Noh), Tokyo: Kadokawa Shoten, 1963, pp. 96f.
78 Nose, *op. cit.*, I, p. 227.
79 *Ibid.*, p. 295.
80 An anthology of Japanese poetry edited by Kino Tsurayuki in 905.
81 Especially in relation to Yeats's understanding of the Noh, Zeami's own definition of the word must be faithfully adhered to. To bring various historical meanings of the word into the discussion of the Yeats-Noh relationship only causes confusion. A good example is Wilson's study in which the term 'yugen' is taken to mean 'ideal beauty' and 'mysterious calm', in which senses Zeami never used the term.
82 Nose, *op. cit.*, pp. 358f.
83 *Ibid.*, p. 193.
84 The reference is to the third essay, which is really a dialogue between Zeami and his father, Kannami.
85 Nose, *op. cit.*, p. 112.
86 *Ibid.*, p. 13.
87 *Ibid.*, p. 362.

88 *Ibid.*
89 *Ibid.*, p. 365.
90 *Ibid.*
91 *Ibid.*, p. 151.
92 *Ibid.*, p. 213.
93 *Ibid.*, pp. 651f.
94 *Ibid.*, p. 601.
95 *Ibid.*, p. 169.
96 *Ibid.*, pp. 169f.
97 Toyoichiro Nogami, *Noh: Kenkyu To Hakken* (The Noh: Studies and Discoveries), Tokyo: Iwanami, 1930, p. 3.
98 Nose, *op. cit.*, p. 169.
99 Hubert Heffner, 'Towards a Definition of Form in Drama', *Classical Drama and Its Influence*, edited by M. J. Anderson, London: Methuen, 1965, p. 153.
100 S. H. Butcher, *op. cit*, pp. 25f.
101 *Ibid.*, p. 29.
102 *Ibid.*
103 Sir Philip Sidney, *The Defense of Poesey*, Boston: Ginn Co., 1890, p. 28.
104 *Essays and Introduction*, p. 224.
105 The *Joruri* is a puppet drama which has its own tradition; its genesis is hidden in the mist of history. The most famous of all Japanese dramatists' that Yeats mentions in his essay 'Certain Noble Plays of Japan' is Chikamatsu Monzaemon, *Joruri* dramatist who lived from 1653 to 1724. He is often called the Shakespeare of Japan.
106 Alladyce Nicoll, *British Drama, an Historical Survey from the Beginning to the Present Time*, London: George G. Harper, 1953, p. 410.
107 *Essays and Introductions*, p. 230.
108 *Ibid.*, p. 226.
109 Nose, *op. cit.*, pp. 46f.
110 *Ibid.*, II, p. 565.
111 *Essays and Introductions*, p. 231.
112 *Letters*, p. 309.
113 *Essays and Introductions*, p. 170.
114 *Ibid.*, p. 14.
115 *Ibid.*, p. 20.
116 *Letters*, p. 374.
117 *Ibid.*, p. 841.
118 *Ibid.*, p. 441.
119 *Essays and Introductions*, p. 231.
120 *Ibid.*, p. 233.
121 Frank Kermode notes an anti-intellectual tendency of Yeats's symbolism in his book *Romantic Image*. The idea of the 'thinking body' has a parallel in Yeats's general view of an ideal culture — that a culture must have a unity that finds its expression in every piece of art and furniture around a single image as if it has been wrought by a single mind.
122 *Plays and Controversies*, p. 212.
123 *Essays and Introductions*, p. 223.
124 *Letters*, p. 625.
125 *Essays and Introductions*, p. 229.
126 *Ibid.*, p. 235.

6: The Flower That Never Bloomed

1   Richard Taylor suggests that Yeats learned little from the *Kyogen*. (See his *The Drama of W. B. Yeats: Irish Myth and Japanese Nō*, New Haven and London: Yale University Press, 1976, p. 78). However, the parallelism between Yeats's distinction of the *tragic* from *the comic* and the Japanese distinction between the *Noh* and the *Kyogen* is too conspicuous to be dismissed. Furthermore, it must not be forgotten that Yeats tried his hand at the *Kyogen* in 'The Cat and the Moon'.

2   Nose, *op. cit*, II, p. 273.
3   Yoshio Araki and Sennojo Shigeyama, *Kyogen*, Osaka: Sogensha, 1956, p. 123.
4   *Essays and Introductions*, p. 240.
5   *Autobiographies*, p. 471.
6   *Ibid*.
7   *Ibid*.
8   *Ibid*.
9   Mario Yokomichi and Shozo Masuda, *Noh To Kyogen* (The Noh and the Kyogen), Osaka: Daidoshoin, 1959, p. 237.
10 *Essays and Introductions*, p. 14.
11 *Ibid*., p. 19.
12 *Ibid*., pp. 267f.
13 *Ibid*., p. 527.
14 *Ibid*., p. 529.
15 Wilson, *Yeats's Iconography*, pp. 237ff.
16 Helen Vendler, *op. cit*., pp. 190ff.
17 *Ibid*., p. 91.
18 *A Vision*, p. 135.
19 See *A Vision*, p. 136, for a description of the being of Phase 15 living out of phase, seeking to live through antithetical phases as if they were primary.
20 *Ibid*., p. 196.
21 *The Collected Poems*, p. 184 ('The Second Coming').
22 *A Vision*, p. 268.
23 The Collected Poems, pp. 211f. ('Leda and the Swan').
24 *Essays and Introductions*, p. 268.
25 *Ibid*., p. 21.
26 *Plays and Controversies*, p. 213.
27 See Hiro Ishibashi, *Yeats and the Noh: Types of Japanese Beauty and Their Reflection in Yeats's Plays. Yeats Centenary Papers*, edited by Anthony Kerrigan, Dublin: The Dolmen Press, 1966; also Richard Taylor, in reference to *At the Hawk's Well, The Drama of W. B. Yeats: Irish Myth and Japanese Nō*, p. 129.
28 Akira Maruoka, *Gendai No Noh* (The Noh Today), Tokyo: Nogaku Shorin, 1954, pp. 14f.
29 Helen Vendler, *op. cit*., p. 208.
30 Wilson assigns Emer to Phase 22 but Eithne Inguba to Phase 14, taking a cue from Fand's reference to Cuchulain's earthly loves and also from the cry of the sea when Eithne enters the fisherman's hut like 'an Aphrodite'. (Wilson, *Yeats's Iconography*, p. 109.) However, it should be noted that Fand's reference is not made to one woman but to 'many a woman/ That did not reach beyond the human' (*The Collected Plays*, p. 291), and that when Eithne enters the fisherman's hut, Emer is also at the scene.
31 *A Vision*, p. 131.

32 *Ibid.*, p. 136.
33 *Ibid.*
34 Wilson, *op. cit.*, p. 126.
35 Helen Vendler, *op. cit.*, p. 234.
36 *A Vision*, p. 136.
37 *Essays and Introductions*, p. 292.
38 *Ibid.*
39 Wilson, *op. cit.*, p. 110.
40 *Ibid.*, p. 84.
41 Mankichi Wada, *Yokyoku Senshaku* (Selected and Annotated Noh Texts), Tokyo: Sankaido, 1950, p. 140.
42 Wilson, *op. cit.*, p. 85.
43 Wada, *op. cit.*, pp. 142f.
44 Wilson, *op. cit.*, p. 218.
45a *Collected Plays*, p. 282.
45 Shotaro Oshima, *W. B. Yeats and Japan*, Tokyo: Hokuseido, 1965, p. 59.
46 John Rees Moore, *Masks of Love and Death, Yeats as Dramatist*, Ithaca and London: Cornell University Press, 1971, p. 233. Richard Taylor, *op. cit.*, 155.
47 Some philosophical (Buddhist) interpretations of the Noh are offered by Japanese scholars. Mamoru Iwami says that the Noh dramatises the Buddhist concept of Maya by the *shite's* performance. See Mamoru Iwami, *Nihon Geido To Bukkyo No Kokoro* (The Japanese Art and the Heart of Buddhism), Kyoto: Nagata Bunshodo, 1958, p. 117.
48 Wilson, op. cit., p. 167.
49 *Ibid.*, p. 191.
50 Helen Vendler, *op. cit.*, p. 174.
51 *Ibid.*, p. 173.
52 Nathan, Leonard E., *The Tragic Drama of William Butler Yeats, Figures in a Dance*, New York: Columbia University Press, 1965, p. 204.
53 Nathan's authority here is a passage in *A Vision*, which I shall later quote (see p. 174). In the passage Yeats says that the man in Christ was antithetical like his age; But *Calvary* does not dramatise Christ the antithetical man but the antithetical Son.
54 Peter Ure, *Yeats the Playwright, a Commentary on Character and Design in the Major Plays*, New York: Barnes & Noble, 1963, p. 119.
55 *Ibid.*, p. 117; Nathan, *op. cit.*, p. 202.
56 *A Vision*, p. 239.
57 For a discussion of the bird-symbolism of the play, see Wilson's *Yeats's Iconography*, Chapter V and Yeats's own explanation in his notes to the play in *Plays and Controversies*, p. 459.
58 *A Vision*, p. 275.
59 *Ibid.*, p. 239.
60 *Ibid.*, p. 240.

7: Conclusion

1 *A Vision*, p. 142.
2 *Ibid.*, p. 141.
3 *Mythologies*, p. 358.
4 Compare his poem, 'Gratitude to the Unknown Instructors':

> What they undertook to do
> They brought to pass;
> All things hang like a drop of dew
> Upon a blade of grass

with a passage from D. T. Suzuki's book: 'When you have satori you are able to reveal a palatial mansion made of precious stones on a single blade of grass. . . .' (*Essays in Zen Buddhism*, London: Rider & Co., 1950, p. 34.)

5 Virginia Moore notes similarities between Yeats and the Existentialist thinkers; it seems to me, however, that the important Existentialist concept of the 'Absolute Choice' or 'project' is practically absent from Yeats's system. See Virginia Moore, *The Unicorn, William Butler Yeats's Search for Reality*, New York: Macmillan, 1954, p. 345.

6 *On the Boiler*, Dublin: The Cuala Press, 1938, pp. 22f.

7 *Letters*, pp. 917f.

INDEX